Challenges of Raising Youth:

Nurturing Teenagers in a Digital World

By

Professor Dr Nazir Ahmad

M.Phil (London) PhD (London), DBMS, MCILIP (Manchester)
Ex-Head of Learning Resources, Southwark College, London
Ex-Professor King Abdul Aziz University, Jeddah, Saudi Arabia
Honorary Visiting Professor, Bayburt University, Turkiye

Radiant Valley
West Midlands, U.K.

Challenges of Raising Youth:
Nurturing Teenagers in a Digital World

Copyright © 2020 Dr Nazir Ahmad

First Published in the United Kingdom: 1442/2020
Reprinted 2023

Published & Distributed by

Radiant Valley,
Castle Bromwich, B36 8JN
West Midlands, United Kingdom

Website: www.radiant-valley.com
Email: info@radiant-valley.com
**   drnahmad3@hotmail.com**

[Place direct orders for this book]

Printed and bound in the United Kingdom

Ahmad, Nazir
Challenges of Raising Youth: Nurturing Teenagers in a Digital World.
Radiant Valley, 2020.

Cataloguing in Publication Data for this book is available from:

The British Library, United Kingdom.

ISBN: 978-0-9957147-0-0

In The Name of Allah The Most Gracious The Most Merciful

TABLE OF CONTENTS

POEMS

LIST OF PLATES

FOREWORD

It is a great pleasure to read through all nine chapters of this painstakingly researched and meticulously written book for the benefit of students, teachers, and the general public who might be concerned with the ethical, psychological, social, and rational development of teenagers. I have known Dr. Nazir for several decades who has gifted memory and prolifically penetrating writing skills, penned many scholarly books, including Saunders's all-pervading biography, intellectually tracing our ancestral roots in West Midlands, U.K. While I was at Australia House, London, he undertook research on Aboriginal rights, presented a paper on Dr Alan Gilchrist in the company of Simon Digby at Oxford and gave a scholarly talk about Thomas Carlyle at SOAS in the presence of Professor Staveley, B.C. Bloomfield, K.C. Butler, and Professor J.D. Pearson.

I have found it interesting, inspiring, and thought-provoking publication that enlightens, informs, and expands our knowledge of issues, questions, and challenges, and significant trepidations confronting the young generation today.

Each chapter gives a concise overview of the adolescents' behaviour, aptitudes, and propensities. There is a pressing need for proper training and education in the sphere of social media, cyber surfing, and social learning. The book will inspire parents to improve the household atmosphere and the teachers to imbed values and virtues in students for caring and sharing knowledge.

Notably, strength-based innovations can promote youth social and academic health, permitting freedom for making the right choices and sound decisions.

Peter H Saunders
Ex-Flinders University Staff
Seacombe Heights, South Australia

PREFACE

Coexistence in the digital world is a reality for interpersonal relationships, empowering youngsters to initiate emotional connections, making psychological adjustments, and developing caring perceptions for others. Childrearing practices and co-parenting strategies evolve the creation of the warm environment, consistent physical and mental growth, and school-based character-building programmes to ensure embedding of virtues and values.

Dr. Ahmad emphasises the significance of youth wellbeing exemplified in many Western countries, including Turkey, where laws are in place for the parallel moral and academic outcome at college and university level, combining merits of, empathy, compassion, and competence. Teenagers are the hope for just, diverse, and disparate societies in which we train them to make prudent choices, wise decisions, and impartial judgements. Cyber awareness helps safe online surfing, protection, and prevention from evil attacks, asserts the author, He mentions initiatives launched by Costa, McDonald, and ASDA for the promotion of literacy skills, inspiring reading habits, and encouraging socialisation.

Digital media are interwoven into the fabrics of young lives, facilitating intimacy, sharing knowledge and feelings, and enhancing social connectedness. The education sector identifies adolescents' strengths and weaknesses, devises far-reaching programmes e.g., Singapore,

European Union, U.S.A., and Turkey and then, finances and monitors the execution for achieving national targets.

The author diligently highlights difficulties of shared-parenting, single mothers, and unloved children's behaviour, attitudes, violence scenarios and addresses challenges and countermeasures necessary for youth wellness. Dr. Ahmad underlines measures to heal youth moral deficit and inculcate behaviour, that can support the healthy transition to adulthood

This book is remarkably a useful read for social psychologists, school and university teachers, and students of sociology and social welfare.

Professor Dr. Mutlu Turkmen
Vice Rector
Dean Faculty of Health Sciences
Dean Faculty of Business Administration
Head of Coaching Department, Physical Education & Sports College.
Bayburt University, Turkey.

President of International Bocce Federation (CBI)
President of Turkish Bocce Bowling & Darts Federation

ACKNOWLEDGEMENTS

I wish to express my deepest gratitude and special thanks to the following individuals:

I am grateful to Mr. Fiesal Mahroof (Assistant Principal, WMG), with whom I held countless meetings and discussed behaviour, manners, and etiquette of young students. I listened attentively about his professional handling of complex bullying incidents in his Academy for Young Engineers. Their youth social welfare training programmes, including ethical education, knowledge sharing, and student engagement in extracurricular activities. He explained the complexities of parenting and the impact on academic achievements. He also briefed me on the application of British Cyberbullying prevention laws and schools' protection mechanisms for pupil safety and moral development. Mr. Mahroof's precise understanding and educational expertise are priceless and have helped me to incorporate practical and rational ideas in my book.

I am equally grateful to my daughter, Dr. Simra Mahroof, who enlightened me about qualitative and ethnographic studies in the field of training of youth in multicultural and multilingual societies. Her invaluable knowledge and experience of motherhood responsibilities in raising happy and vibrant children stimulated my thinking and shaped my research direction. I am greatly impressed by how much you genuinely care about the wellbeing of your children and the close-knit family.

My thanks are due to my son Aqeel Ahmad (Manager, Flight Operations Training Dept, Qatar Airways, Doha), who utilised his I.T. expertise in designing the cover title and publisher blurb. He researched to discover topics-relevant photographs that scientifically support and augment the textual matter in the book. He also proof-read parts of the book and provided treasured feedback, enabling me to make vital rectifications.

I am also thankful to my youngest son, Dr. Nabeel Ahmad (G.P., Birmingham, West Midlands), who patiently and consistently offered indispensable cooperation during the typing stages, retrieving lost data, accessing reference sources, adjusting citations, organising chapter titles and subheadings of this book.

Finally, I do acknowledge with appreciation the contribution of my son Dr. Adeel Ahmad, as he devoted precious time and energy in revising two chapters of this book with commendable resilience, suppleness, and scholarship.

Last but not least, my wife Farah Ahmad, who exhibited endurance, courage, and serenity during my long hours of scholarships, research, and writing. Indeed, I spent hundreds of sleepless study nights to focus, imagine, conceive, and write while she demonstrated patience.

INTRODUCTION

Our children are an invaluable asset for the present and future hopes of a global society free from linguistic preferences, racial susceptibilities, cultural propensities, and religious sensitivities. Their role is indispensable in decreasing inequalities, minimising social disparities, and reducing extreme economic conditions. Our vibrant kids are lively and pulsating prospects for people and optimistic expectations for posterity on account of their vast potentials and capacities. We rely on their competences to pleasantly address the encounters of innovative cyber, internet, and online technologies to deal with the digitised world effectively.

We, as parents, caregivers, teachers, and service providers, have a demanding, and yet challenging task of childrearing encompassing home atmosphere, breastfeeding, involved fathering, intimate mothering, and compassionate grooming. It is a bumpy ride to nurture values, cherish positive thoughts, permit total freedom, and build nice etiquettes, satisfying behaviour, and productive capabilities. Dutch mums are rearing the happiest kids owing to natural calmness and delightfully relaxed perception. They are indulgent and prioritise remarkably well. Free societies face moral and social issues ranging from family splits, dilemmas of single mothers, financial constraints, and lone fathers influencing child upbringing in a robust and amicable environment. Former U.S. President Barrack Obama (New York Times, 15 June 2008) reprimanded American fathers for their wilful neglect of kids since too many fathers were missing from too many lives and too many homes. The British Prime Minister David Cameron (The Guardian, 15 June 2008) echoed that fathers' absence from families caused social snags ranging from unlawful activities to inferior school accomplishments. However, lone fathers in Australia quietly suffer from the impact of separation in middle age, causing distress and sorrow. They experience difficulties in maintaining contact with biological offspring, depriving the innocent vital paternal affection. Kids from single-parent families remain perplexed and increasingly baffled, aspiring true love in a fragile connection with non-biological fathers. The latter sometimes lack desired unruffled temperament, calmness, and tolerance in raising step kids.

Qualified nannies in the West and unqualified housemaids in the Arab world look after infants in unique but different ways impacting cognitive, motor, and thinking skills. The transition from the cuddling of kindergarten to a primary school is crucially significant for animated shared-parenting and the recreational nurturing of kids. Better still for raising lovely children in coordinated mother-father joint care, love, and adoration, parenting styles, whether Authoritarian, Authoritative, or Permissive, unveil both shortcomings and proficiencies impacting kids' aptitudes and knacks.

Digital awareness know-how, including online learning tools, assist teens' perceptions about unseen challenges of the digital world. We embrace the arduous task of rendering proper training for preparing teenagers well capable of overcoming hurdles, behaving justly, and meeting the intermittent contests with flexibility and perseverance. Observation of adolescent behaviour beyond the school walls offers evidence of their desirable and undesirable exploits. In social media, our children are exposed to internet platforms such as Facebook, 1.9 billion active users, Twitter 329 million clients; LinkedIn having four hundred million end-users; Google ten million customers. The teens get effected by intriguing sugary communication, overemotional and nuisance messages, and intimidating harassment texts that inflict socio-psychological damage. Social media impacts numerous modes over youth live because it generates educational value that amplifies and prolongs learning produces content for steering kids to get polished, entertaining, and insightful. The power of shared knowledge is a potent antiseptic with an enriched perceptiveness of correlation to rudimentary human values of compassion and care.

Cyber belligerence targeting innocent girls, humble boys, and vulnerable youth causes physical pain, psychological distress, and emotional agony. It is a relentless mocking and potential source of embarrassment, amounting to an individual's humiliation and defamation. Both parents and schools have the responsibility to teach our impending youth sensitivities of cyberspace operations, encryption mechanism, and online safety measures. Exemplary initiatives include Germany's Medienpass NRW, 2017; Singapore's Unmute Daniel 2018; Slovenia's Better Internet for Kids, 2019; and

Netherland's Better Internet for Kids. Italian Safety Internet Centre targets young gamers, and Unite Kingdom's Online Safety Live, E-Safety for Schools, and Thinkuknow are reachable for the wellbeing of adolescents in a virtual cyber world. Whether digital or physical, both types of bullying are lamentable, negatively causing mental harm and social agitation.

Without necessary regulations, a society reprobates into turmoil, disorder, and lawlessness, thus streamlining the passage for scamps to dehumanise the human values. On account of widespread cyber bullying in Europe, USA, New Zealand, and Singapore, effective cyber laws for the protection of the public are in place to safeguard immature, naïve, and simple-minded segments of the population. The Australian government has built an astoundingly, sophisticated cyber safety mechanism. We have a robust chain of British innovative online mischief detection and protection tools currently implemented across the country.

Our youth tend to set their scruples dismantling social norms, pursuing licentious and irreverent practices for pleasure and sensual gratification. They engage in social activities for the sake of attaining exhilaration and happiness, albeit some exploits are immoral acts. We should infuse in our teenagers' attributes of kindness, openness, and reliability. German and Dutch youth, in general, possess traits of candidness and trustworthiness (Erikson, 1959).

Secularism has been an increasingly acceptable form of our culture that admirably suits the aspirations of majority populations. Secular acuities have inflicted considerable damage on the social, moral, and decent perceptions of a pragmatic society. The sociologists and psychologists raised severe concerns about ethical decay, impelling governments to introduce values training and proper guidance in the school curriculum through rehearsals and presentations, workshops and seminars, and theatrical performances. Since the 1990s, teens consistently developed through relationship reflections and emotional self-restraint, the candidness to experience mannerism and friendly interaction with peers accommodating cultural diversity and social integrity. Genetic endowment and environment are the two factors rampant in influencing youth behaviour and dealing with others. With the sizeable Christian population, the Turkish Model for values teaching is commendably optimistic, incorporating secular and non-secular elements, guaranteeing freedom to all communities in their social and cultural varieties and way of life.

The question remains, how do we raise autonomous, confident, and glad kids? Intriguing research findings by Mac Acosta and Michele Hutchinson (The Telegraph, January 7, 2017) emphatically declare that Dutch parents, especially mothers, do successfully raise the world's happiest children. The kids anxiously need social education beginning with pigeon feeding, wrapping gifts, making comic characters to designing greeting cards for people with special needs. In-school acting shows, musical sessions, and thoughtful games inspire learning and improve retention powers. Socialisation expedites understanding of hypotheses and ideas when peers participate in knowledge co-construction. We impart social education to change youth habits and lifestyles enumerating cross-cultural variations. Joint exercise and shared learning improve critical thinking and simplifies decision-making abilities.

Learning is a social activity (Lindeman, 1926), and knowledge acquisition through engagement and participation (Dewey, 1963) is a noble act because the students learn more when they can talk to one another and be keenly involved. (Hurst et al. 2013). One of the basic human needs is to have fun and enjoy studies (Glasser, 1993). Social interaction motivates peers to reflect, resolve, and achieve more in groups than in seclusion. Through a pleasant learning environment, teenagers become prolific writers and creative thinkers. Resultantly, pupils' involvement in education is a predictor of personal development, and they allocate (Austin, 1999) substantial energy into studying and interaction with classmates and faculty members. Also, social relationships created during college years affirms (Wayt, 2012) have an invaluable impact on their success in academic studies. Social learning has become a significant part of innovative education at the Glasgow School of Art. (Tom Inns, 2017) We teach values that are a piece of cultural evidence (Opler, 1954), a way of life (Morris, 1956), and criteria for performance for social behaviour (Williams, 1968). Value is an element common to a series of situations that is capable of arousing an understandable response in the youth. (Linton, 1945).

In short, youth social engagement with college mates edifies their sensitivities about social values, boundaries, and pleasurable interconnections. Family-friendly caring, thought sharing, and frank interactive dialogue imbibes in progenies and teenagers the beloved trust, necessary confidence, and emotional stability for demonstrating patience in adversity, sobriety in an argument, diligence in creativity, and ingenuity in making a difference in others' lives

CHAPTER I

CHILD REARING PRACTICES & REFLECTIONS

Child-rearing practices vary considerably owing to cultural, social, and economic conditions, parental commitment, and aspirations. Fathers' pre-occupation, working mother's self-absorption, and partial neglect in childcare have an unfavourable impact on child grooming in the early years of development. It is a bumpy ride to nurture values and cherish positive thoughts in offspring who develop understanding and thoughtfulness through observations and actions of parents and sometimes grandparents in a multicultural, multilingual, and multi-ethnic world. The child-rearing task becomes exceedingly more intricate when a toddler views mischievous and strange occurrence in the surroundings and then poses questions as to why does harm vulnerable minors give pleasure to some and pain to others. Moreover, why do gratification and discomfort, delight, and distress exist side by side? A harmonious family brought up cultivates praise-worthy habits, enriches perceptions and promotes etiquette in adolescents. One must not overlook parental responsibilities in a decent household in which kids feel safe and comfortable. As far as childrearing is concerned, maternal or paternal comfort should not be the top priority since children get ignored and wellbeing neglected at the cost of night outs and weekend breaks. All children learn from what they see, feel, hear, and watch and then conduct experiments imitating elders for the sake of fun and amusement. Sometimes, emulations and replications turn out against the aspirations and expectations of innocuous broods. Unsupervised activities and playful events can go wrong for the children resulting in harm and hurt.

In many European countries, Child Care Centres accommodate kids from 0-2 years of age whose parents are customarily in full-time employment. On the top of the list are Denmark (65 percent0, Netherlands (56 per cent), and Iceland (55 per cent), where mother or father drop toddlers at these centres before heading for work. Nearly 100 per cent of adolescents in France, Spain, and Belgium age 3-5 years attend nurseries before entering mainstream primary education. No more than 50 per cent of Greek, Polish and Swiss kids go to kindergarten schools, permitting both parents to earn their living to share the financial burden. (Raz-Yurovich, 2012, pp.12-13). In Germany, day-care is publicly provided as professional couples with progeny fully benefit from this facility. Such care is not comparable to motherly love and emotional involvement for the well-being of children. Informal childrearing is very common in the Netherlands, Greece, and Germany, where blood relations and even neighbours and female friends take care of them for a certain number of hours.

Banning of physical violence against children is not a new trend in the Western world, and even in the Asian-Arab countries and in the Far East. They have abandoned the use of the cane and any other form of physical punishment. In many African countries, however, the bamboo and wicker are kept beside the teacher's desk to instil fear in the mind of naughty and disruptive students. It is undesirable to use a stick for imposing discipline in both primary and secondary schools. The Scottish parliament legislation banned the smacking of children, applauded by some but despised by others in social media. Jamie Gillies from the campaign group 'Be Reasonable' says that 'seeking to further the protection of children is highly commendable, but a smacking ban is not the way to do it' (The Daily Telegraph, 5 October 2019. London, p.25.). For young mothers, the child-rearing experience is an ideal time to cuddle, love, and occasionally give a light smack to make the toddler understand the limits and avoid inflicting self-harm by touching the hot cattle or the iron. Under-five kids innocently make mistakes, and repeated verbal warnings at times, go unnoticed, and they do the same thing again and again. Harsh physical spank would create fear, making the child inattentive and belligerent. A mother compassionately explains various things to make the child realize what is right and what is wrong and what is not in his/her best interest? Consciousness develops slowly and steadily and comes with age supported by consistent motherly instructions and empathetic fatherly adoration. Under all circumstances, avoid a simple slap or a lighter spank; otherwise, the child gets used to receiving physical punishment. The significant point of infant training is that he/she follows the guidance out of respect for the mother rather than out of fear as young as two-year-old begins to observe most of the things happening around the house and attempts to emulate mother and father. The parental role becomes increasingly important for keeping a watch over all activities, offering plenty of reassurance for consistent growth, making kids more thoughtful, ruminative, and reflective.

Nannies Childrearing Skills

Childrearing is a strenuous refinement geared towards unrelenting struggles to incite kids' growth and to nurture cognitive, motor, and social skills. The primary objective is to promote adolescents' capability to think, perceive, and ask questions as the mother listens with patience and perseverance. Female domestic servants in the United Arab Emirates serve as convenient childcare nannies. Gulf oil-rich countries hire unqualified housemaids from the Philippines, Thailand, Sri Lanka, Syria, Morocco, and Lebanon to look after infants. They also perform many other duties in big bungalows. Their daily work schedule includes vacuuming, dusting, scrubbing the floor, washing dishes and baby laundry, ironing and toiling in the kitchen cooking large meals a few times a day. In the morning or afternoon, housemaids accompany madam to shopping malls where they have to drive buggies or push shopping trollies. The exploitative practices cannot be reported at any official platform, lest they lose jobs or face visa cancellation. The poor foreign girls from deprived families continue to bear the burden of excessive workload. Intensive mothering by foreign housemaids is a cultural catastrophe affecting the training of Arab children. Underpaid girls have negligible authority over them in planning their routine activities. Credible mothering entails enormous emotional development, ceaseless self-sacrificing, inimitability, and a far-reaching child-centred upbringing.

It is futile to expect from foreign housemaids, the compassionate and empathetic involvement in attending to toddlers' needs and necessities. No matter how kind-hearted, caring, and considerate the Nannie might be, she cannot be a natural replacement for the biological mother of the child. The cuddle, hug, and snuggle of a loving mother have no parallel in the remarkable childrearing and grooming process. Early stages of nurturing and formative periods instrumentally shape the kid's mind and personality. Heavy reliance on housemaids for fostering core values and furthering beliefs is not a commendable proposition. Dr Shaikha Obaid Al-Tunaji, a professor in the Department of Foundations of Education, UAE University, has expressed concern about this unreported sensitive issue and urgency of tackling it. Dr Shaikha has suggested the establishment of Early Child Care Centres in all parts of the UAE staffed by fully trained caregiving personnel. Furthermore, Arab women, in general, are not mindful of the significance of parental participation in the cognitive, physical, and socio-psychological development of their children. Besides, there is little awareness among young mothers about post-natal training.

Perceptibly, nannies do not possess parental power and influence, so the kids look down upon them as despicable workers. Such values and norms reinforce the class system. In Western countries where elite families employ nannies for grooming kids, doing domestic chores, and chauffeuring them to school. Teaching values to children has been replaced by building values into them, and preparing them to compete academically, contends Schwartz (1993). In the United States, middle and upper-class couples holding senior professional and executive positions engage caring child girls who are verified to be acquiescent and compliant. The Filipinas are suitable nannies in aristocratic circles, but US diplomatic families equally prefer the Latinas young girls. They are well-disciplined and trustworthy nannies who render excellent childrearing services to American kids. Most of them are reliable, dependable, and considerate towards host families and their adolescents. In the past, they had to surrender their passports on arrival (Smith, 2002) to ensure that they do not flee.

Although, some wealthy employers unhesitatingly build up intimate relationships with nannies who find it difficult to resist the advances. Helena, in her article 'Slaves in the land of the free,' elaborates this point. Yet the 21+ nannies do not wish to lose lucrative jobs and possible chance of finding a suitable American partner for permanent settlement. Childminding is a bridging occupation that provides appropriate socialization experience for Latinas and Filipinas nannies. They happily serve American middle-upper and upper-class dual-career couples. A misconception prevails in the U.S. about these maids as outright vibrant, unkind, reticent, outspoken, and Erotic girls. The U.S. government issues four types of care worker visas to facilitate their employment to young girls from Europe.

1) A3 Visa to work for ambassadors, diplomats, counsellor, officers, public ministers, and their families.

2) G5 Visa to work for officers and employees of international organizations, foreign missions, and their families.

3) B1 Visas to accompany US citizens who reside abroad but are visiting the USA temporarily for no more than four years.

4) J1 Visa is used to bring young European women as nannies or au pairs with educational and cultural exchange. Each of these nannies is required to attend orientation sessions.

In the Netherlands, professional working couples do not engage nannies for childrearing but send their kids to Child Care Centres. The housewives take care of their children during maternity leave and then, enrol them at childcare venues where robust nurturing programmes make toddlers more confident. (Heckman, 1974). Combining work and family life is a feasible strategy for childrearing and well-being as it can minimise the time restraint for both partners (Oppenheimer, 1977), who can amicably share all domestic chores. Gender equality in the family and female contribution to run the household increased living standards and strengthens intimate relations.

Home Atmosphere

Home Atmosphere matters a lot for the child; he does what he sees, practices what he/she observes, and utters what he/she hears? Argumentative parents frequently assert about trivial matters in the presence of minors that indirectly transforms kid's thinking. If parents show anger quite often, the kid will develop rage and fury and demonstrate it in the school by hounding others. When you begin entirely to rely on God and live by the faith, the Omnipotent takes care of your genuine needs, look after you and never let you down, although small incidents do occur as a check upon patience and contentment. Your calmness keeps going while you surmount all odds with perseverance and resolution. If we help the needy and cause no hurt to others, it brings inner satisfaction and spiritual enlightenment. It is worth reading Darrell Tunnigley's book entitled, 'Unreachable': a true story. Lancaster 2011. ISBN. 978-185240 5892). He is just 40-year old, an ex-convict between the age of 17-21, amazingly turned his life around by identifying the true God with the simple guidance of two ladies at the Chapel Inside a prison complex. He learned to control fury, exercise self-restraint when confronted, walked away from a bully in the prison yard, gave up drugs and smoking, practised patience and learned how mouth and anger could drag you in big trouble. Those of my readers belonging to Christian faith might be interested in delving into the initiatives of Darrell such as 'Faith Works' Xcel Youth Ministries' Progressive Social Inclusion Project' and 'Tearfund' co-jointly advanced by Mark Finch and Mr

Tunningley. However, curious explorers of Truth might wish to know more about the teachings of Prophet Jesus. The real Bible in which Prophet Jesus professed the arrival of the Last Prophet of Almighty God and that Prophet, my Christian brothers, was Prophet Muhammad (peace be upon both of them). The latter received Divine Revelation in the form of the Holy Qur'an. I ask my Christian brothers to get hold of a translation of the Qur'an by M. Marmaduke Pickthall, an Englishman of exceptional standing. Please do read it with open mind and generous heart.

Teenagers have a different set of social issues in the age of the latest innovations as child gamblers are spending pocket money on videogames and slot machines. Anne Longfield, the UK Children's Commissioner, is attempting to introduce a total ban on loot boxes and voiced concern about the unlicensed 'Skins gambling sites' because children have access to age-restricted products. As Lizzie Roberts reposts that child gambling harm is to be reversed, and it is a collective responsibility for all stakeholders to work together. (The Daily Telegraph, Buckingham Palace Road, London. 24 October 2019. P.14.). Another burning issue is the rape and grooming of children,76204 in the last 12 months, out of which 16733 involved kids under 10-years of age. One of the important reasons is the paedophiles' use of social media to exploit and entice innocents. Undeniably, the online pornography Bill makes it mandatory for social websites to remove the manipulative, devious, and abusive substances and stop child access to pornography.

Thinkers unanimously agree that round-the-clock social media is negatively contributing to a mental health crisis among kids. The sedentary lifestyles leave little time for regular exercise and mindfulness. Whatever the nature of your faith may be, meditation and prayer before bed would help the child to have a good night's sleep, albeit secular-minded atheists could think of other avenues that help the kids to enjoy deep-sleep. The present writer's childhood experience point to the fact that praying regularly and keeping eyes fixed on Almighty God would work wonders in terms of staying on the right path. It would increase concentration, develop a healthy mind, and body coupled with positive and productive outcomes. Intellectual nourishment is nurtured in the classroom, school gym, and play areas as well.

Children are not evil-minded by birth; neither do they inherit mischief, deceitfulness, and treachery. Youth may wish to get away and escape from family chaos. They notice dilemmas at home caused due to absent father or mother struggling to adjust with a new partner who might be abusive and arrogant towards stepchildren. The vulnerable kid finds it disturbing to get along amicably with a stepmother or stepfather. Hastily taken parental decisions owing to irreconcilable differences, tear the hopes of innocent toddlers apart. As early as ten or eleven years of age, the neglectful kids try to get hold of amphetamine or ecstasy to feel better and forget about untimely social-psychological worries. To feed such bad habits, they turn to theft without feeling any remorse and guilt. It begins with stealing cash from a father or an earring from mum's cabinet. When this experiment succeeds, the next stage is to look for like-minded children in the locality and then jointly plan pilfering strategies ranging from shops, supermarkets, and adjacent residents. It is easy to get away with any minor, unlawful incidents since the legal system rarely apprehends underage children. Despite digital tags and chips attached to each item on display in superstores, smart kids skilfully nick desired articles and promptly leave the premises without being detected. They have perceived ingenious techniques of thievery and frequently get away with pillaged products.

On October 22, 2019, a man appeared before the Fujairah Misdemeanour Court in the United Arab Emirates for slapping a boy causing minor injury. The man was in the toilet of a supermarket when a naughty boy repeatedly knocked at the door and then pushed it to open, thus making the man irritated and embarrassed. As the man came out, a group of boys, including the perpetrator, laughed hysterically to tease him. It was at this point; the man slapped once to discipline him. The judge, however, imposed 20 thousand dirhams fine and handed one month suspended jail sentence to the Gulf citizen for this act of cruelty. (Khaleej Times, 22 October 2019 and 30 October 2019). Here, the rights of teenagers irrespective of the magnitude of mischievous, seem to be supreme over the respectability of adults. Let us assume the man in the toilet was a judge of the Gulf Supreme Court or a close associate of an influential member of the royal family of the UAE, what would have the verdict of this case? There is no mention of the parents of the teenager and the domestic environment. Hefty fine awarded to the man in court indicates the affluent background of the boy and his upbringing in an affluent and prosperous household.

Child Rearing Styles

Child-rearing styles differ widely in different societies depending on the nature of child protection laws, implementation criteria, care-givers' attitudes, parental expectations, adequate resources, and the role of social media networking platforms in the grooming of teenagers to become worthy members of the communities. In the race of technological and human resources development, Western countries compete in producing the best talents, distinguished scholars, eminent inventors, renowned research scientists, and lead thinkers. It starts from initial toddler commode training to attentive listening, thinking, speaking, imitating, reading, and writing. Potty training for a baby begins at the age of just 12 months as mothers discern facial expressions or if a toddler points the finger to his/her tummy, a sign of bellyache or a little cry that alerts the sensitive mother to head straight to the toilet. In some cultures, mothers sparingly use nappies for a couple of years or even longer. Delayed potty training is associated with painful nappy rashes and pimples, causing itching and sores. A diaper-free kid who sits on a toilet seat for urination and poop would not get blister, lesions, and infections. Recent research findings involving Chinese, Japanese, German, U.S.A., British, and South Asian mothers clearly show variations in the commencement of toddler potty education schedule as the average time frame is between 18 months and 30 months.

Correspondingly, eating habits, and sleeping manners are dissimilar across the globe. South Korean children, from the beginning, learn to endure thirst and hunger patiently. Both the French and South Korean kids wait for mealtime and then sit around the table with the family to eat available food without choice. On the other hand, American children continue to eat appetizers, crisps, chocolates, and biscuits throughout the day and feel no desire for a proper meal with their parents. No wonder America has the highest obesity rate, followed by several European countries. Most children in oil-rich Arab states, eat all types of junk food, snacks, nibbles, and drink varieties of mangoes, banana, and pineapple milkshake before and after school. As a result, the vast majority of them are obese and overweight. In the absence of smoking restrictions, adolescents do not hesitate to smoke, adversely affecting body fitness and general health.

A two-year-old brood learns etiquette of washing, bathing, tooth cleaning, dressing up, combing hair, wearing socks and shoes, and sitting around the dining table for meals. The kids learn to hold a knife and fork, acquire cleaning habits, and adopt the practice of throwing litter in the bin. Disobedient kids do not conform to the desired guidelines causing unnecessary frustration for their parents. Domestically, minor issues arise owing to non-compliance of rules set by the conscious families. For instance, children as young as four or five-year-olds are supposed to tidy toy boxes, clean the room, and place the pots and plates in the kitchen sink after a meal. Wise mothers do not reprimand children for not putting away things but sensibly administer light punishment such as sitting on the stairway or in a room for a while. Innocents may forget to implement instructions for being careless, lazy, tired, and weary. These are habits, not considered acts of disobedience or stubbornness. Especially in a loving and warm family atmosphere, toddlers are very responsive and receptive to their parents. The Duchess of Cambridge Kate Williams (wife of future British King Williams) believes a descent playground is a paradise for children, and she goes on to say that 'spending time outdoors plays a pivotal role for the future health and happiness of youngsters. She has developed an "Early Years Project" in cooperation with her three kids, Prince George, Princess Charlotte and Prince Louise for studying how babyhood experiences have a direct connection with the problems, some face as adults such as social rejection and addiction. (Daily Mail, September 4, 2019, p.23.) Developing a social life outside of school such as art classes, sports, cycling in the afternoon, material arts, bowling, fencing helps kids gain confidence and improve behaviour. Any activity is a positive social experience that acts as an outlet for an adolescent to show resilience in tackling minor incidents head-on.

What makes the child mentally and physically strong is the quality of parental care, attention and understanding of his/her emotional development. Freedom of jumping, running, playing, falling and getting hurt are natural activities, but one should be careful about the disproportionate motivation of the kids. Parents should study the system devised by Italian educator Maria Montessori (1870-1952) and gain knowledge of childrearing presented in a care guidance portfolio by Hungarian lady Emmi Pikler (1902-1984). Body movements are necessary for motor development and cognitive progress.

Children develop some competencies and acquire meticulous freedoms and restraints at a certain age. They may be at risk from outsiders, but can equally be at risk from parents, step-parents, brothers and sisters or step-brothers and relatives for several reasons. The heightened risk to kids most likely comes from intimacies that increase manifold from strangers when they step outside the house. In the past, such threats were relatively low as Hillman reported that in 1971, eighty per cent of 7-8-year-old children happily walked to school on their own. In 1990, however, only nine per cent were going to school alone. The situation is not much different today as the present writer who lived opposite the mixed school confirms it. Hardly five per cent or fewer children walk to school alone because mothers are seen holding their hands and saying good-bye at the school gate. It is a psychologically protective mechanism in which parents ensure the safety of their children and erect a safeguard against any unexpected horrific incident. Impulsiveness and lack of concentration along with quickness caused fatal road crossing accidents involving school-going children.

Interestingly, Roald Dahl shares his 1922 experience of cycling to school in the city of Glamorgan. His excitement cantered around tricycle that he enthusiastically rode to school daily with his eldest sister riding beside her. Dahl says, "We used to race at enormous tricycle speeds down the middle of the road, and, then, most glorious of all when we came to a corner, we would lean to one side and take it on two wheels. All this, you must realise, was in the good old days when the sight of a motor-car on the street was an event, and it was quite safe for tiny children to go tricycling and whooping their way to school in the centre of the highway." In these days, cycling to school has dramatically decreased due to heavy traffic, busy life, and high speed. Each household in multicultural urban areas possesses several cars, big taxies, 12 to 18 seater vans, and delivery trucks all parked on the footpaths, making it hazardous to walk or ride a bike. People generally prefer escorting kids to school, avoiding road-crossing vulnerabilities.

Other valid reasons might be the more car ownership, frequent bus service, affordable taxi ride and inhabitants residing far away from schools. It is also possible in multi-ethnic societies, some parents are overprotective, accompanying kids to school, keeping them home under surveillance, allowing limited tv viewing and granting regulated autonomy. The British Government produced guidelines released by the National Society for the

Prevention of Cruelty to Children are valid today. Kids as young as eight-year-olds are too young to go to school alone and seven-year-olds are too young for unaccompanied visits to the shops. It is generally proclaimed that the three to nine-year-old kids are little devils in one breath and little angels in the next. They might engage in age-inappropriate behaviour due to their awareness gained through internet and television programmes. Children need recreation, social activities and parental love to minimise isolation. If the mother is overworked and tired, she would be less responsive to kids' needs. They are innocent but fully capable of viewing, retaining, and imitating pictures and actions. Onerous lies with the sensible parents who earnestly set the boundaries exercising caution but giving desired freedom for their satisfaction.

Anyhow, the mother, in particular, has to set reasonable boundaries indicating acceptable limits. If the adolescents make negligible errors, they are neither ridiculed nor admonished since slipups are hardly deliberate and frequently unintentional, The parents should continue to act as affectionate mentors for kids to develop their full potential, restoring confidence. A study conducted by Zevenbergen et al. of Polish and American mothers revealed a variation between two different styles of bringing up kids. The Polish mothers give emotional support and share stories with their offspring and also, talk about past occurrences which enable kids to distinguish between uprightness and wickedness. American mothers use chronicles to teach morals and help kids remember about the lives of significant people. Dr Spock (1973, p. 1.) advocates young mothers preferably adopt 'a more relaxed vision one that acknowledges kids autonomy'', should loosen their authority and give them space to grow and even let them make mistakes. He is in favour of promoting leniency and laxness rather than harshness and callousness that undermines self-esteem and confidence. In the USA, before World War II, parents were required to discipline their kids. John Watson after World War II bluntly asserted that there should be adequate punishment for parents committing 'psychological murder'. He was concerned about the emotional damage and neglectful attitude of parents who were preoccupied with handling personal, social, economic matters due to high separation and divorce rates and infidelities. Betrayals and disloyalties were fairly common as the war had shattered family lives resulting in separations and breakups. According to de Tocqueville, (1990, p.192), American children considered independence a certain right and fathers and sons treated each other with far less formality than in Europe. The U.S. children were liberated from parental influence and home restraint, and therefore, they lacked graciousness and courtesy in interaction with others. One of the fundamental reasons is the absence of noble tradition says de Guronski (1857, p.381.) like their European counterparts. The steadfast and hardworking kids enjoy robust relations with their parents as they are rarely reprimanded and admonished. English children in the presence of strangers are reserved and relatively shy and tend to be accommodating in the school environment where UK born Asian children of educated parents compete in educational pursuits. In a diverse and multi-ethnic society, child upbringing reflects many features of various cultures and the way we relate to each other ethically and morally. Paula Fass, (2013), former Professor of History at the University of California, Berkley asserts that "the success of our children seems to be on everyone's minds as we look around the world where economies are faster, students seem smarter and their work habits stronger". She believes that our children can adapt to varying conditions and move beyond their parents' comprehension to generate and originate. We need to give our kids more latitude in an all-inclusive and diverse society so that they learn to use their judgement and make judiciously wise decisions and equip themselves to operate safely on social media internet platforms.

Breastfeeding Practices

Assertive young mothers of today are hugely independent compared to their counterparts in the previous century due to male ascendency in all spheres of human endeavour. This traditional hegemony has undergone an unprecedented change that has genuinely challenged the male dominance in the intellectual, economic, political and social fields. In the Western world, the young ladies avoid breastfeeding for not only keeping physically attractive but for the sake of professional career that does not permit sufficient spare time for the slow pace of breastfeeding many times a day and night.

Besides, personal comfort, social activities and personal biological intimacy prevent young mothers to commit since alternatives to breastfeeding are readily available for middle-class and affluent families. Different cultures have different norms of childrearing depending on mothers' employment status, family background, societal beliefs, parental expectations and degree of self-sacrifice in the upbringing process. A group of researchers including Dr Elizabeth Nixon of Children's Research Centre, Trinity College Dublin, Ireland interviewed 14 Irish, 13 Polish and 13 young Nigerian mothers about their childrearing and breastfeeding experiences and found the Irish parents more agreeable as compared to the other two. Notable was the fact that 49 per cent Irish and 83 per cent of non-Irish ladies favoured breastfeeding.

An increasing number of women in Europe find breastfeeding excruciating and arduous partly because it calls for a lot of serenity and forbearance. Young mothers are employed and cannot afford time for adequately feeding the baby several times a day and well into the night. On the contrary, United Arab Emirates Child's Rights Law 2014, makes it mandatory for mothers to breastfeed a child until the age of 2 years. Interestingly, young ladies can be seen feeding toddlers at Dubai Mall, Dubai Marina Mall and Mirdif City Centre, openly flaunting their flesh without hesitation. World Health Organisation reports 'Globally, less than 40 per cent of infants under six months of age are breastfed. Although it is not compulsory in Scotland, the Breastfeeding Act 2005 gives women the right to breastfeed a child for 24 months, and employers permit short breaks for such mothers to fulfil this noble act. Japanese infants are apathetic whereas Danes and Germans are stoical since they are primarily bottle-fed due to mothers' full-time work commitments and the belief that such babies' cray far less than those on breastfeeding. The British mothers find nerve-shattering the wailing of newly born babies but after imbibing mothers' milk sleep for long stretches in prams. According to medical research in baby feeding, breast milk is the best nourishment for infants in the first few months.

Among the South Asians and East European immigrant in the United Kingdom, husband or partner seems to be the traditional wage earner and the wife being the caregiver, devoting more time for upbringing toddlers. Childrearing is a complex chemistry of tricky interaction between parents and toddlers as they demand tremendous affectionate support in the early years.

Child Etiquettes & Impatience

Various cultures have diverse child protocols and have wide variations in Western, Asian and African continents. Within each culture, one can observe further disparities in affluent, middle-class, working-class academic, and non-academic communities in which kids are nurtured by some perhaps illiterate, others erudite and highly educated professional mothers. For example, the stigma of wealth makes kids economically secure. Still, Rachel Sherman (2017) in her book "Uneasy Street: the anxieties of affluence, has expressed fear that children from the prosperous background are 'selfish, self-satisfied' and are spoiled broods. There is no concrete evidence or globally gathered quantitative data to support this presumption. It may be reasonably accurate in individual families. Higher education has always been the privilege of wealthy, powerful and aristocratic ruling elites who can afford to pay colossal tuition fees and monumental living and travelling expenses to send the youngster to world-renowned universities in USA, Australia, Canada and Europe. Albeit, a few lucky ones, including the present writer, do manage to simultaneously work for living and study at institutes such as University College London, Oxford and Yale. Admittedly, utilitarian, erudite, well-read and solicitous parents do foretell and foresee the significance of their directives that ultimately lead their kids to achieve the objectives set for them. French parents are pretty strict in making their children compliant and yielding to instructions. Their mother would yell at them if they don't behave since pulling kid's hair or light beating on the back seat of the car is not uncommon. Mothers browbeat psychologically into submission so that they become exuberant high-spirited. A French kid can be disruptive and may circumvent the parents, infuriate the teacher and embitter classmates, albeit he/she is likely to be cheerful, buoyant and carefree. Pascal- Emmanuel Gobry (2012) surprisingly concedes, that she would not like her daughter to attend any French school and instead prefer home-schooling because psychological, physical and verbal bullying is prevalent in schools. There are over 700,000 kids bullied every year in most schools across the country. Poor attendance, absconding from classes, asking mothers to change the school or staying at home being sick, unwell and sad are some of the signs concerning school environment. Kids face intimidation, classmates tearing clothes, ripping books, and nudging and elbowing make the atmosphere unbearable. Marie-Jose Gava author of 'Halte au har element a l'ecole' runs Place de la Mediation- a network to help educational institutions to overcome school-based intimidation and coercion.

Other significant components are the mother's background, mind-set and time investment in child grooming since birth. For instance, Scottish, Irish, Welsh and English toddlers' queue at school dinner halls, bus stops airport check-in counters, bookstores and theatres. Civility and moral superiority of being British illustrate a sense of order and decorum. Politeness and courteousness are two distinct traits of well-groomed kids even in chaotic situations at concerts, balls and festivals or carnivals. Grown-up teens do sometimes become eager, desolate and impatient at football grounds, amusement parks and discotheques where crowds misbehave and cause harm to others. Frustrations are also visible at airport security checks where queues get longer when someone takes time to empty pockets, remove the watch, belt and shoes. The violent drunken youth are apprehended, and hooligans detained ensuring, law and order in society. The law enforcement officials effectively and consciously, control public disturbances. Childcare is at the forefront of US senators political campaign agenda due to presidential elections looming in 2020. Senator

Elizabeth Warren has introduced the Universal Child Care and Early Learning Act in the Congress for open debate. (Anna North, 2019). Access to affordable, high-quality care should be the right for all US families rather than a privilege for the wealthy people. The school districts and overcrowded urban areas would get federal government funding and support to set up day-care homes and care centres for married, separated, cohabited, and lone parents' kids.

Professionally successful parents, enjoying affluence, prosperity, and comfort, have high academic expectations from their kids. They are accustomed to cosiness and luxury and show little interest in pursuing pure scientific subjects and even less inclined to study legal and medical disciplines. In both China and Japan, child-rearing is very stringent involving taxing schedule of concentrated studies with idealistic anticipations of children's progression, academic achievements and educational feats. Debra Waters (2019) calls this authoritarian style a Tiger Parenting that equally causes discontentment and unhappiness. Chua Liang in 'Battle Hymn of the Tiger Mother' commends Tiger Parenting for a productive career primarily to fulfil parental aspirations. Dr Madeline Levine 'Teach your Child Well' has presented a counterargument by reflecting that affluent family teens are "overstretched into performing well", disregarding conviviality that leaves the kids emotionally perturbed and psychologically distressed. Dr Levine questions in her book why the kids from wealthy families unable to do well academically, are depressed and anxious and turn to drugs and alcohol for solace. The child does not get the opportunity of demonstrating credibility and creativity in non-academic subjects. Obviously, "There is not something quite right about our parenting," says Levine because the parents cannot prepare every child for admission to Cambridge, University College London, Yale and Harvard Universities.

The very first test of toddler's patience and manners begins at 5-years of age when he/she faces the transition from cuddling and relaxed atmosphere of the nursery to a primary school where etiquettes and class discipline are paramount, and formal learning occurs. Here, kids intermingle with other broods of the same age group. They are harmless and innocent but expect genuine affection and care from nursery teachers. Some children show an inclination for learning, but others take no interest in classroom lessons. Pupils cannot study science subjects through parental pressure. They might not memorise tables, solve simple sums, learn to read and write. The primary school kids age 5 to 11 are under no obligation to complete homework or participate in other educational activities. The elementary school adolescents belonging to broken families, single mothers, orphans, with disturbing background, feel agitated and distracted. Lack of interest in learning and restless nature make them commit acts of public disorder. While at school, their violent acts leave much to be desired. The violence issue is at the forefront of an unhappy background of toddlers in many countries. For example, a child under the age of 10-years in Oslo primary school gets upset, goes to the school kitchen, secretly obtains a knife and threatens his teacher. As classmates intercede to protect the teacher, he injures two other kids. The school authorities take the wounded children to an emergency clinic for treatment. Astoundingly, it is a first to fourth grades very modern Brynseng School in Oslo, Norway, opened in 2017. Steffen Handal, the Leader of the Trade Union Federation, concedes that ferocity is widespread in primary schools in Norway since teachers are subject to a rising degree of viciousness. Arbeidstilsynet, a regulatory agency survey of 93 primary and junior high schools in South-eastern Norway pointed out a major factor in this troublesome scenario, was the lack of a mechanism in 90 per cent school to prevent violent kids from committing odious acts against teachers and pupils. (The Independent Barents Observer, March 20, 2019). Another shocking incident occurred at the Stovner High School in Groruddalen, Oslo, where a student had brought in an axe and an iron rod, and he threatened a school mate raising the alarm among teaching staff. The principal Terje Wold informed the newspaper editor of Dagsavisen, he felt a sense of disquiet that students and teachers could be injured. He also mentioned that he had previously seized weapons from many students and intervened to stop vehement bickering among pupils. (The Independent Barents Observer, September 28, 2017). Yet in another Oslo school, police were called in to sequester an electric shock-pistol from a bewildered student. The situation in many schools remains tense because student gangs are operating on the premises committing arson and sabotage. These are unhappy kids affected by the doomed domestic environment.

When children get together in the local playgrounds at weekends, they do all sorts of unpleasant things, and some go to nearby superstores for stealing chocolates or other eatable items. Presumably, their parents or guardians have appointments with the hairstylist, meeting with an old friend or purchasing dresses, home accessories, outfits and uniforms.

As Oliver Wheaton (The Independent, English daily, UK, May 26, 2018) reported that self-service checkouts at supermarkets have become stealing hub costing millions of pounds in lost revenues leading to redundancies and outlet closures. On electronic tills, option carrot is ticked which are very cheap and then, expensive avocados are weighed as an individual bought 18 kg carrots in one go but got away with pricey avocados. (Voucher CodesPro.co.uk) have reported that people in the UK, young and old stole £3.2 billion worth of food from self-service tills in 2017. Similarly, customers scan costly grapes as cheap carrots, swipe prime steaks as discounted potatoes, and young girls remove stickers from inexpensive on-sale products and fix these on expensive cosmetics. (The Guardian, UK, May 20, 2018) Pilfering from a self-checkout machine is fairly common, and even the children do not hesitate to bag the items that fail to scan. Spike in shoplifting has been largely due to legislation in 2014 which stated that the police would not pursue thief shoplifting items worth less than £200.

Notwithstanding that, London Metropolitan Police, since 2017, abandoned any theft investigation for items worth less than £50 value. Teenagers do not hesitate to pinch fresh sandwiches from Sainsbury and other major stores, and now they fix TV screens right above the sandwich cabinets to deter petty thieves. To prevent shoplifting, Australia has espoused 3D sensors maintaining virtual cart of items for each buyer. Also, artificial intelligence platforms are in operation for the detection of products; a customer picks up and puts back. Asda supermarket store uses Edesix Video Badges to stem the rising rate of food theft.

How far the parents should ignore misbehaviour of kids on school premises as well as at home such as a boy pushing his food off the dining table, a spiteful toddler breaking a toy, a vindictive girl hitting another girl at playtime, a resentful youth expressing bitterness for unfair treatment by another chum. While playing hide, and seek at break time, a buddy slips on a banana skin, then blames pal and struck him, causing bodily harm. Although a teacher's intervention for reconciliation achieves the desired result, the injury sustained by the victim does not minimise the tension. The friendly meeting with parents yields nothing on account of total denial for the wrongdoing. Each family permits permissive upbringing, but lack prudence and practicality and the problem remains unsolved. In such complex settings, a possible scenario is that no one would emerge impeccable because families do not discuss tolerance and forbearance with their broods. Supposedly, overbearing perceptiveness in opulent families predetermines the conduct of teenagers. They are considered insensitive towards the sentiments of school fellows or acquaintances in the community venues. Lack of tenderness in temperament causes hurt to others. Recalcitrant and rebellious youngsters amusingly defy any sort of behavioural instructions seeking pleasure in cheekiness, rudeness, and disrespect. Numerous technologically driven pupils-teacher, parent-kids' programmes have been devised by sociologists to improve the behaviour of uncooperative and perverse children. It is not an easy undertaking for the teacher to coax haughty and arrogant children and expecting quick progress. Changing the mindset of disgruntled and unhappy youth requires a great deal of patience and endurance, planning and training to give them real hope and promising potential. In this context, social media providers, intellectuals, educators, faith leaders, community personnel. celebrities, athletes, caregivers, parents and teachers must contribute time, efforts and resources to instil confidence and offer optimism to the young generation. More philanthropist like Bill Gates and Warren Buffet need to pool their resources and services for the ethical, social, educational and economic wellbeing of teenagers across the globe.

Naturally, parents are concerned about any unpleasant and unsafe activity that may affect children's intellectual and physical growth. As young adolescents seek out audacious experiences for the sake of excitement, making mistakes that sometimes land them in trouble. But they learn from slip-ups and flaws as long as such blunders do not involve violence and law-breaking. So, risk-taking is not abnormal, albeit a tendency to act hastily and to miscalculate potential danger is hereditary. Interest in innovation makes them feel thrilled and electrified, and in the process, build new friendships and widen their social circle. Some kids have superior spatial skills than others and rationalise their judgements to understand abstract concepts. In the elitist perception, gifted children with particular academic abilities outperform in intellectual pursuits. They are blessed with a retentive memory, vivid imagination and set high standards of achievement. Gifted children are vibrant, energetic and focused, having the resilience to concentrate on a specific subject for a long time. The parents can watch out for early signs of toddler's learning skills, thoughtful inventiveness and creativity. The keen school teachers can equally identify in brilliant kids, the pace of learning, the power of analytical thinking and academic endeavour to excel. Exceptionally bright children can enhance their wisdom, perception and knowledge through thought-provoking learning experiences and develop the potential for building a harmonious and peaceful globe.

CHAPTER II

FATHERHOOD & SHARED-PARENTING

Family fragmentations owing to enormous divorce rates, increased co-habitation, proportionately splitting couples, crumbling relationships, absconding mothers and deserting fathers have radically influenced the traditional parenting of innocent children. The predicament of lone fathers, dilemmas of single mothers, unforeseen changes in household structures and dubious co-parenting arrangements have drawn the attention of lawmakers to review, debate and approve regulations and ensure enforcement for a preferred outcome.

In modern societies, non-resident, co-resident, biological and stepfathers are parenting kids born to ex-wives, partners or female friends. With more and more ladies working full-time, men/husbands/partners and casual associates have adopted "caregiver role and become 'stay at home' fathers" (Doucet, 2006). Therefore, fathering responsibilities are changing (Morgan, 2004), notwithstanding that, "involved fathering has become prominent. (Collier & Sheldon, 2006). A few decades ago, fathers did not have any emotional involvement with children. (Dermott, 2008). For robust childcare, both parents should have a meaningful relationship with their offspring even after the unfortunate episode of separation and divorce.

Non-Resident Biological Fathers

FATHERHOOD (Poem)

Our Kids Need Loving Fathers

As Much as Affectionate Mothers

Have Sisters and Little Brothers

Ensured Safeguard from Others

Lone Fatherhood, is Mere Isolation

Ill-timed Desertion, Causes Indignation

Blocked Access to Kids Exasperation

Genuine Fathers Feel Vexation

No Quick Fix for Such Irritation

Join Associations for Consolation

Separation, Source of Invisible Grief

Child Custody Battle, Brings No Relief

Bear with Sorrow, Loss of Attachment

No Rational Solution for Detachment

Female Rights Are Undoubtedly Supreme

Infringement Would be the Wildest Dream

Sufferers Are the Blameless Broods

Affects Morality, Their Unheard Scream

Best of Life, No Turbulence or Trial

Give Them Back, An Innocent Smile

[Composed by DR NAZIR AHMAD, 3 May 2020]

Non-Resident Biological Fathers should continue to maintain biological ties with kids based on agreeable co-parenting arrangements. On account of academic achievements, young ladies in their 20's and 30's are gainfully employed in promising fields. They are not willing to sacrifice lucrative jobs and rewarding career for the sake of monotonous household chores and childcare. The women expect their husbands to share domestic work and childcare. In working-class families where men earn little or have no worthwhile employment, they do babysit at home and perform housekeeping duties. At the same time, women work fulltime in supermarkets, offices and food outlets. The middle-class professionals and technically trained men who have lost jobs due to redundancies and top business and industrial closures, feel embarrassed in a changing scenario where women are the breadwinners, and the men have become Stay at home fathers. Many men are uncomfortable with their extensive contribution to unexciting, repetitive childcare activities. Marriage institution has declined, and the vast majority of couples are living together as partners. As the frustration creeps in, one of the partners move out, and the legal procedure begins for the child/children custody.

As the number of no-resident biological fathers has immensely increased in the West, the childcare arrangements have become hot issues between two biological parents. The mother with a new partner and children from the former partner needs time for adjustment before entering into a suitable child-biological father contact. Indeed, involved fathers wish to devote quality time to their biological kids because "knowing and understanding is the crux of intimacy" says Jamieson. (1998, p.19.). Ominously, caring activities flow from an emotional connection constituting the fathering role. (Dermott, 2008, p.142). Persistent traditional connotations of "fatherhood have shifted or been challenged." (Williams, 1998, p.63) . In the present century, cultural impediments to paternal engrossment in childcare threaten to limit men's real immersion in parenting. Supporting fathers' involvement in their kids' lives is a vital element in the maintenance of healthy families and communities. Sometimes mother with their kids moves to another city creating difficulty for the father to travel a long distance, costing a lot of money and time.

In many cases, non-resident fathers have no link and rapport with their children. On the one hand, they become lonely due to the loss of a female companion and on the other, they badly miss children. Moreover, kids with single mothers suffer from a lack of paternal affection and love and quite often get involved in malicious and playful actions. While others deliberately disassociate from their children to avoid financial and caring responsibilities. It was in this context that ex-President of USA Barrack

Obama in his historic speech on Fathers' Day, June 2008, at Apostolic Church of God in Chicago reprimanded Afro-American fathers for their wilful neglect of kids and emphasised that "What makes you a man is not the ability to have a child- it is the courage to raise one" since too many fathers are missing- missing from too many lives and too many homes. They have abandoned their responsibilities, acting like boys instead of men".(The New York Times, 15 June 2008). In an interview with Suzanne Malveaux, CNN White House Correspondent, Obama remarked that his father deserted him and his mother when he was two years old. He went on to say that he would be a good father to his children and if he could give them anything, "I would give them that rock, that foundation on which to build their lives and "I would be a presence in my children's lives". Simultaneously, The British Prime Minister David Cameron valued Obama's remarks and reiterated that a "responsibility revolution" was urgently needed in the U.K. and raised his concern about family breakdown. David Cameron, however, conceded that his parenting skills 'are a work in progress'. (The Guardian, 15 June 2008). Father's absence from families causes social problems ranging from crime and delinquency to poor school achievement. Undeniably, children raised in two-parent families perform well on measures of educational attainment and psychological adjustment than kids raised in single-parent families.

Non-resident biological fathers are also called Lone Fathers who face monetary, housing and health problems. They have low self-esteem, loss of confidence and feelings of isolation and seclusion. Western communities have negative attitudes, and people look at them with suspicion. (O'Brien, 1982) They find it challenging to meet the constant demands of children, causing frustration and anxiety. While others prefer to stay in touch with former biological children, joining them in social activities and helping them in sporting competitions. Admittedly, they cannot be a replacement for mothers, as was confirmed by Doucet (2006, p.219). She interviewed 118 Canadian men responsible for childcare. Most of these men were kind, compassionate and decent fathers but not mothers. She raised the point that while conversing with caregiving fathers, it was not always clear what the essence of fathering is, what is specific for men is that "it is not mothering" (Doucet, 2006, p.217.). Fathering of biological children after couple's breakup is becoming diverse and multifaceted in Western societies. Increased job opportunities for women (Dermott, 2008) have brought demographic changes in childcare as well as a decrease in formal marriages and consequently, increase in living together.

Lone fathers quietly suffer from the impact of separation and divorce owing to the loss of beloved partner and children. It is an inexpressible painful experience causing distress, agony and shock. Notably, men are not always at fault when abandoned by their partner, desirous of seeking a new exciting relationship. Right-minded fathers are anxious to keep open lines of communication with their children. Fathers' emotional and material wellbeing shapes their fathering capacities and involvement as various theories of post-divorce fathering predict. (Braven et al., 2005b; Lehr & MacMillan, 2001)). Winchester (1999, p.94) drawing on interviews with members of the Lone Fathers Association, Australia, concludes, while discussing intense emotional matters with them, it shows feelings of frustration and deepens sensitive scars of breakups. There is systematic discrimination against fathers and a sense of helplessness concerning the judicial system (Lehr & MacMillan, 2001, p.376).

It is inappropriate to depict separated and divorced women as opportunistic, deceitful and spiteful because they have got rid of abusive and violent partners. It is equally wrong to assume that all girls are dishonest and prone to making untruthful accusations of internal violence.

Fathers and Fatherhood

Once a famous US psychologist proclaimed that maternity is a matter of fact, but paternity is a matter of opinion. When A Salford-based Bio clinics Group, UK undertook the delicate task of examining 5000 DNA results between January 2014 and June 2016, it was concluded that forty-eight percent of British men were not the biological fathers. If a woman co-habited with two men on the same night and then, conceived, the fatherhood became controversial. (Manchester Evening News, 3 January 2017. Professor Cumming says that DNA tests have been revealing awkward family secrets. (Metro,

I June 2019). Genetic testing emerged in the 1960s but got perfected in the 1990s.

Professor Michael Gilding has raised such concerns about Australian fatherhood denials. Misattributed paternity is not uncommon in many secular societies. In the Elizabethan England, the weight of shame from illegitimacy was dumped squarely on the innocent kid. In those days various terms were coined such as spurious, natural, misbegotten, imputed (father denies fatherhood), reputed (father admits fathering), filius nullius(son of a stranger), and ignotus (Father unknown). Even the permutations of coupling created difficulties for the Church. In the 1770s. Dr Samuel Johnson rightly felt the need for female chastity. He declared that 'we hang a thief for stealing a sheep, but the unchastity of a woman transfers sheep, and farm and all from the right owner' to a woman who compromised the trust. In 1610, under James I, the law stated that 'every lewd woman who shall have any bastard which may be chargeable to the Parish, the Justice of the Peace may commit such woman to the house of correction for one year. As the dispute arose about naming the illegitimate child upon christening, Ear James in 1643, ruled that such kids be entered under their mother's name.

Owing to the increasing fashion of partnerships and drastically reduced culture of marriages, biological fathers are considered essential for positive child growth. The contours of family life have witnessed structural changes in the vast majority of households.

PARENTING SITUATIONS (Poem)

Marriage is Abandoned in Favour of Free Life
Cohabitation is the Norm, Instead of a Wife

Society Rejects a Domineering Husband
Women Would Rather, Have a Good Friend

Since Wife Became the Breadwinner
Psychologically, Woman Was The Winner

She Struggled But Claimed Equal Rights
Changed State Laws, With Rational Fight

Bounded Nuclear Family, Concept of the Past
Privileges were For Men; It Could Never Last

New Market Structure, Women Got Employed
More Jobs For Girls, Men Became Unemployed
Textile, Cotton Mills, Female Were Deployed
Outdoor Life Mostly, Women Fully Enjoyed

Household Routines Got Utterly Changed
Men Took Responsibility, Tasks Rearranged

Question Still Remained, For Kids Growth
The burden of The Brought-up Fell on Both

Marriages Declined, Co-habiting Increased
Intimacy Improved, But Trust Decreased

Multiple Relationships Took The Hold
Youth Affairs Turned Fragile and Bold

Unstable Companionships Affected Innocent
Partners Disputes, Rows, Wedged Adolescent

If One Spouse Left, the Other Became Depressed
Wrangling Between The Two, Child Was Depressed

Woman With Kids Facing isolation
Financially Hard, But No Consolation

The Child Misses His Real Father
Who Has Become Biological Father

His Memory is Fresh; Feelings Are Low
Which One to Blame, He Does Not Know

Misunderstanding Was The Root Cause
Let Us Concentrate With a Little Pause

Misapprehension The Inherent Source
Who Could Find Out In Due Course

Bickering and Arguing, Family Life Dilutes
Anger and Quarrelling, Kid's Mind Pollutes

Under Such Scenarios, Violence Erupts
Setting Like These, Child Brain Corrupts

If the Child Happens To be a Girl
She is Loving daughter Like A Pearl

She Becomes a Disturbed Child
Who Grew Up, But Hardly Smiled

At School, They Call a Troubled Kid
Biological Parents Must Open the Lid
What Prompted Her To Be Rough and Wild
That She Never Giggled or Ever Smiled

Lone Fathers or Single Mothers

Biological Fathers or Step Mothers

They Are Solely the Main Players

In Training Their Kids, None Others

[Composed by DR NAZIR AHMAD, 12 June 2020]

Role of Stepfathers in Childcare

It is not unusual in many cases when a mother cohabits with a third or fourth partner, her kids from former companions live under one roof since their biological fathers had left to find new mates. Evidence suggests, British working-class stepfathers to assume an all-encompassing outlook to consider all children, whether natural or step kids as their own and attempt to build up a healthy relationship. Resident stepfathers shoulder a critical role in the lives of the broken family's children who are naturally attached to and emotionally involved with their father. On occasions, stepfathers are perplexed to confront children of their new female partner who abruptly reject affectionate gestures and make him feel unwanted. In other instances, they are considered violent, aggressive and even abusive towards stepchildren. Over two decades ago, Burgess (1997) reported that one in six stepfathers had sensual intimacy with stepdaughters. Frosh (2002) and Cawson et al. (2000) research findings assert that sexual abuse is committed mostly by siblings or adolescent family members, recurrently by stepbrothers and nephews. It is disturbing to note incidents of voluptuous violence which Daley & Wilson (1994) believe "is inherently problematic for child welfare.

Cohabitation in some civilisations is not appropriate based on beliefs, moralities and ideologies. Still, in Western societies, revised laws and ethical standards seem to support and facilitate the sustained association of two individuals without the necessity of tying the knot. This connection lasts up to the point that both male and female partners are entirely happy and satisfied in the relationship. Friendship is in the context of 'interpersonal equality and emotional intimacy'. (Giddens, 1992, p.130). Cohabitation and childbirth outside of marriage in the liberal West is not an odd or strange phenomenon. Serial monogamy and sporadically changing partners are neither peculiar nor weird but a socially acceptable standard. However, such sensual relationships produce children with many intermittent intimacies. In this environment, childbearing in a stable household is unsustainable as these progenies despise sense of belonging in intermingled family make-up.

Every time, one partner leaves the co-resident, the other one moves in to resume cohabitation. In the spirit of fatherhood, the non-genetic related males are called social fathers. In a single household, one child may be from previous husband/partner, the other could be from the present resident boyfriend, while the third kid might be the result of a social relationship with a neighbour. Three kids from three different fathers find it confusing to understand the meaning of genuine parental affection.

Frequently, they are bewildered, perplexed and baffled about their predicament and do aspire true love and paternal warmth. Some stepfathers face difficulties in establishing links with co-resident stepchildren and cannot form emotional bonds. They are taken for granted when stepchildren ask for expensive toys, clothes and trainers. Fragile relationship with step kids harms childrearing. Good and compassionate stepfathers do attempt to develop a fatherly association with innocent children and devote precious time in their leisure and educational activities. In some instances, children despise the presence of a stranger in the house, albeit the mother's new partner, since they miss their genetic father. All adolescents need a safe and comfortable unified family home to grow, prosper, enhance confidence and self-esteem. They are naturally affected by unpleasant family disputes and arguments. Mothers are emotionally close to their children and in case of family breakups, get custody of kids. Equitable rights campaigns have empowered women to expect better treatment from their husbands. Many ladies in the West work fulltime and contribute to running the household. They are financially independent and do not want their partners to dictate unacceptable term or show arrogance in any matters.

Shared Parenting

The concept of shared-parenting has gained popularity as biological fathers are expected to shoulder higher responsibility for childrearing after the couple's separation. The emotional attachment should not diminish even after divorce. Regular contacts can sustain a child-father relationship. Non-resident fathers should be available for a weekly meeting with broods to fulfil their nurturing and caring roles. In Europe and the USA, mostly white married or co-habitant partners, express egalitarian attitude towards parenting, are democratic and treat each other with respect. Fathers experience substantial touching issues in the wake of split-up. (Lehr & MacMillan, 2001). To facilitate shared parenting, the Canberra Fathers and Children's Services in Australia (CANRACS) provides accommodation and support to homeless fathers with accompanying children. This service provision stems from another service run by the Lone Fathers' Association. Astonishingly, they offer refuge for men fleeing domestic violence. According to Professor Michael Flood of University of Wollongong, NSW, Australia, 'Painful experiences of divorce and separation...produce a steady stream of men who can be recruited into fathers' rights groups' (2012, p.1.). Other organisations supporting separated fathers include Men's Confraternity and Fatherhood Foundation, Men's Rights Agency, Fathers Without Rights and Shared Parenting Council, Australia. In 1997, the Australian Federal Government started financial incentive to lone fathers for supporting ex-partners, biological children and stepchildren. The following year in

1998, Men and Family Initiative was launched to reinforce and underpin the responsibility of fathers in families and children's lives.

Kids conceived by sperm donation or born due to extramarital relations; the mother must brief the child or children about his/her real biological father. In many instances, child custody problems erupt after marriage break down. Joint custody must be one of the sustainable solutions, although mother mainly succeeds in winning over the children. To intensify the father's involvement, the U.S government had amplified 'Responsible Fatherhood Initiative. The former US President Bill Clinton inaugurated it in 1995 to increase fathers' contacts with their biological children. Three years later, in 1998, the U.K. government started 'Father Direct" Initiative to maximise parental participation in childcare. (Featherstone, 2003, p.245.)

When his wife/partner forsakes a 40-year old spouse, he is overawed with sorrow, anguish and pain and feels psychologically anxious, lonely and isolated. He could not have anticipated sudden desertion and abandonment. The loss of wife and kids leaves an indelible and ineffaceable impact on his mind.

The quality of parenting and family relationships do have a profound impact on kids' wellbeing and intercedes the influence of fathers. Youngsters brought-up in nuptial families with high encounters may experience as many glitches as broods of divorced, separated or never-married parents. Indeed, living together is very convenient for young couples instead of formal marriage and then, divorce due to family altercations, tussles and rows. Notwithstanding that, mammoth divorce settlements have scared the professional and affluent men to avoid legal marriages. Material assets play a major part in the child growth process. There is evidence that children raised by highly educated, well-to-do unwed mothers predictably do better emotionally, economically and socially than the children reared by two married parents with slighter educational and economic resources. (Stacey, 1998, p.70) Undoubtedly, when the domestic clash is severe, prolonged and explicit, divorce represents a getaway says Amato (2000, p.1278), from an unpleasant home atmosphere for children. Under these circumstances, kids' get disheartened and show little interest in school-based educational activities. They are affected by emotionally frozen parental relationships. The family breakup owing to marriage breakdown or partners heading in opposite directions is the darkest and gloomiest episode in the lives of two individuals. It is equally murkiest for children in that household who face a traumatic situation in an adolescent. They know full well that the tumultuous custody battle has yet to come (Bertoia and Drakich, 1993). The presence or absence of shared parenting exerts a key influence on a child's welfare and health.

In shared-parenting, focused care and father's attachment with kids has several benefits as long as stepfathers are not involved in abusive behaviour towards female partners. (Jaffee,et.al., 2003, p.111). In Australian society, unwed fathers' anti-social conduct adversely affects children who deserve affection from stepfathers. (Rickard, 2002, p.2). Involved dads whether genetic or otherwise are a blessing, but neglectful fathers are a threat to the kids' wellbeing. Boys are like to resemble fathers, especially their genetic dads and keen to have a warm and cordial relationship. In all intents and purposes, the mother's role is crucial in raising sons because, in Western culture, girls receive more attention and care as compared to their brothers. ((Howard, J, 2001. P.157). However, mothers as sole parents do come across behavioural issues with their sons, particularly in the absence of biological fathers. Ideally, mother and father should equally share the obligation, unify social capital and improve mentoring style for raising kids. Adolescents in shared parenthood receive breezes of physical and social stimulation from fathers, rhythmic and calming love from mothers. Building healthier families in which children prosper, paternal active and involved partaking in sharing parental obligations is of great significance. Fathers need the training to look after newly born infants if the female partner is fulltime employed. In the USA, they have hospital-based sessions called' Boot Camps for New Dads' in which experienced nurses and midwives impart baby care training. The Father time sessions are held as part of antenatal classes. In the changing world, economic and job situations, opportunities for women have been on the rise due to which formal parental education should be made available for prospective genetic fathers to fulfil their childcare duties better. Cultural norms, interpersonal relations and leisure circles are an obstacle to genetic fathers' involvement in shared parenting. Arguably, fathers can or cannot nurture like mothers since affection of the later has no parallel in the history of humanity. The present write believes with a personal experience that equivalent is a comparable emotional attachment, tremendous self-sacrifice and selflessness in rearing progenies. Mother and father take care of broods in unique but intersecting ways. If mothers play games and rough house with children, while father hugs, utters rhymes and spends quality time with kids.

Perceptibly, there are several chores which are exclusively the domain of fathers, including being role models for sons. (Popenoe, 1996). Other blood relations such as grandfathers, maternal and paternal uncles, older brothers and also non-biological stepfathers can visibly contribute to children's wellbeing in parenting or quasi-parenting positions. Noticeably, a wide variety of family structures can complement and support productive family outcomes. (Silverstein and Auerbach, 1999, p.397.). Undoubtedly, emotional connection and credible caretaking relationship are the most vital variable in the promotion of positive child development. Genetic fathers and stepfathers can offer material assistance, encouragement and support for building confidence and discipline in children's everyday lives.

If the guy is unkind with her spouse and unable to meet her social and biological aspirations, she feels free to move on without prior warning lest he seeks violent revenge for rejection. The couple's relationship depends on mutual pleasure and happiness. However, middle-aged white men are more likely to lose their female partner for a shortage of spark and exhilaration in cherished cohabitation. The laws offer her safeguards and uphold her wishes with the provision of counselling and reconciliation. Ostensibly, ladies are in the driving seat leading the societal transformation of family life. Unsurprisingly, divorce rates in the Arab world have quadrupled. This augmentation is due to educated girls fighting for better treatment and equal rights. The Arab men are confounded and mystified by women, despite high living standards, demanding more social freedom and elimination of obedience. Paradoxically, European, American and Australian women enjoy complete freedom from male ascendancy and claim fare share in the parliament, local councils, managerial and executive positions in governmental and private organisations. They believe in intimacy and love and continue to strive for 100 per cent gender equality in all spheres of human activity, including piloting the commercial and air force planes.

In contemporary democratic societies, outmoded and conventional tactics of childrearing are no longer applicable. Orthodox harsh parenting practices says Amato & Fowler (2002), strictness, and constraining the expression of negative emotions (Schaefer & Bell, 1958) are not acceptable in the Western countries since they have changed to egalitarian styles of parenting. (Oppenheimer, 2004). Harsh parenting has an unhealthy impact on kids' development. (Baumrind, 1966). In 1990's

Swedish parents used punitive measures to discipline children. (Stattinet al.al 1995), but during the last two decades, they have adopted a moderate attitude towards adolescents. Research results indicate a dramatic increase in kindness and decrease in parents' directive control, and over time, parents permitted children to express annoyance towards them. Parents 'role transformed from stereotyped forms of fathers as decision-makers and mothers as caregivers to both parents sharing decisions and garnering respect from children. In Asian and African countries, parents claim compliance and use corporal punishment if necessary, to command respect from their children. Mothers are empathetic, but fathers do not hesitate to hit their children to discipline them. (Michael, 1987; Hosley & Montemayor, 1997) European societies are more relaxed and soft for children. (Galdin, 1978). Physical punishment is the hallmark of authoritarian parenting. (Baumrind, 1991). Parental directedness (Robinson et al. 1995) is a degree of control over children's behaviour.

Parental attitude, quality involvement, unruffled temperament, natural calmness, and investment of family time are some of the characteristics for raising happy kids. Blond, tall and slim Dutch mums hardly lose their calm, patiently listen and render fruitful support that makes the children the most comfortable in the world. Dutch mums are delightfully relaxed, lenient and indulgent, and hardly shout at the broods. Their social networks are relatively small, love privacy, prefer Dutch products and avoid lavishness in merriments. They are not fussy about branded items and seem careful about lushness, luxury, and the swapping of gifts at Birthday parties, bicentenaries, and Christmas events. Most functions involving children are well structured, held primarily at home with limited invitees. The UNICEF Report 2013 reinforced the research findings reported in the European Journal of Developmental Psychology that Dutch babies laugh and smile, infants are calm and sleep well. Dutch mums prioritise extremely well, work part-time and devote more time to the kids' wellbeing, comfort and emotional health. Fathers are equally conscious about the cheerfulness of their broods who enjoy paternal affection and attention at the long weekends since dads squeeze job commitment into 4-days a week. Building social skills takes precedence over academic achievements in other European parents.

Raising teenage boys and girls is a challenging experience for parents struggling to comprehend the intricacies of social media ventures. Connected nurturing relationship with carefree kids does not exist due to the web culture enticing young brains towards unexplored avenues. The bedroom privacy presents an escape route for the navigation of vulgarities and crudities. Parental unpretentious concern about the unrevealed and infinite use of technological devices may be justified, but intrusion in the brood's jurisdiction might cause argument and conflict. The sensitive parents want to impart the best training for building lives of teenagers to become worthy individuals. Abundant arguments favour a rigid style of grooming while other research scholars and sociologists support relaxed and liberal methods. Historically, commanding procedures were prevalent in many races across the globe owing to dependence on the breadwinner- usually a male head of the family. Obedience and respectfulness were child assets who relied on father for the fulfilment of basic needs such as food, shelter, learning and welfare. The state laws were stringent in Western countries where a 17-year old teenager got severely punished for stealing bread. Under British rule, he would be put on a ship to Australia to complete his sentence. Typical genuine households-imposed strictness for teenagers to be compliant without questioning parental authority.

Contemporary communication technologies have revolutionised the discernment of youth reaction to parental disciplinary benchmarks and moral touchstones. Interaction with the outside world cultivates freedom of thought, encourages self-belief and fosters openness in our present generation. Academic accomplishment is not the sole criteria to be successful in life; other avenues of creativity in which youth can outshine have proved to be more promising and praiseworthy. Arts education is merging with scientific subjects to promote artistic talents, and there is an overwhelming desire to convert STEM (Science, Technology, Engineering, and Mathematics) into STEAM (Science, Technology, Engineering, Arts, and Mathematics). Currently, 25000 lecturers and professors are teaching 'History of Arts' at a university level in the United States. School dropouts are valued members of Western societies, leaving an indelible impact as distinguished entrepreneurs, movie artists, imminent athletes, illustrious female designers, comedians and theatre performers. Knowledge co-construction strategies have transformed traditional teaching into shared learning benefiting all learners irrespective of economic, social and racial background. The classroom is not a monotonous hub but an experimental laboratory in which pupils contribute instrumental notions, present new initiatives and discuss topics for enhanced learning. Curiosity unfolds when kids ask questions requiring caringly envisaged explanations. They all join in the problem-solving rational discourse, learning along how mixed ability children equally derive benefit and gain knowledge.

Mums' role before and after school remains prominent for the cognitive and social development of her kids, permitting sufficient freedom and allowing arguing with them without compromising respectability and dignity. Conceding to teenagers' genuine demands for social activities with certain restraints but not yielding to undesirable blackmail seem to be a moderate parenting strategy. It is impracticable to employ any specific stratagem in all family structures at all times. Cultural norms, societal expectations, primordial thoughts and governmental policies have considerable influence on the applicability of parenting practices. In some

Even today, authoritative style is prevalent in Japanese, Singaporean and Cuban families where dependant kids are required to abide by stringent rules laid down by parents, grandparents and elder kinfolks. Paternal guidance is invaluable, but children must obey instructions with little room for negotiation and defiance is not stomached. Intellectual endeavours, scholarly pursuits and academic attainments are at the forefront of kids progress. Teenaged youth have far less time for recreational activities on account of a hectic educational schedule. Dedicated learners are the high achievers who gain expertise in financial, medical, engineering, technological and managerial disciplines, thus occupying lucrative high-pitched positions. The Harvard, Yale, London, Cambridge and Oxford produced enlightened youngsters guide the world in formulating economic, defence, social, political and administrative policies.

These academic achievers are in the minority, whereas a vast majority of youngsters do not bother to enter universities, adopting other options for building their lives. There is a fair proportion of youth who leave school without any formal qualifications but succeed in other fields. A few examples of notable individuals who abandoned schooling in their teens will suffice to elaborate this point. Jennifer Lawrence, an Oscar-winning actress, is a middle school dropout who struggled in early education but proved her acting skills in Hollywood. Hilary Swank, a talkative, cheerful girl was too cool for high school who did not like to follow the rules and yet again, gained prominence as Hollywood actress winning an Academy Award. Likewise, Christina Applegate quit high school, followed the footsteps of her parents, mum, an actress and dad, a recorder producer. She quickly achieved eminence in Hollywood movies as an actress and dancer, won Young Artist Award at the age of 17, and altogether 14 T.V. and film awards in her showbiz career. Christina was honoured twice with Grand Emmy Award first in 2004 and then in 2019. Ryan Gosling is a school dropout, pursued music and acting winning Golden Globe Award. Harry Styles, an English singer and actor, is also a high school dropout who is still operating in popular movies. Keanu Reeves, a Canadian actor, was expelled from a school of arts for being disorderly and boisterous, and as yet, gained many film awards.

About parental concern for childrearing, we turn back to the real problem of indiscipline and failure to obey rules. Two Iranian professors Fahimeh Niaraki and Hassan Rahimi (2013) at Farhangian University, Tehran researched by distributing questionnaires to 180 Iranian parents of high school teenagers. Research results showed authoritative style was more appropriate as compared to authoritarian and permissive modes of upbringing. Authoritative parenting indicated far better psychological health outcome. The researchers conceded that it was illogical to expect youngsters could meet adult standards of discipline overnight. It is a slow and smooth process surmounting newly emerging kids' social issues and tackling with sensitivity, serenity and sympathy. Under no circumstances should the parents lose calm, composure and serenity. Head-on confrontation with a child on any matter would complicate the situation. A liberal approach and a positive attitude can have a constructive effect on their perceptions. The kids' mental stability, sanity and rational wellbeing would be improved. They would become level-headed, exercise reason and logic to make a sound judgment. Such kids are not just reflective and prudent but show common sense in solving social issues. A study of "Baumrind's Parenting Typology" underpins this style as it has encouraging augmentation to explore invisible faculties of the adolescent. Open and free exchange of dialogue occurs between mums and kids who can comfortably raise controversial issues and receive an amenable response. The children do have reasonably high self-esteem. (Milevsky et al. 2007). Fathers are approachable and attentive listeners, receptive to children's candid needs. The role of parents is basically to sway, educate and control their kids while remaining supportive and responsive but not bowing to extravagant expectations. Diana Baumrind's "Classification 1971" categorises parenting styles into Control, Explanation, Matureness, Order and Nurturance, that leads to three main modes, namely authoritative, authoritarian, and permissive. However, pleasant and courteous home atmosphere portraying cordiality and kind-heartedness are admirable facets for rearing psychologically healthy children.

In the last century, well into the 1950s, authoritarian parenting was prevalent in Europe and the USA. Strangely, authoritarian style is still practised in African, Asian and some Latin America. Strict parents demand total obedience and frequently use corporal punishment, show little fondness and most render harsh treatment to their broods. In such families, says Diana Baumrind, (1991) kids are less cheerful and prone to anxiety, strain and nervousness. They are allowed minimal freedom to explore and experiment. The mum and dad hope of academic success are profoundly high, but communication lever is exceptionally stumpy. Their self-esteem is at the lower end of the scale (Rebecca et al., 2006; Martinez et al., 2007). Egyptian, Iranian and Asian fathers are authoritarian but mothers, mostly housewives, show kindness to their children. (Rudy & Grusec, 2006). A study involving 118 Vietnamese Australians and 120 Anglo-Australians of children between the ages of 11 to 18 years (Herz & Gullone, 1999) revealed that overprotectiveness caused lower self-esteem. A decade earlier, (Bunn et al., 1988) had studied 230 college teenage students and confirmed the fact that rigid parenting style adversely impacted self-esteem as it was directly proportional to the authoritative style of parenting.

The authoritarian parents give orders, impose directives, deny emotional openness and ensure strict enactment of rules without compassion. However, expectations are high, but parent-child communication is negligible, and while making a decision, fathers do not consider the needs of kids. Instead of paying attention to their necessities, parents prefer to smack and slap them. In Western democratic societies, the parental childrearing attitudes, perceptions and practices have significantly changed, and the teenagers are very confident in exercising judgment and making decisions.

Children are relatively independent and enjoy autonomy in permissive parenting. The parents are more thoughtful and less emotional, permitting kids to hold a conversation in a friendly manner. The parents are neither careless nor neglectful of kids' candid demands. Dictatorial parenting is impracticable, undesirable and unrealistic and detrimental to children's psychological, social and ethical health. Corporal punishment, including ear twisting, slapping or hitting with a bamboo, causes emotional and physical damage. It is counter-productive to adolescent's welfare, mental fitness and happiness. Today's open-minded and generous parents aspire to build a well-connected cherished relationship with their children capable of logical thinking, self-control, and exercising self-regulatory restraint.

Recreational Nurturing

Make learning fun for kids is a beautiful approach through recreational nurturing which conscientious parent should consider for their mental, social and physical health. The significance of frivolous outdoor undertakings has a unique value for the wellbeing of broods who, frequently find classroom attendance dull and dreary. In May 2016, the British government rolled out a programme entitled "Towards an Active Nation" accentuating usefulness of physical activity such as 'Walking for Leisure', Simple smooth walk has a powerful impact on youth mental and bodily wellbeing. For youngsters and small kids, walking is a thrill-seeking commotion and an exploration exercise in the desolate natural environment. It is a real amusement that allows them to inhale fresh air and enjoy freedom. A 20-minutes brisk walk is refreshing for the young mind as it improves fitness, reduces disquiet and uneasiness. Small children may not be able to cope with long walks, but shorter walks with a slow pace can inspire them to explore and learn. For instance, accompanying parents should make a list of items that might be discovered along the way and collected by the kids. These items might be- a feather, small pebble, red leaf, a bone, a cane, a silver coin, a chocolate wrapper and any unusual object. The child who finds the most get a reward, and the one who discovers a unique artefact, or relic also receives a present. This incentive would inspire the walkers to focus on finding designated items and fully enjoy even the longest walk.

It would be fascinating for kids to make them stop after now and then and ask them to turn over rocks, small logs, or a piece of bark to observe what is lurking underneath. They will be amazed to see spiders, worms, and woodlice galore and if you possess a magnifying glass, look closely and give a short talk about the biology of insects. Let the kids take photographs to discuss it later at home.

Apart from the above-cited parenting styles, the present writer would dare to bring in a recreational aspect of child's life generally ignored by the parents. On account of exceedingly high expectations for children, the focus is primarily on academic accomplishment. Parents, especially fathers, should set aside a few hours on alternative weekends to accompany teenagers for a country walk- a gigantic psychological health-boosting adventure so refreshing for mind and soul. Even the kids who despise classroom instruction and the school dropouts would greatly benefit from audacious walks of varying lengths in mountain country. The children as young as 7 or 8 years old could walk at a leisurely pace with their young mothers, appreciating beautiful sceneries along the way. Some of the walks are mostly wooded shore as is the case in Windermere (Lakeland, Lake District, England) where your kids can enjoy views across the lake to mountains. The woods are marvellous places to take children for a splendid walk to discover new things, observe stunningly spectacular views, touch beautiful plans and smell wildlife. The adolescents can freely move around, picking up a variety of objects along the way such as twigs, stems and pine cones. If they have a blank A4 paper, yap rubbing and foliage rubbing will fun for small kids. Under parental supervision, they can play hide and seek, climb trees, practice balancing knacks on dropped logs.

In the United Kingdom, there are government-developed walkways, cycleways and bridleways. In North Wales, Cwm Idwal, Lyn Idwal is world-famous for its rock formation, and a 3-mile walk is a challenge for the youth. Precipice Circular walk offers a fantastic view, pastures, lakeside. Pembrokeshire is well known for coastal walks and strolls in West Wales whereas South Wales; waterfalls appear fascinating at Sgwd Gwladus, river Pyrdalin plunging six meters to form the lady falls. In the North of

England, Lyme Park, Disley, Stockport is a 14-acre deer park with ample chance for walking and cycling.

Interestingly, the local council provides free bus service between Hazel Grove and Lyme Park. One may walk around the fantastic gardens and enjoy the sound of streams and fountains. There is a traditional Timber yard Café that sells on the premises made hot and cold snacks, soups and a wide variety of muffins, croissants and cupcakes. Equally tasty is the Earl Grey English tea and superbly prepared exceptional coffee and latte. Both in the Peak District and the Lake District are exquisite pathways through the woodlands. In Derbyshire, Peak District presents an excellent opportunity for rock climbing, a palpable activity for developing shared cohesion and collective solidarity.

In Scotland, Hillwalking, rambling and long-distance promenades are prevalent activities for youngsters. Adventure seekers take a captivating Glencoe, 16-miles route beginning from Fort William for mountaineering, skiing and cycling. Along these pathways, there are steep-sided Munros, bumpy tracks, jagged paths, typical slopes and delicate descents. Spring is the perfect time to visit Walberswik National Natural Reserve. This exciting walk is one for twitches with avocets, godwits, pintails and Wigeons among the sightings.

Community Initiatives

World-renowned food chains McDonald's and Costa apply creative ingenuities that inspire kids to enjoy delicious cuisine with their parents, especially at the weekends, and simultaneously secure book prizes and other gifts on offer. Chipmunk 52 stores across Australia, New Zealand and Indonesia, warmly welcome children under 11 at indoor lavishly laid out play areas including safe and broader space for parents to hold kids' birthday parties. Book Trust U.K. gives away five million books free to babies and young children every year. In 2012, McDonald's allied with British publisher HarperCollins to produce child-centred books aimed explicitly at pubescents aged three and above. Michael Morpurgo's nine million copies of free distribution inspired kids to enjoy reading. Its Happy Meals strategy is to stimulate kids' interest in books and reading because 'Reading is for Everyone'. Many parents either cannot afford or do not have the desire to visit libraries or bookshops. Until recently, a Happy Kids Meal pack received by children at McDonald's contains a book and a toy to take home. McDonald, all famous food chain celebrated its 40th anniversary in 2019 and re-released some of its popular toys, e.g., Ty Beanie Babies, Patti, the Platypus and Tamagotchi.

COSTA Foundation is one of the most remarkable private enterprises in the Western world, extending its charitable ambitions to the African, Central American, and many other countries across the globe. Beginning in 2006, it fastidiously assumed the task of supporting remotely located coffee-growing communities in countries such as Columbia, Costa Rica, Ethiopia, Guatemala, Honduras, Peru, Uganda, and Vietnam. Costa has transformed 85,000 lives, 600 classrooms, and eighty-four schools in ten countries located in three continents. During the last fourteen years (until September 2020), it has forged partnerships with the Plan International U.K., Imagine 1Day and many other charitable volunteer organisation. Costa Foundation enthusiastically dispenses extracurricular ingenuities that terrifically augment gender fairness and eco-friendly awareness. Among the earliest creativities, it introduced the very first project at Awash Kolati Primary School in close collaboration with the Imagine! Day in Ethiopia that was subsequently extended to other institutes of learning, e.g. Bule High, Haru High, Churso High, and Mesay Kassaye Dano High School. From the outset, Costa has provided resources for the provision of clean water, fresh vegetable, and fruits for improving health and hygienic conditions of people. The emphasis is placed on sanitisation and pollution-free atmosphere in which children attend schools, participate in the play-to-learn games. Pupils receive free sports equipment to keep and re-use for practising in the playground. The nurses regularly carry out health checks at schools and administer appropriate First-aid on-the-spot treatment to reduce infections and sustain pupil health.

Costa, on the other hand, allocates a space mounting on the wall, eye-catching posters, pictures and placards inviting parents' attention towards child-led local community events and educational programmes to promote learning. Sainsbury is a familiar name among the top few British market with a large number of vast stores across the United Kingdom. Getting kids reading is one of the many social initiatives opening Reading Corners in several supermarket locations. Famous kids' authors such as Tom Percival, Rosie Greening and Joe Berger personally attend the World Book Day to read to children. Sainsbury, a Make-Believe Stimulator, is committed to raising literacy levels in younger children. Other ventures aimed at improving reading capabilities share the same goals, such as 'Read On' and "Vision for Literacy Campaign". Save the Children charity participates and supports children reading well at the age of eleven, an achievable target by 2025.

IKEA is a Scandinavian chain across the globe, and each jumbo store has a "Smaland" (crèche), a purpose-built play area where children can feel the Swedish forest atmosphere. They are fully supervised freely by expert staff, while they paint, draw pictures, jump or read books. A vital opportunity for kids to be creative and imaginative for satisfying their sense of curiosity while parents go further into the store for browsing and shopping. The tools include crayons, colours, papers, cardboards, beads, adhesive tape and writing paper at no cost. The kids can demonstrate artistic ability, express creativity and draw pictures. Brood between 4 to 10 years old is not allowed to use the play area. The real incentive is the food at reasonable prices for adults and minors. Freshly prepared Delicious items include Swedish meatballs, cinnamon bun, pastries, desserts, cookies and frozen yoghurt.

Fathers are as essential components of adolescent nurturing as much as caring mothers who infuse cheer in their lives. If dad applauds the offspring for attainment, mum permeates a sense of awareness and permits freedom of action and choice of friends. Paternal optimism inculcates confidence and boosts kids' self-esteem through interpersonal interaction, open dialogue and understanding. Maternal connection with daughters should be two-fold, respecting their wishes with friendly correlations and safeguarding their innocence with a compassionate approach. A watchful eye on classmates and school friends, and knowledge of their family background may reduce chances of adrift among children. Single mothers or stepfathers, mums in partnership and biological dads, they have to bear the responsibility of upbringing adolescents that demands a degree of self-sacrifice, altruism and selflessness. Our youth are the seekers of knowledge, hopes of destitute, builders of economies, guarantors of prosperity and sponsors of peace in the world around us. What intellectuals and thinkers will sow today; future generations will reap tomorrow?

CHAPTER III

THE POWER OF SOCIAL MEDIA

Powerful social media is a blessing in disguise, or a harmful medium for the young cohort is debatable. Socialisation channel or a learning hub, it has considerable sway on the acuities and beliefs of adolescents. Almost all juveniles believe in complete freedom, total independence and unrestricted, unsupervised access to the cyberspace. Whatever the nature of media influence may be, digital awareness education for youth wellness is not only crucial but also a learning necessity.

It is imperative to comprehend youth activities on social media websites to understand the inherent dynamics that contribute to the emotional, physical and mental health of teenagers. The intensity of use, time duration on the web, frequency of cyber utilisation and the level of youth social involvement for exploration and experimentation would determine the degree of impact on the wellbeing of youngsters. A cursory glance on some of the most popular websites along with youth activities would divulge the tricks and deceits affecting modern societies and contemporary mind-sets in a world of ever-changing technologies. Nonetheless, convictions and beliefs have been replaced by human-made rules and regulations guaranteeing infinite freedom of expression and the fortification of human rights. The misuse of social media entails unreasonable exploitation of autonomy, the selfish benefit of obscurity and egocentric advantage of anonymity. Youth health protection is paramount for a prosperous, peaceful and thriving world. Although some states and non-governmental organisations are formulating laws and implementing regulations for the positive, productive and restricted and selective use of social media websites, a lot more needs to be done by the community associations, faith organisations and educational institutions. In addition to explaining the intricacies of website operations, the youth should be enlightened about the cyber laws and cyber safety regulations for safeguarding personal privacy, emotional dignity and self-esteem.

In the world of robust, vigorous and enormous competition for tempting and seducing the cyber consumers, the number of end-users, marketing strategies and effectiveness of the websites determine the popularity. For instance, *Facebook* (est.2004) boasts over 1.59 billion monthly active users. It is a significant medium for youth connectivity in addition to extortionate utilisation by a colossal number of businesses for the promotion of their products and services. *Twitter* (est.2006) based at San Francisco, California, offers an internet platform to more than 320 million monthly users and acts as an interaction model of business communities. Initially, Jack Dorsey started working at home in the evenings and at weekends on SMS base communication platform and then put forward his design to Evan Williams and his friend Biz Stone. It has a user-driven functionality in the shape of retweets. Reid Hoffman launched *LinkedIn* on May 5, 2003 (founded on December 14, 2002) long before the establishment of some eminent social media sites. Four hundred million registered followers have corroborated its usefulness for networking. The multilingual 24-languages service to the end-user worldwide makes it the most functional medium. Another universally renowned website *Google* was inaugurated on December 15, 2011, swiftly joining the high-performing social media networks, singularly attracting five million customers around the globe. The owners, however, had already acquired *YouTube* in November 2006 for $1.65 billion, which is an efficient search engine comprising digital bulletin boards. PayPal employees created this site in February 2005, now claims to have one billion users each month. There is an obsession for girls to post videos of themselves soliciting viewers' opinion about prettiness. The girls typically formulate self-image based on feedback that may or may not be the accurate reflection of their personality. Popularity seeking conduct can be misused by a grown-up stranger to seduce a teenage female with praiseworthy tweets and colourful sycophancy remarks. The kids are thrilled with appreciative feedback but get stressed on account of critical reaction. Sexualised body images of girls who post selfies can encourage paedophiles to take advantage of female innocence.

Some girls on the social media unconsciously criticise their physical features, height and weight, offering respondents a chance to post depressing comments. Others face sexual exploitation at the hands of evil-minded individuals who appraise pornographic images on the net. Several websites operated by compassionate, selfless and dedicated ladies are a source of consolation.

Famous Hollywood actress Geena Davies who made a fantastic film "Thelma & Louise" in 1991, has created "Geena Davis Institute on Gender in the Media" to promote a realistic image of women and girls. She tweeted on 29 September 2019, that 'the lives of women and girls are at stake' and social media must do more to recognise the role of women as leaders, managers and equally brilliant partners as men in many emerging fields of technological development. The girls should also promote their image of what are they capable of achieving rather than how pretty they look? The girls must not become slaves of technology and mere objects of beauty. An American lady Jennifer Siebel Newsom founded "The Representation Project" for combating wrongful portrayal of young girls that their value lies in youthfulness, beauty, and sexuality. Under this project, Jennifer launched some online hashtag platforms such as hashtag 'Askhermore' which inspires ladies to call out sexist reporting. In a similar Hashtag 'SmartsGirlsAsk' the girls ask the companies to achieve gender fairness and parity and not to objectify women as erotic objects and advertisement symbols.

Similarly, *Instagram* commenced operations in October 2010 with 400 million clients, and *Pinterest* came into the competition in March 2010 and later, Facebook acquired it (formerly FaceMash).

In February 2007, David Karp founded Tumblr targeting youth for sharing photos, videos, audios and permitting re-blogging activity for a large number of contents. Interestingly, variety and more extensive choices make it a fascinating medium of social divulgence. Equally, captivating is an online image and video hosting site *Flicker* (created in February 2004) now owned by Yahoo which is used by millions of youngsters internationally. It has customers in 63 countries who freely share photos, images, metaphors and smiles. A brainchild of roommates Alexis Ohanian and Steve Huffman of the University of Virginia, USA, is called *Reddit*, developed and presented on June 23, 2005, as a merrymaking dissipation, presumably for the college students rather than the general public. The recreational orientation of this social media site attracted both male and female teenagers in more significant number, connecting around 300 million monthly visitors. Correspondingly, three Stanford University students Reggie Brown, Evan Spiegel and Bobby Murphy launched *Snapchat* in September 2011, enticing over one million social media patrons in a short space of time. Most stupendous, likeable and highly operational website is *WhatsApp*, an instant messaging platform used regularly by one billion individuals globally.

Charlie Cheever and Adam D'Angelo while working for *Facebook*, intuitively devised an idea of creating a youth-friendly question-and-answer social website called *Quora*, founded in June 2009, which serves 100 million users. In June 2012, a video-sharing website *Vine* was presented, soon taken over by all-famous *Twitter*. In the course of rapid cyberspace innovations, there appeared in March 2015, *Periscope*, a video streaming social networking platform developed by Joe Bernstein and Kayvon Beykpour. Another social media site *BigSugar* (founded 2007) allows users to share videos, mount podcast, articles and blogging. There is *Delicious* (est. 2003) online podium that offers services for preserving and sharing bookmarks, claiming 180 million URLs.

Among the educational sites is a compulsive browser and reader called *Digg* (Est, November 2004) online site which chooses absorbing narratives and exciting anecdotes for the viewers. Moreover, a user-friendly internet app meant for mobile devices is *Viber* (est. December 2010). Its spontaneous success lies in its widespread use by 600 million registered clients. A search engine *StumbleUpon* came into the market in June 2018 for informational and merriment purposes. This online hub has moved onto *MIX* that displays contents chosen by like-minded youngsters. For instance, it conveys knowledge-oriented stories such as:

Internet Posts from:

SMITHSONIANMAG.COM

1) Could a rusty bridge generate electricity?

2) Drinking tea was once considered an irresponsible, reckless pursuit for women.

3) Drivers encounter a human-size jellyfish off the coast of England.

4) Americans are among the most stressed-out people in the world.

5) A summer hailstorm buried the Mexican city of Guadalajara under the ice.

6) The farm boy who invented television.

7) People have been using big data since the 1600s.

WELLANDGOOD.COM - Real talk: how much sugar should a healthy person eat in a day?

NYTIMES.COM - Summer in the city is hot, but some neighbourhoods suffer more.

NEW YORKER. COM - The changing climate inside the world's largest bat colony.

How social media shapes our identity?

FATHERLY.COM - Cooking with pre-schoolers.

FASTCOMPANY.COM - How successful people make decisions differently?

OZ.COM - Why does it still take six hours to fly across the US?

WIRED.COM - Here is what space looks like to the human eye.

The simplest method of making a connection with anyone is posting a mawkish and overemotional message on a social website or submitting an intriguing sugary communication that would tempt the innocent victim to respond. Naturally, social media online have given the perpetrator a sounder and sturdier path for bullying potential prey by quickly becoming a friend. In the case of female contact, the chances of harassment are apparent. Instant messaging is a perpetual nuisance since it has the prospect of chasing an innocent girl from school to her home. Tokunaga (2010) has provided an eye-opening picture of how teenagers are affected when followed from home to school. Mckenna and Bargh (1999) have studied the socio-psychological side of impact on the victims, whereas Gross et al. (2002) have focused on the safety and welfare of adolescents. Juvonen and Gross have vibrantly documented several notable and excruciating experiences of school kids (2008). Emotional disturbance is a cause for great concern (Cowie, 2013) as it lowers self-esteem, perturbs conduct and lowers the morale of the victim. (O'Moore & Kirkham, 2001). Many parents have long realised their kids' uneasiness at home and consistently raised a concern about the consequences of cyberbullying. (Dehue et al., 2008).

Generally, youth from affluent families are less inclined to pursue scientific, technical and medical education which can be tedious due to long years of dedicated studies. Most affluent people in developing economies enumerate social status and living standard through profiteering, wealth accumulation, huge bungalows, and luxury fleet of cars. Consequently, the youngsters enjoying their superior status, tend to relish the opulent lifestyle and explore all channels of societal gratifications. They turn to social media websites to satisfy their growing appetite for fun and amusement. On the contrary, Social media also teaches high school students the art of learning to learn, improve academic grades, seek admission to rewarding occupations, raise standards of living for a better future. Nonetheless, the teenagers entering colleges feel the freedom of choice, socialisation autonomy and free from parental time-management restrictions as was the case in school days. Here, an individual can enjoy life, intermingle with college mates, fraternise with new chums, discover unknown avenues of the social set up and forge sensually indulging attachments. Within the college atmosphere, there are some study-focused souls, determined to gain knowledge and climb the intellectual ladder for making a positive contribution to society. As yet, pleasure-seekers are bored with exhaustive learning and use the whole time in experimentation and amusement. So, a vast majority of youth find solace from boredom and relief from strenuous studies through the 24 hours a day and 7-days a week available social media platform. On the positive side, social cyberspace is heaven for isolated and secluded youth who can communicate to form amicable friendships. On the negative side, online connectivity carries many ills leading to cyberstalking, bullying and intimidation of innocent teenagers that sometimes results in suicides, depression and frustration.

Teenagers Behaviour & Perceptions

It is a demanding task to prepare teenagers capable of surmounting snags, dealing justly, behaving judiciously and meeting the challenges with resilience in their teen years. Teachers need to impart precise training at school and the parents to provide friendly atmosphere at home for the accomplishment of noble goal. Protecting victims of bullying is as significant as the prevention of bullying in the society to restore confidence, self-respect and self-esteem. Surveys and quantitative studies do matter, but informal intermittent communication with students, teachers and parents disclose valuable information. Observations of teenage behaviour beyond the school walls offer thought-provoking evidence of their attitudes and manners.

Based on qualitative, observational, retrospective and reflective research related to social status, social classes, and social perceptions of youngsters, an attentive theme emerges. It Indicates that cerebral, psychological, spiritual, ethical and ideological characteristics have substantial clout on the human mind, temperament and disposition. The youth frame of mind is the mirror of their behaviour, individualism, egotism and empathy. The tendency of dealing justly, fairly and equitably with friends and acquaintances is the result of the domestic and social environment. The habits of self-importance and arrogance stem from the desire to dominate, overshadow and control class fellows and schoolmates. Bullying for a proud young teenager is an amusement and hilarity without due regard to the feelings of others. Once bullying bludgeon is released unchecked, snowballing takes the roots and begins to damage the inner fabrics of the school atmosphere. The emotions are the replication of personal temperament, proneness to do good or the propensity to inflict harm.

About the social class structure, the people in the poverty table are unlikely to protest against the economic oppression and more likely to accept the imposed injustices of the system in democratic societies. The individuals or groups may grumble but feel helpless in uplifting the socio-economic conditions. Mostly, ethnic minorities and third-generation immigrants in Europe, USA, Australia and Canada are comparatively low in social status. Some brilliant kids do attempt to compete with bright indigenous youth in the fields of High-Tec, Medicine, Engineering, accountancy and other scientific professions. For the labour classes, including both the native and immigrant populations, the problems of housing, health, jobs and living standards are not dissimilar. Globally, the economic conditions continue to impact the behaviour, character and habits of the youth population. Family, societal and monetary settings influence the feelings and manners of youth and their interpersonal relations in schools and local surroundings. The modes of the upbringing of upper-class kids make them better-behaved and conservative in their approach towards others. It does not necessarily mean all are disciplined and not spoiled due to lavish and luxurious flair of living. It is a proven fact that some gifted children belong to the poor working class, yet still, they excel in their chosen field of academic interest. They are equally genius and talented, but many cannot climb the higher education ladder on account of stringent financial resources.

Youngsters from the middle-classes and upper middle-classes achieve better, educationally in schools and universities and manage to secure professionally rewarding occupations. Aries and Seider (2007) found that affluent students were mindful of the educational benefits which they enjoyed due to monetary standing in the society. Manifestly, economically better off youth fared well in school and pursued higher studies to attain professional qualifications. In UK grammar school, 11+ test for admission open to all social classes attracts able and determined youth of both wealthy white and ethnic minority communities. Conversely, economically disadvantaged youth are denied the chance of entering universities and thus, fail to get worthwhile employment in any field of socially significant.

When we talk about attitudes, kindness is an attribute of lower classes, narrates Piff et al. (2010) since they seem to be inclined to help others than upper-class counterparts. Concerning democratic values, lower-class people appeared to be generous and willing to contribute funds in charitable pursuits. (Van Lang, De Bruin, Otten, Joireman, 1997) Widening the gap between rich and the poor has enhanced youth frustration in European societies despite genuine state initiatives to reduce inequalities, increase job opportunities, and promote living conditions for the deprived communities. David Lockwood (1960) argued at the time that the "extreme poverty produced a way of life that was not by necessity shared by other sections of the working class who were wealthier". Presumably, skilled workers in the spheres of engineering and construction managed to earn more than the ordinary labourers. His views on administrative, clerical staff in England were unique, as he maintained that they suffered from false consciousness for not aligning with working classes. (Lockwood, 1958) They found it insulting to join the all famous Trade and General Workers Union U.K.

Even in European countries, second-generation immigrants have varied hopes and involvements compared to their parents. The colour of the skin is not the only issue in social class disparities; the white immigrants such as Turkish communities in the Netherlands and Germany face difficulties. Candidly speaking, from the Netherlands to Switzerland where white Turkish people reside mostly in urban housing units, vacated by white flight to up-market neighbourhoods, anti-immigrant sentiments also exist in prosperous native white areas without sizeable immigrant communities. (Daneygier, Rafaela M, 2013, pp1-2). This resentment is the result of socio-economic imbalance, reduced job opportunities and slowing down economies of European countries.

However, in those days, demand for manual labour was very high when in 1965, the Vauxhall factory in Luton, England, offered £5 reward to their employees for bringing in a recruit to work in the company. (Devine, 1992, p.9). In the early 1960s, "keeping yourself to yourself" and being decent rather than bumpy were vital traits of the weekly waged class lifestyles. Goldthorpe and

Lockwood felt that the division between manual and non-manual workers and their families was evident in terms of housing, relations with neighbours, friendship groups and involvement in associations. (1963, p.142). They also described the weakening of standard forms of class consciousness and class behaviour within the local community. (Goldthorpe & Lockwood, 1963, p.157). From 1970 onwards, the need for factory labour declined due to closure of textile and other manufacturing factories in the United Kingdom. For instance, the car production stopped at Vauxhall, and the plant was closed in 2002. In South Reddish, Stockport, a cotton factory Spur Doubling Mill in which the present writer worked as a spinner in 1969). The factory closed permanently in early 1972, and the vast building demolished. Until recently, new low-paid occupations have emerged such as care workers, social workers, cleaners, fast food home delivery personnel, leaflet distributors, restaurant waiters and waitresses, school dinner ladies, cooks, domestic helpers, cherry pickers and gardeners. The situation is not much different in other industrialised countries concerning the jobs for the lower middle classes. Online shopping trend has developed a new type of workforce, ensuring next-day parcel delivery. They use cars, vans and trucks to efficiently supply the packed products to every household at the doorsteps.

In the past two decades, millions of people from East European countries such as Romania, Poland, Latvia, Check Republic, Slovenia, Estonia, Lithuania and Portugal have entered the United Kingdom with their European

Union Passports. The White English native population have been affected due to long waiting times for doctors and hospital appointments, housing shortage, school admissions and employment. Many skilled and semi-skilled jobs have been taken over by the wave of new EU settlers. It was the economic set back that caused Brexit in which White British native population overwhelmingly voted to leave the European Union.

In the last century, begging was non-existent in Great Britain. Yet, during the previous fifteen years, the present writers' observations in the course of travelling around UK cities, are a clear testimony of the proliferation of widespread begging. You can notice White East European beggars at coach stations, railway stations, petrol stations, car parks, traffic lights, outside huge supermarkets such as Tesco, Asda, LD, Liddle, Morrison, Marks and Spencer, cash machines, McDonald's and on the footpaths asking for "change please". Even a typical occupation has emerged as some of them nick shopping trollies from supermarkets and walk around the affluent housing estates picking up metal pieces, electrical items, household accessories. Some even have vans looking for furniture, fridges, and TV's left outside the properties.

Unsurprisingly, the migration of white Europeans to more prosperous lands such as USA, Canada, Australia and New Zealand has never been a contentious subject for the sociologist, economists and research scholars. For example, between 1870 and 1914, the period of Great Transatlantic Migration, 14 million Italians left Italy for the

United States and happily settled in Chicago, New York, Boston, Texas and Washington DC. Some of them are traditional Catholics, attend churches regularly, others are secular in their outlook. They work, study, gain employment, get married and lead respectable lives. Regrettably, controversies erupt when the Western intellectuals, research scholars and sociologist professors discuss the migration of Asians, Arabs and African into European countries and the USA or Canada. No matter how much these 1st, 2nd and 3rd generation immigrants contribute through highest academic achievements, unstinted hard work and total dedication to uplift the Western economies, they are considered foreigners and ethnic minorities.

Currently, class origins are more significant than the ethnic heritages on account of political, social and demographic changes occurring in the industrialised economies. In short, the communities that make a difference in promoting the fiscal conditions of the European states are well respected because they work hard, achieve excellence in demanding fields and make a positive input in the society. Understandably, the lethargic lot belonging to any race, sect, belief or nation face diverse socio-economic problems. The welfare states have to cater to their needs as well by creating training opportunities following their abilities, faculties and skills.

Digital Awareness Education

Understanding of meaningful safety measures and online user cognizance are fundamental to the thoughtful navigation of social media sites. The schools are on the forefront of digital awareness education through classroom instructions and experimentation, lesson plans and curriculum development. Selective dissemination of digital awareness information for parents and youngsters is the responsibility of local, national and international bodies, albeit schools can make a substantial contribution to the promotion of cyber mindfulness. The activities in schools may involve cyber-safety workshops, monthly seminars, weekly discussions about the adverse effects of bullying and open debates on the challenges of recreational media. Many different configurations of bullying take place in a wide variety of manifestations, leaving a detrimental effect on the individual, hurting feelings and devastating emotions. The harm is cosmic that stupendously shatters self-esteem, minimises self-confidence, increases vulnerability and undermines morality. The teenagers are not mature enough to intuitionally realise the impending sensitivities of cyberspace operations. Educational awareness for youth has become a top priority for several social media websites. Instagram with "Hashtag Awkward Years Campaign" and 'Hashtag Stop bullying on Twitter' has taken the initiative to curb an endemic of online abuse. Boys ostentatiously use indecent words, rude language, and vulgar phrases to intimidate girls who suffer in silence, affecting their educational focus and progress.

Germany is the most susceptible country in the European Union with constant and prolonged internet access and high-tech digital devices in households. (Feng et al. 2017). The government has, therefore, enhanced online safety through several digital education programmes such as "Medienpass NRW". It develops internet literacy and augments the use of social media websites. (Kammerl & Hasebrink, 2013). While on online devices, the social domain of small children remains exposed without the know-how of consequences. In many instances, the adolescents leave the Media website profile public, innocently unaware of the magnitude of risk, problems and coping strategies. (Livingston & Helsper, 2017) and as a result, unknowingly suffer chat room victimisation. (Katzer et al. 2009). Many developing countries are unable to use cyber technologies for financial reasons, and even the literacy rate in some states is deplorable. Social and digital media infiltration has negative consequences because falcons have the tools to follow cyber victims. The virtual chase penetrates the preys everywhere ranging from private apartments, supermarkets, libraries to hostels and shared digs. It turns the lifestyle of especially young girls into a living hell. The gullible girls should be aware of the significance of 'mother and daughter relationship' in dealing with cyber strangers either by blocking the site or interfering with an effective response to hurtful text and threatening message. Safeguarding passwords is a precautionary measure to avoid the commotion of privacy.

In Singapore, "Unmute Daniel" digital awareness movement has been very successful, advising teenagers to open the Shazam app (2018) on their smartphones. It presents real-life scenarios and instruction for teachers, parent and kids. The bullies using digital resources for defamatory statements, scandal-mongering assertions, and malicious expressions are cybercrimes in Singapore. (Willingham, Catherine, 2018). Equally unlawful are conspicuous text messages that make the recipients endure psychic lowness and fragility.

Given adolescent welfare, Netherland government has established Safer Internet Centre and allocate three full working days each year for scholarly debates, research presentations, police law enforcement reports and interactive workshop for teachers. They have a free online teaching programme about the digital world for primary and secondary education. They have developed a cross-media game for the classroom and to be used at home in which topics cover information skills, virtual reality, online behaviour and imaging. Also, Veiliginternetten and Bureau Jeugd en Media have produced animated videos about sexting for parents and teachers to be knowledgeable and be prepared to deal with this sensitive issue. Likewise, Singapore Ministry of Education has launched an all-inclusive cyber Wellness programme for the security and reassurance of internet users. They must use common sense to pinpoint online risks, evaluate and reflect on the cyber behaviour and act appropriately to protect themselves. They implement thoughtfully designed and carefully prepared curriculum in all schools across Singapore. Indeed, bullies have to learn to live with the past that continues to chase them after positively changed perceptions. The classmates sporadically call their names online for a long time. Although cyber

protection mechanism implemented by concerned stakeholders do reduce online bullying. A 15-year old girl stayed for a month at a rehabilitation centre in Singapore, but weekly counselling sessions helped her recuperate and salvage the admirable image. Before her psychotherapy treatment, the girl faced predicament online for no less than three years, says Dr Carol Balhetchet of Singapore Children's Society. She tweeted afterwards that old school mates called her reprehensible names and posted messages "Don't befriend with that hooligan" She simply ignored all the unpleasant communication and got on with her life, building new relationships.
[https://www.asiaone.com/health/cyberbullying-rise-among-children]

Undue flattery of female physical features is nothing more than a fantasy and illusion, and this kind of online behaviour entices innocent girls into emotional and excitable cyber acts. Digital contamination taints the tender-hearted unblemished brainpower of adolescents. Digital alertness will augment consciousness for a pristine mind to resist the temptation and challenges of social media. Bully's vulgar phrasing, on the net, causes embarrassment with demeaning tweets and indecent words. Foul-mouthed utterances are common in cyberbullying that can cause annoyance and resentment and instigate an embroiled reaction from the victim. You must remember that bullies are quite frequently victims of bullying themselves, says, Cecile Swart who runs a campaign at Riverside College, Cape Town, South Africa.

Digital platforms are used for harassment, leaving no trace of the scoundrel, and it is difficult to detect, impermeable to investigate and exceedingly arduous to track the rascal. The social media initiatives for digital safety awareness projects involving parents, community leaders and educators can produce tangible results. It would improve know-how, amplify victim perspectives and invigorate the voice of silent souls.

Pernicious social media appears to be increasingly more inimical for teen girls than boys owing to several unfavourable stimuli which causes sleep disorder. Many innocent website addicts are potential targets for bullies with vindictive nature and malicious intentions. The British youth make perpetual use of cell phones and other social media platforms for exchanging messages, sending photos and sharing toxic, sinister and malignant contents. The seductive and tantalising dialogue between male and female teens allures inexperienced girls who fall prey to the astute stalkers. In the United Kingdom, parents have the facility of accessing "Stopbullying.gov", a solicitously envisaged website to oversee teens' digital undertakings by the family members. Advisory service is available to preclude cyberbullying incidents and retrench the undesirable use of kids' internet practices. The UK Safer Internet Centre was set up in 1995 to give voice and advice to parents, teachers and children, empowering them to make better use of the internet. It has two partners, namely Childnet International, Internet Watch Foundation and SWGIL. It is one of the 31 Safer Internet Centres in the European Union. They have an anonymous helpline to report child sexual abuse, obnoxious imagery and objectionable videos. The Childnet hold competitions at various venues to raise awareness of positive internet use. For instance, on 2 July 2019, Film competition was held entitled "Future of the Internet". The top two documentaries showed thoughtful messaging, displaying kindness and supporting diversity. [https://www.betterinternetforkids.eu/web/portal/pract ice/awareness/detail?=4823954]

Latvia is one of the highly affected countries in which children fall victim to cyber assaults, physical and verbal bullying in educational institutes. Every third child faces bullying in schools, 37 per cent admit unpleasant experience in classrooms, and one fifth concedes that bullying occurred online. [https://nekluse.lv/wp-content/uploads/2019/07/survey-about-bullying].
Latvian Safer Internet Centre has established a hub to stem the wave of bullying through [Hashtag Nekluse.lv] social project raising awareness of parents and teachers within the framework of Globally Shapers Riga Hub. [http"//www.globalshapersriga.com]. Unfortunately, the non-stop online presence harms the biological needs of boys and girls. For example, ninety-nine per cent of U.S. boys age 2-17 years and 94 per cent of girls regularly play video games and are at the great menace of developing an addiction. (Sentile et al. 2017). As early as 1998, Kraut et al. had raised the alarm about the disproportionate use of social media and its adverse impact on the emotional health of the young population. They predicted that the internet could change the lives of people as television had

done in the 1950s and 1960s. They measured the psychological impact of 169 internet users and discovered that communication within the family members had decreased and social relationships declined. However, the latest U.S. SMART Act, i.e. Social Media Addiction Reduction Technology would compel media organisations to adopt practical measures for the substantial reduction of risks concerning 'internet addiction and psychological exploitation'. (No more Snapstreaks and Autoplay, BBC 10 Sep.2019)

Although parents should not shy off passing cyber literacy skills to their progeny, the classroom teachers and the school librarians should short digital learning workshops as part of 'Learning to Learn" extracurricular activities. These extramural illustrated talks supported by videos will generate youth interest in furthering the knowledge of dealing with online risks and digital ability to deactivate fake and simulated accounts. The kids must not download a virus on their device by clicking on the wrong flicker or a commercial enticement. Also, unsafe is the posting of exposed selfies and attention-seeking portraits on the web, which can be maliciously accessed by evil-minded individuals and then, passed on to friends and foes in the school and beyond.

Youth enlightenment programmes are specifically developed for kids in Australia through the multiple websites and yearly held National Day of Action since 2010. On 15 March 2019, the Australian Prime Minister conveyed a message to the nation, loud and clear that

"Bullying is not O.K." because over 2.4 million teenagers attend 5,726 schools, and one in five has experienced some sort of bullying. Students and parents receive instructions to access particular websites to enhance awareness and increase their knowledge of online technologies. The online sites include:

www.bullyinggoaway.gov.au.; www.esafety.gov.au.; www.studentwellbeinghub. Edu.au.; www.beyou.edu.au.; www.relationships.org.au/what-we-do/research/online-survey/march-2018-bullying-in-schools.

Cyber technology, cell phones and digital media have ripped human values apart, robbed privacy, infiltrated homes, permeated youth dreams, saturated personal relationships and shattered time-management schedules. Cyber addiction has surpassed all boundaries and superseded drug addiction, binge drinking and a substantial number of supports. The Kids have lost paternal touch, detaching sentimentally from caring and affectionate family members and seeking refuge in social media sites for photo sharing, dialogue exchange and fruitless rivalry and antagonism that leads to bullying. Time is ripe to stem the tide of a digital technological revolution with the spread of digital knowledge to save the moral, social and psychological wellness of present and future generations.

Online Learning Tools

We are living in a less prognostic world in which parents have to invest productively in kids' infanthood, putting in place appropriate safeguard against instantaneous threats to their wellbeing. We should plan ahead for any unexpected incidents which might perturb kids' advance towards tangibly and emotionally healthy maturity. Social networks are part and parcel of our lives which are heavily used mediums among all segments of a society. These online networks are not going to disappear in the foreseeable future and therefore, we have to accept social media culture in its existing form. We should be prepared to embrace new innovations which might be in the pipeline as inventors and media owners are competing with each other to acquire bigger share of the world market. What matters is the productive use of websites by our children? Imposing ban, applying censorship and snooping or taking away digital devices would not do any good, it might inflict more harm, mistrust and qualm within a happy family. Although, many parents in both the industrialised states and third world countries do permit youngsters to keep smartphone at all times, some of them do try to check the contents and the modes of texting which is considered a sheer violation of privacy. Senior family members whether mum, brother or elder sisters keep an eye on the cyber activities of young girls. They want to prevent unpredictable harassment and cyber intimidation by checking kid's phones. The social media websites such as Google, Facebook, Instagram, Twitter and many other newly created sites have system in place to protect user's privacy through encryption. But such encryption makes it impossible for both parents and law enforcement officials to get access to child predators digital communication. End-to-end encryption scrambles messages in such a way that they can be deciphered only by the sender and the intended recipient. In the latest mobile technology developments, encryption is a very impressive digital tool for tenable privacy and ensures concealment of text messaging.

Social media is a way to advocate and enhance kids' learning and discussing school projects. Many valuable subjects are posted on the web such as health information as children can learn how to protect themselves from certain diseases. What suitable measures should be taken to maintain good health and what protective and medically tested products are available in the market? The kids can express online their opinions on delicate topics of health and safety, ailments and infections. They can put forward their viewpoint about cyber violence, physical viciousness and drug abuse. They can openly raise concerns about use of weapons in school shootings, possession of lethal firearms and related matters. The teenagers can cooperatively voice serious anxieties about gun control regulations. They can mount on the net personal photos and creative pieces of writing, literary expressions and interesting proverbs. Some youngsters can use imagination to transmit decent self-composed poems to convey messages of lasting value. Both boys and teenage girls can use ingenuity in the composition of beautiful verses reflecting social aspects of everyday life. They can engage in productive conversation with like-minded schoolmates and can actively participate in live chats online about morality, values and traditions. They can discuss rules and regulations that impact feelings about certain restrictions. Social media can be used to form pressure groups who can daringly debate environmental issues impacting humanity. They can lobby politicians and government officials and ask them to ensure child safety from paedophiles and evil-minded individuals. There are many websites who are well known for educational endeavours and specifically help kids to hone their skills in mathematics and pure sciences. These educational programmes reach out to teenagers. Locally, social media plays commendable role as a medium of communication for youngsters. They can effectively contribute in local policy forums and can also share personal videos. Online networking removes shyness develops understanding and promotes child confidence. It gives them a voice for the freedom of expression and a platform to be heard and noticed. Youth on the web can start charitable projects for the needy and the poor, destitute and impoverished. Finally, social media is a hub for recreation and leisure where youth can have fun, share jokes and enjoy amusing stories.

It is a learning tool in many ways and a powerful expression outlet for both the teenage girls and boys. They can also learn necessary technical skills to shape their digital lives. kids can access contents that may help learn new practical skills such as 'do it yourself', cycle repair kits, bookbinding, dress mending, making dolls, creating puppets, assembling Lego pieces and designing models. They can also learn the methods of building wooden antiques, etching designs on timber, engravings on silver pots and etching drawings.

The youngsters can evaluate the intentions of others, whether beneficial or harmful, before continuing to hold a conversation. Girls, in particular, can freely ask sensitive questions and sensibly analyse replies reflecting the respondent's truthfulness. Frank communication may reveal whether a person is reliable and straightforward, cheater or deceptive. An elusive teen would hesitate to divulge accurate whereabouts to a female web user. The innocent kid feels innocuous at home, away from strangers. If foul play is suspected, kids can block further contact, and the personal profile should remain secret, never agreeing to a face-to-face meeting without taking mum or dad into confidence. The children follow home-made rules for internet use and online time management. Too much digital media use consumes a great deal of precious time, allowing a little break for physical exercise at the local gym or a brisk walk in the nearby park.

Challenges of Digital World

Cyberbullying or cyberstalking Is a behaviour presented through digital media to intimidate the target, trap the susceptible, entice the innocent into performing acts of vulgarity and use offensive language to hurt the recipient. The most dangerous aspect of the cyber resource is that the digital message stays online for an unlimited period, reaching the audience far away, recurring frequently and inflicting incalculable emotional damage to the victims. Quite often, the teenagers form social bonds for thrill and excitement, exchange intimate and revealing photographs, post fanatical memos and share highly personal details. The relationship breakups create resentment, making youngsters edgy, irritated and disturbed. As such, former chums use social media platforms for intimidating and hurting those with whom they had in the past, shared personal stories, highly private tales, and sensitive secrets, and even photographs in delicate settings. After termination of friendships, they turn against closest friends, causing psychological bitterness through the misuse of digital media diverging intimate details, posting objectionable photos, and writing obnoxious linguistic taunts. Such images of innocent girls displayed on websites become a potential source of embarrassment. A topless photograph of an adolescent girl on MySpace or Facebook could be enormously harmful, distressing and stressful. Mental torment is far worse than the physical pain and agony that bullies perpetrate. Victims unintentionally become resentful, sober children turn indignant, and well-behaved kids sometimes assume the role of frightful bullies on account of inner indignation caused by fun-seeking, excitement-pursuing school mates

Digital use spontaneously multiplied in many European countries since the beginning of the present century. The think-tank in most EU states immediately felt the necessity of evaluating consequences for the youngsters who enjoy unrestricted and unsupervised access to online resources, and yet, cannot foresee the possible negative side of social media. The meeting in

Brussels enabled European leaders to put some measures in place for the productive use of speedily proliferating social sites such as Facebook, Twitter, My Space, YouTube etc. The European Commissioner Neelie Kroes, in 2011, impressed upon all EU states to engage a team of Digital experts for ensuring optimum use of digital resources. Before this endeavour, the Dutch had in 1995, founded Meldpunt Kinderporno on the Internet much earlier than any other member state. It was fully supported by the Netherland Ministry of Security and Justice to combat sexual exploitation of children. Internet child pornography has always been a burning issue in the European Union. Though many countries, through their NGO's, have succeeded in curtailing child pornography but failed to achieve total restraint. During the 1980s and 1990s, the bookstalls and newspaper stand at European railway stations, bus and coach stations, airports and main shopping centres, a huge diversity of colourful sexually enticing magazines were displayed, and the publishing industry was making billions of euros, pounds and Swiss francs. In the recent past, new technological advancements, screen time on the internet, social media sites, and smart devices have replaced the printed version of dubious discourteous literature. The cyberspace is shaping the behaviour of youngsters who are notoriously excessive users of social media sites. The traditional class structure has vanished in the face of openness, online social chats, unlimited WhatsApp natters, Facebook-based friendships and interpersonal relationships, discovering new partnerships via Twitter and Myspace.

The native White British men are increasingly seeking and developing lifelong personal relationships with Philippine, Chinese, Polish and Serbian girls. The European football top teams are paying colossal sums to recruit best players from Brazil, Argentina and Portugal.

The preliminary step taken in the Netherland was the establishment of INFORMATION SOCIETY which was a Safer Internet Centre Platform run by Information Scientists, researchers from universities, and educationists from schools. They launched several wide-ranging initiatives. First the launch of a website for safer internet usage veiliginternetten.nl for the general public to obtain information and advice to ensure online safety, guidance for Wi-Fi use and advisory tips for parents to help children learn the effectiveness of internet application. For children, in particular, a website Meldknop was introduced to assist them in dealing with bullying attacks, inapt sexual behaviour, swindles and mental provocations. Other initiatives are the provision of Expertisebureau Online Kindermisbruik, [online child abuse], De Kindertelefoon and Pestweb [bullying]. Also, Mediawijzer.net, a Dutch Centre of Expertise for Media Literacy, set up a platform for increasing digital awareness of pre-school children. Other participants taking steps included "SamenDigiwijzer" an initiative of CodePact; Medi.e.ijzer.net; Koninklijke Bibliotheek [i.e. National Library of the Netherlands] and Kennisnet. One of the latest best media projects for Dutch children is "Golden Hummingbird" Golden@penstaart. The Media masters devised as a cross-media game is useful for classroom use.

It consists of a fruitful conversation between teachers, parents and school children about virtual reality, games, blogging, imaging and cyberbullying activities. While playing the game, kids learn information skills, online conduct and negative allusions of social media. Mijin Kind Online has developed good websites for children under the age of 8. Even they teach small kids how to formulate a secret password, memorise it and never share this with anybody else, including close friends. [www.saferinternetcentre.nl]. All school-going children should be digitally literate to resist the challenges of social media and bravely face embarrassing encounters related to online bullying. The kids should be capable of effectively dealing with a demeaning tweet and intimidating messages. The girls, in particular, have to handle with courage any vulgar phrasing and indecent terminologies. Conversely, girls receive fanatic postings and flattery remarks admiring their physical features are nothing more than fantasy and illusion.

CHAPTER IV
CYBER AGGRESSION & BULLYING

In all categories of schools, whether state, private or grammar, minor incidents of fun and merriment do happen among same-age children. The relaxed and haughty kids participate in funny jokes by mocking one another for the sake of amusement. Even conventional peer-to-peer pushing, and propelling do not create hostility. Still, elbowing and jostling generate anger, whereas hitting and knocking down a classmate can lead to bitterness and hatred. These actions and reactions are various forms of physical bullying giving rise to aggressive behaviour. Playful activities such as throwing snowballs at each other during Christmas season and flinging paper-plains at other kids in the forecourts are harmless and inoffensive tricks for joy, thrill and delight. Yet, taunting, jeering and insulting remarks about another kid are provocative that fall in the domain of verbal bullying. An English proverb 'a sword wound heals but a tongue wound festers' is a true aphorism. Socially loftier, aggressive, and bodily robust teenagers customarily exhibit oppressive behaviour in the school environment. They seek gratification by jeering and taunting others which are considerably unreceptive and meek. Frequently, unintentional passing remarks about the dress or shoes of a shy pupil by a classmate are exceedingly annoying. It irritates and embitters the affected child and leaves him/her disillusioned and alienated in the school. The docile nature of compliant and humble kids becomes their weakness among a group of belligerent mates. Even a few Loud-mouthed children tactfully get away with verbal bullying in the absence of witnesses who tend to side with the provoker rather than the victim. However, school teachers, administrators and counsellors do take notice, adopt feasible measures for peer-to-peer reconciliation, offer training to both the aggressor and the victim and succeed in overcoming the bullying infection. The staff are personally present, well capable of taking appropriate measures to prevent future bullying incidents in their schools.

Nevertheless, during the last few decades, we have entered a new era of online, on-air communication, internet interaction and instantaneous messaging via social media sites, cell phones and emails. Consequently, cyberbullying has dramatically replaced the conventional forms of face-to-face bullying at schools and other institutes of education.

Over 15 years ago, research scholar Marilyn Campbell (2005) opined that "Cyberbullying is merely a new form of traditional bullying that has adapted to new technologies". Realistically speaking, cyberbullying is a dangerous endemic that causes immense emotional impairment to the victim. Yet, the perpetrator remains anonymous, unaffected and beyond the jurisdiction of legal, social and psychological accountability. In effect, the research scholars and academics have painstakingly conducted qualitative and quantitative studies throughout the past fifty years to inform the stakeholders and enlighten the decision-makers, resulting in meaningful initiatives undertaken globally by various government and semi-government bodies.

Research articles on this delicate theme have appeared in journals ranging from *Journal of School Violence*; Child Abuse & Neglect; Aggressive Behaviour; *Youth Studies Australia*; *Cyber/psychology & Behaviour*; *Aggression & Violence Behaviour* and *Sex Roles* to *Prevention Science* and several socio-psychology related professional periodicals. For instance, the PsycINFO database has cited 245 research articles which appeared from 1975-2000 in reputable professional journals. Between 2000 and 2010, 1458 articles were correlated to school violence and bullying. Several masters and doctoral thesis have comprehensively covered bullying studies. Crothers & Levinson, 2004; Griffin & Gross, 2004, have stressed the need for accurate assessment of a bullying situation.

Cyber abuse is a deliberate unfriendly mindset with the intent of causing hurt to feeble teenagers by posting degrading and demoralising information. The helpless youngsters as young as 7-year old are capable of freely using smartphones, tablets and laptops for the sake of pleasure. Their online indulgence makes it easy for perpetrators to communicate anonymously, butter up, trap and tease the innocent. A cyberbullying victimisation study of 14-17year-old kids across 7 European countries discovered that the bullying was the highest in Romania followed by Greece, Germany, Poland, Netherlands,

Iceland and Spain. In this research, 13708 teenagers completed the questionnaire. The crucial questions asked were the parental educational level, marital status, monitoring of internet use and the time kids spent in front of the screen. (Tsitsika, A.K. 2018; https://bmcpublichealth.biomedcentral.com/articles/10.1186/s12889-018-5682-4).

Likewise, Ortega et al., (2012) studied cyberbullying intensity and emotional reaction of children age 9-16 in UK, Italy and Spain. Online risks for the youth were far greater than the positive side of thrill, new relationships and the unexplored bonds of love. Although kids despise any kind of cyberspace supervision, a certain degree of parental digital use monitoring was necessary. As such, threatening messages and malicious rumours put an undue psychological strain on the victim that eventually affects his/her learning focus at school. To widen the geographical scope of cyberbullying and extrication the features of aggression, Gorzig and Olafsson (2012) conducted the study of 25 European countries. Dr Goriz of the London School of Economics and Political Science and Dr Olafsson analysed a large sample of 12641 boys and 12501 girls asking questions about teasing, hitting, kicking and pushing of mates and also whether they have ever sent a photo or video to someone online. Cyberbullying had the weakest relationships with too risky online activities in Romania and the U.K., but most influential in the Netherlands. Also, girls are more prone to relational aggression than boys. (Coyne et al., 2006)

Professor Gokhan Atik of Ankara University has emphasised the application of self-reported instruments for the collection of data. So far, tools used by Turkish scholars for measuring the intensity and breadth of bullying include Bully Scale developed by Kutlu (2005) to calculate verbal, physical and relational forms of bullying. Another one is a Bullying Survey created by Kepenkci and Cinkir (2006), which asks respondents explicitly about the frequency of bullying occurrence. Then, the Turkish version of Colorado School Climate Survey adapted by Kartal and Bilgin (2009) which included a checklist of bullying behaviour. This list is in no way complete as new forms of bullying have been invented through the clever use of the latest electronic podiums. Gukltekin and Sayil (2005) brilliantly modified "multidimensional Peer Victimization Scale created by Mynard and Joseph in 2000". Turkish researchers used the scale for assessing victimization of 11-16 years old pupils in school. It primarily covered bantering, trepidation and relational bullying. To study mistreatment and intimidation of pupils, Dalek in 2002 and Tipirdamaz-Sipahi in 2008, produced a translated version of "Olweus Bully/Victim Questionnaire (1983). and (Olweus 1996, p.9) produced a revised self-reported questionnaire to assess the forms, patterns and processes of bullying in Turkish schools. Another such instrument has been Calik (2007) School Bullying Inventory; also, School Relations Attitude Scale, Koc (2006) and then, developed by Piskin (2010) entitled "Peer Bullying Survey". Koc's PhD thesis was entitled "Predicting bullying levels of high school students" submitted at Ghazi University, Ankara. Submissive and obedient pupils express themselves in a non-assertive manner (Alberti & Emmons, 1970) and while remaining non-hostile, they mostly overlook their own needs. Atik et al. (2012, p.202) reported that the main form of the bullying encountered by victims was verbal as the preys showed modesty which in itself was a risk factor for victimisation in peer groups. The kids possessing compliance and modest nature became soft targets for the perpetrators. A study in 2018 conducted by Van Geel et al. involving a more significant number of students focused on a specific question, i.e., Does peer victimisation predict low self-esteem or does low self-esteem predict peer victimisation? The first part of the investigative problem included 16230 students, and the second part of the problem comprised 16394 youth confirming the impact on peer abuse with long-lasting adverse effects on self-esteem.

Undeniably, Turkey is a collectivist society; infrequently pupils join together for fun targeting a particular kid who might be misfit due to docile nature. His/her unassuming and meek character makes him the prime prey for the impish teenagers in the school. The children at 14+ appear in a nationwide exam for entrance into higher secondary schools. So, the best academic performers get a place in well-behaved career-oriented schools. In these selective schools, similar to the British Grammar schools, the discipline is admirable, and teaching is splendidly magnificent. The present researcher asked a teacher in Istanbul about overall kids' behaviour and bullying. He promptly replied, although a certain degree of bullying issue exists, it is in no way a serious matter. If occasional incidents occur, the teachers have the right training to contain unpleasant situations. They keep an eye on perpetrators' intentions and movements, preventing them from choosing naïve classmates for bullying or harassment. Usually, bully incidents are related to pupils who enjoy backbiting, name-calling, trash-talking. The Turkish girls, in particular, face psychological bullying when they do not fancy a pestering and stalking by an unlikeable boy. [https://www.quora.com. how-common-is-bullying-in-Turkey. 28 May 2018.] The magnitude, gravity, and nature of bullying in schools present challenges to the teachers, parents and society. National strategies, appropriate regulation enforcement, local initiatives, and in-school tactics help tackle the issue. Individual peer-to-peer bullying should be dealt with by the school counsellors to recuperate any unpleasantness, thereby improving the credibility of the school. If obnoxiousness prevails more widely, the school itself should prepare a bullying prevention programme to root out the undesirable evil. However, the present writer has visited Turkey half a dozen times (between 2012-2019) and curiously observed after-school pupils' behaviour, spoken to some parents, teachers, lawyers, and bank officials. I have moved around shopping centres, open markets, spend some time in libraries, museums, parks and gardens; amazingly, the behaviour, manners, conduct and etiquettes of Turkish teenagers are admirable. Not everyone would agree with my observations and reflections of Turkish kids as a whole, but comparatively, they are honest, well-disciplined, meticulous and well-organised people.

In African countries, there is considerable emphasis on protecting female chastity. Cyber-related violence is targeted at girls and young women and with rising use of the internet, cyber-security is at the forefront of national forums. Online erotic pestering, shadowing, illicit use and handling of personal contents such as leakages of sensual metaphors are a blatant feature of cyber intimidation. The young girls make offensive comments about high school or college mates. When chums get together online, they choose an easy-going going victim to coerce her and make nasty remarks to cause anger and resentment. Social networks such as Snapchat, Twitter, Facebook and Instagram are the avenues used by perpetrators to bully innocent girls. David Sam et al., (2019) research on 'Cyberbullying victimization among high school and university students in Ghana' concluded that all respondents who took part in the investigation conceded to experiencing bullying online several times. It also had a psychological impact on their general health and wellbeing. The cyberbullying problem is even worst in other African states where laws have helped curtail the damage caused by cyber aggression. Both Tanzania and Nigeria passed the law in 2015, followed by Uganda and Botswana in 2017 and then Kenya in 2018. Having identified cyber belligerence, a social endemic, South Africa in October 2019 has criminalised non-consensual pornography. These governmental sponsored steps to combat cyber violence and cybercrime offer hope to the youngsters. Zimbabwe, in particular, the situation is precarious since girls are the crucial object of cyber violence and are callously slut-shamed and often called 'Here', a vulgar word to vitiate ladies in the society. Girls should have the courage to retaliate the bullies with harsh language deterring them from instigating further extortion. The concerned authorities in Botswana and Uganda are in the process of drafting regulations for the prevention of revenge pornography and false information posted on the internet. The task on hand is to educate young boys and girls to evaluate social media shared communication before posting personal photographs. Failure to recognise the negative side of cyber communication, they should be prepared to face the consequences which might well be lethal and unbearable. The perpetrator could potentially ruin your life and destroy your promising future.

The progression from a toddler to adolescent evolves a few stages when kids need to foster abilities, secure autonomy and accept obligations. As Scott (1999) states that they should "develop competencies" but there are "Blurring of boundaries between youth and adulthood" (Reisinger, 2012. P.96.). In the past, teenagers were under the managerial "gaze of teachers, parents, scout leaders, psychologists and juvenile justice" (Lesko, 2012, p.75.) In the current century, kids are more confident, free and control personal space without parental snooping and teachers' meddling. The laws give them more protection, and even parental authority has slackened, allowing social workers to intervene in family disputes and arguments. Mounting secularisation, new racial multiplicity, the upsurge in social media use and independence have made youth more assertive and self-assured. It is difficult to control internet use and social behaviour on the media platforms where relational aggression usually occurs, gossip takes place, humiliation befalls, and anxiety develops. The shy kids hesitate to inform parents, and they are not mature to identify the motives of the bully. Unable to handle interpersonal conflicts, children feel sad, depressed and miserable. Under the circumstances, either they start to eat a lot and gain weight or eat little, become skinny, but emotional damage lingers on for many years. The culprits of cyberbullying turn bold and aggressive, causing socio-psychological harm to innocent victims. Many compulsive bullies grow up to get involved in unlawful activities such as thuggery, substance use and violence. They have little interest in education, learning or academic pursuits.

All bullies are very popular in their youth groups and exert undue influence over classmates around them, but never lose an opportunity to insult others, and wield authority for self-respect. When parents move to another city or state for career advancement or other family reasons, the children have to adjust to the environment in the new school. If they have been the target of bullying in the previous school, it is highly likely for them to become victims again. (Brendgen & Poulin, 2018). Peer victimisation is prevalent in many scenarios (Cooley & Fite, 2016). Even in the new school where recent admissions bring kids of different backgrounds together, and they make new friends, exchange mobile number for cyber links, the teachers are not fully aware of such contacts. However, what role teachers can play to prevent relational aggression before it occurs. (Weyns, et al., 2017). Atherton et al. (2017) have accentuated various pathways between relational aggression and kids' temperament, which can be a guide to perceive the mind-set of troubled children. Bullying is undoubtedly a complicated social phenomenon (Barboza et al., 2009) swayed by distinct features of the broods' school environment, family circumstances and the modes of upbringing.

School-Based Bullying

Bullying is undesirable belligerence with the intent of causing harm to another classmate. Normally nudging, striking and hitting takes place during school recess times or in the playing fields. There is a clear difference between playful joking and scornful taunting for pleasure. Research into kids' movements suggests that boys crack ignominious jokes, chat wildly and make fun of a noble chum. It upsets the victim but brings joy and laughter for other kids. Hilarious gags are funny and repulsive titters are considered unpalatable for victims of bullying. It is ridiculous to satirise an innocent youth possessing immaculate manners and virtuous qualities. Impersonating another youngster is disturbing and offensive indeed. Girls are particularly sensitive except for a few naughtiest who seek delight in the process of teasing. The victim has three options namely, walk away without uttering a word, secondly, show courage to confront the bully with a firm stance, thirdly,

Informing parents, teachers or school counsellors. The educational focus is disturbed, concentration wanes, and interest in lessons fades. In the classroom, naughty peers use bodily signs to distract the attention of other children. They might cross arms to convey a concealed message, roll eyes and make an obscene gesture with fingers. Family instability prevents girls from opening up and communicating bullying stress to their mothers. They keep silent and do not inform their teachers about unfortunate incidents. In stable families, girls feel secure and usually disclose school-based unpleasant episodes to parents in a subtle and supportive domestic environment. Some emotional hurt boys give an adequate response by inflicting bodily harm to the perpetrator who, out of rage, may turn to a fistfight. Teachers intervene to protect the kids and prevent unexpected obtrusive reprisals. When two or more friends inflict severe pain as a punishment on a class fellow to compel him to use, buy or supply drugs, the situation gets worse due to no-cooperation of the cohort. His denial to become accomplice makes him vulnerable to bullies. In many countries, including Malaysia, physical bullying is indeed a crime that carries imprisonment and hefty fines. Several deadly corporal cases have come to light in Malaysia.

Bullies' Conduct and Protocols

Bullying and Cyber Safety (Poem)

Bullying Stems from Domestic Strife
Husband Leaves Children and Wife
Choice She Makes to Lead Her Life
Unpredictable Future, Stressful Life

If She Decides to Go On a Date
Genuine Effort In Search of a Mate
Children Embrace a Brand New Fate
Dislike Step-Father, Begin to Hate
Kids' Behaviour Spills Over In Street
Initially, Do They Remain Discrete

Extract Excitement With Little Pain
Nothing to Lose Nothing to Gain
Out and About in Sun and Rain
Harassment Infliction Without Refrain

Internet Bullying, A Despicable Act
How Do a Child Properly React
Online Learning Tools, They Require
Safety Mechanism Skill They Desire

How Do We Encounter Cyberstalkers

Penetrate Social Media Just Like Hawkers

Surf The Networks, Pushers and Vendors

Entice With Messages, Fake Pretenders

We Teach Our Children, Ward Off Dangers

Cyberbullying Protection From Any Strangers

Subsist Cyber Laws to Punish The Evil

Place Filters for Information Retrieval

Stay On Cyber Air, Safe and Glad

Restrict Your Stay, Don't Get Mad

[Composed by DR NAZIR AHMAD, 1st May 2020]

Naturally, bullies learn from the home, locality and social environment and then, act according to personal experiences within the family and youth practices in the area. Local groupings and casual friendships influence kids' behaviours and attitudes. For instances, if parents are separated, divorced, and a new partner appears on the domestic scene, the kid is likely to be restless and unsettled. If one of the spouses happens to be in custody for any legal procedures, the child will be nervous and distressed. Unemployed parents on account of sickness, redundancy bring economic hardships and adversely affect the young children in the family. All these factors have an unpleasant impact on the tender brain, making him/her agitated, irritated and dismayed. While at school, internal restlessness turns into anger, and that takes the form of aggressive conduct, teasing and bantering classmates. With a smartphone in hand, text messaging commences for initiating friendships, and if the response is not favourable, bully becomes troubled. In effect, the rejection means the posting of threatening communication. Habitually, cyberstalking individuals tend to remain anonymous and unreachable. Spiteful gossips on the cyberspace and false stories about others bring excitement and ego elation for the perpetrators. The girls and kids from broken families are vulnerable and soft targets for deceitful bullies. The cyberspace bullies are not only false-hearted but also devious who operate fake online accounts and conceal their real identity. Under the disguise of a decent person, they persuade innocent teenagers to open up, exchange flowery dialogue, receive photographs especially from girls, in a compromising position and then, blackmail by repeatedly rotating on cyber sites thus automatically seen by innumerable internet users. In the recent past, excessive use of digital technologies has made lives of innocuous young girls miserable, inadvertently exposing them to persistent online harassment which involves image-based sexual abuse, familiarly called revenge pornography, disseminated without victim's consent. Repeated retribution is a severe cause for great concern that makes it imperative for individuals and families to review cyber safety mechanism.

Moreover, parents should realise that the youthful years between 13 to 19 are a sensitive time of mental growth as the kids acquire perceptive skills in hikes and spikes. They are in the process of traversing social affiliations and simultaneously expect motherly love and care. They are entering into a complex world of countless hues, and as such, their common sense is undeveloped and incapable of making timely decisions. Throughout the teen years, parental guidance and consultation promotes maturity and boosts self-confidence. The limbic system in the brain links sensual information to emotional reactions that lead to temper, panic, eagerness and irresistible attractions.

Usually, children bullied online do not mention it to their parents, who might ban internet use or take away mobile phones. They prefer to remain silent for fear of losing parental trust. In Singapore, some naughty boys pulled down the trousers of another teenager using a school toilet for amusing. The boys instantly made a video of the whole episode on the smartphone and subsequently shared it with other school fellows. The victim did not report to the teacher as it would have provided more fuel for intimidation to the bully. The survey of over 3000 pupils aged 12 to 17 was conducted co-jointly by the Singapore Children's Society and the Institute of Mental Health in 2014 and narrated that one in nine adolescents had experienced cyberbullying. There are three specific methods of bullying in Singapore, a) posting an excruciating video of a mate on the net, b) making online demeaning annotations, c) calling them deleterious names.

[https://www.channelnewsasia.com/news/cnainsider/3-in-4-teens-singapore-cyberbullying-online-survey-10001480]

Some students rightly feel that complaining about bullying would be a sign of conceding defeat and a symbol of weakness for the youth. To overcome cyber-attacks, there is an immense need for parents to prevent cyber-attacks targeting kids for the emotional wellbeing of their children. They should navigate careful parental monitoring and time management for the home-based use of the internet by youngsters who might despise strict rules and stringent supervision. However, a moderate approach with mother or father's amicable involvement, with the kid's selective use of cyberspace could produce encouraging sequels. Secondly, the kids are supposed to develop digital skills for confronting challenging text messages.

Cyberbullying in Singapore and Australia

Surprisingly, Singapore has the third, uppermost ratio of bullying worldwide, although Latvia and New Zealand are the 1st and 2nd in this table. The physical and relational bullying is widespread in many schools. The Organisation for Economic Cooperation and Development sponsored a three-year study on this vital topic. (OECD: 2017). As reported in The Straits Times of Singapore on 2 July 2019, a 14-year old bully who customarily teased others, was a bullying target herself in the school. A video containing complaints against her appeared on the cyber net that remained in circulation for a year. She began to suffer stomach aches and migraines owing to stress caused by the video. Her parents contacted the Singapore government-sponsored helpline "Touch Youth Intervention Programme" who came to her rescue to prevent the worsening health condition of the girl. One of the Cyber usage surveys claims that 85 per cent kids under 13-years have created social media accounts out of which 43 per cent have experienced cyberbullying whereas 16 per cent, girls, in particular, have been involved in online sexual behaviour. The advice stemming from the Touch Youth Intervention is that all school going kids in Singapore, should try to appraise online information and search for the interaction source before committing oneself to online companionship.

Online exploitation of power in relationships through cyber abuse has been prevalent in Australia. Overt and covert bullying incidents have exceeded 45 million across all schools instigated by 543,000 perpetrators. Bullies are said to be at high risk [http://www.livescience.com/11163-bullies-bullying.html] of substance abuse, nervousness and aggression. In March 2018, Australian Relationship Website conducted online research asking about digital awareness of bullying in schools. Only 24 per cent male and 76 per cent female took part in the survey, and the

141

majority conceded that the problem was pretty grievous. They put forward concrete proposals for handling the bullying epidemic. [htpps://www.relationships.org.au/what-we-do/research/online-survey//march-2018]. The annual event is gaining popularity in the country as in 2019, 5726 Australian schools participated in the National Day of Action titled "Bullying No Way! Take Action every day". Social media cyber platforms are accessible for sexual predators suspiciously searching for soft female victims through the chatrooms and websites. For a simple-minded teenage girl, online preposition made by a stranger on a fake account could be fatal. Cyber-attacks have ruined many young female lives in industrialised countries. In one of the bullying occurrences at school in February 2019, the Perth Court issued an order banning a child from keeping 100 meters away from a fellow school mate. In this case, an innocent young girl was violently bullied by a group of girls, persuading her to commit suicide. Another shameful incident took place in October 2018 at Huddersfield school in which a 16-years old British boy tugged the 15-years old victim to the floor, forcefully pouring a bottle of water into his mouth. In an Adelaide school, Australia, a 14-year girl stabbed a 17-years old girl with a knife on the premises, causing minor injuries. With the amiable intervention of the staff, the wounded girl reconciled, showing patience and demonstrating kindness.

Cyberbullying Detection Clues

Signs, hints and traces of cyberbullying are both visible and invisible, apparent and veiled. Online anonymity makes it much harder to uncover the perpetrator who can create a fabricated hate page, a fictitious name and false account for spreading gossip. Observing cyberbullying but remaining quiet is to support the bully inadvertently. The Onlooker of this incident may be defined as a non-participant spectator, but passively witnessing the manifestation without taking any action. Presumably, the bystanders view the intimidating episodes either with regret or amazement and yet, play virtually no role in condemning the wrongdoing. Some observers may feel utterly remorseful for cyber victimisation but do little about it while others may not intercede on account of timidity and fearfulness for reprisal. They may not even highlight concern to the relevant parties such as teachers, families, mentors and counsellors. Courageous watcher can inform and help attenuate the cynical impact on the victim. An abettor is no less guilty than the co-conspirator.

Inaction is to urge the tormentor to mock the victim without the fear of liability. Conclusively, thrill-seeker bystanders are as dangerous as the culprits of cybercrime. Cyber felons use abusive language, slang words, vicious verses, insulting jargon and waffle terminologies. The lingo and blather expressions online are meant to cause emotional damage, psychological impairment and mental despair. Regrettably, girl victims get pestered, sexually harassed, and intimidated not only by male culprits but by fellow female teenagers for vengeance and retaliation. The cyberstalking makes them nervous, scared and petrified when the depiction of innocent girls on the net as prostitute, bitch etc. demean their personality. Such language is disgraceful and insulting as it falls in the domain of character assassination. It is challenging to identify defamation and even more complex to verify slander. The impact of online interaction is different from the effect of school-based bullying, which the teacher can detect by observing the victim' face. A yellow face conveys some unhappy emotions and looks nervous, edgy and tense. On cyberspace, the victim experiences the feelings of sadness, focus disturbance, learning decline, academic frustration, low exam grades and low-self-esteem. Sadistic comments tarnish the thoughts and judgements of the kid. Typically, cyberbullies lack language skills for want of attention and focus on learning. Their online text is likely to reveal spelling errors, grammatical mistakes, broken sentences and use of the second language, e.g. Bromance, 53X, side chick, Snatchchat, Netflix & Chill, and smash. Teens also use coded words to avoid parental attention, and on mobile phones, sneak texting acronyms to conceal cyber messaging from family members.

Reactions from victims can confirm the bullying narrative of selfish and deceitful culprits. The parent-teacher collaboration and vigilance can apprehend the bullies by involving counselling and community services groups. Instead of punishing or detaining the youngsters, psychotherapy, and compassionate treatment of domestically disturbed children would be an ideal step to bring them into the mainstream school environment.

The British school teachers keep a record of the learning performance of each child. If anyone does not bring homework for a couple of weeks, the parents are informed. They are required to follow up with the desired homework, which is a significant segment of learning. The kids get rewards for doing good work in various manners at school. In my recent question-answer session with granddaughter and grandson, I discovered how the procedure works in classrooms. My Granddaughter says, "If I answer a particular question well, so my teacher gives me a free card, a raffle ticket; If I solved a difficult math sum quicker than other classmates, I get one more free card and another raffle ticket. More the raffle tickets, the more are the chances of winning a prize in the prize draw. The prizes include a strawberry jelly pen, a blueberry jelly pen and a sparkly pen. Other instances of gaining a raffle ticket are, listening attentively to the teacher during lessons, give a definitive answer to a question, showing kindness to classmates and helping other kids in the class". [This short communication took place on 24 September 2019 at my Grandchildren's house]

The free access to mobile devices has made teenager more ingenious for they now use disappearing snap chat messages and Finsta (fake Instagram) accounts without parents' knowledge. They move on to different apps and talk freely for the sake of freedom, independence and

145

excitement. The young mothers are finding it difficult to groom well-behaved and well-mannered kids in the presence of cyber and related mobile devices. The supervisory and restraining power of a good mother has been hampered due to tremendous technological advancement in all spheres of mobile and cyber platforms. Exercising freedom without responsibility in the name of liberty and individual emancipation can be incredibly risky for an orderly civilisation in which healthy and weak, rich and poor live in peace and harmony.

Children's autonomy and protection is a burning issue today for all parents as the kids themselves cannot foresee potential risks posed by paedophiles and bullies. In the present climate, parental fears about child safety are fully justified. It is the responsibility of parents to keep a check on night use of smartphones by kids in their adjacent bedroom. Good night sleep is essential for a healthy mind and a happy child. According to a research finding in the United Kingdom, 9 out of 10 teenagers regularly access online resources that affect the wellbeing of youth. Mostly, the children use Instagram, WhatsApp, Twitter and Facebook regularly. The BBC report confirms that 51 per cent girls and 43 per cent of boys have online access three times a day. Limiting screen time and taking teenagers on board about the inherent dangers of strangers' 24/7 use of social media to entice innocent kids would be essential for the safety and cognitive wellbeing of our youngsters.

Cyberbullying Prevention Measures

One of the comprehensive surveys carried out in 2009 in the USA, revealed that ninety-four per cent of 7th grade and forty-eight per cent of 8th-grade students encountered bullying at schools. (Young et al., 2009, p.417.) Demonstrably, the purpose of the wrongdoer is simply to dominate and control (Herrenkohl et al.,p.3) through spiteful acts and influence. The affected student would probably divulge rather than remaining silent "If the parents showed sincere concern and made heartfelt inquiries" (Matsunaga, 2009, p.225.). Typically, when the girls fall out with friends, they tend to punish each other by "maliciously spreading lies and rumours about a peer to damage the peer's group status" (Grotpeter and Click, 1996, p.2329). Concerning relational bullying, the girls pressurise classmates to join them in intimidating a certain girl. The role of parents is to assist the victim in demonstrating self-restraint and patience, avoiding vengeance and verbal retaliation. But parents of bullies should also make their kids understand that "they do not violate the social etiquette of the non-aggressive female" (James and Owens, 2005, p. 72). It is not easy to cope with secretive and enigmatic methods of bullying among girls which cannot be normally detected by the teachers, school counsellors and the psychotherapists. However, the victims need family support, congenial domestic atmosphere and good-natured teachers at schools. They can act as consolers and counsellors and take positive measures, especially to bring peace and amiability within female groups. As such, peace-making channels within the school environment would assuredly produce cordial and refreshing outcomes.

An influx of immigrants since the Second World War, and more appropriately after US-sponsored war imposed on Arab-Islamic countries beginning from 1991 attack on Iraq under the false pretext of Weapons of Mass Destruction, the demographic pattern in Western schools, have undergone unprecedented transformations. The Western nations at present are the centre of the civilised world (Leonard & Grubb, 2014) and many countries in Africa and Asia do recognise it. How far it is superior in terms of justice, equality and diversity, can be judged on merit, application and evidence? Social scientists have forcefully presented arguments for and against the supremacy of Western Civilisation over other Eastern societies and cultures. Consider the present-day paradigm of Finland where the immigrant children have come from Middle Eastern and some Asian countries notably from Iraq, Syria, Somalia and India. Customarily, immigrant kids at Finland schools recurrently encounter hooting, laughter and name-calling. They also routinely face derisive smiles from local kids who relish sneering and mocking of immigrant children during school breaks and playing intervals. Unfortunately, staring and weird looks to cause taunts and heckling of non-white school mates are relatively common occurrences which carry little evidence of apparent bullying. Consequently, the young kids with an immigrant background in Finland rightly feel they are expected to accept "insults and attacks as a humorous incident" (Souto, 2011). Finland has the highest number of incidents related to race-oriented violence and harassment. The naughty and impish Finish children also make negro jokes for dark skin school fellows. The local rascals and scoundrels do not get caught in the absence of valid proof as their appalling and inexcusable activities go unnoticed. They frequently get away with it, for teachers do not wish to create a fuss to protect the reputation of their schools.

Currently, the world is facing unfair competition in the field of trade and business, and the contemporary wave of nationalism is adversely impacting global economies, making youngsters angry, frustrated and bewildered. The global economic powers have the responsibility to cooperate, offer hope to youngsters and bring peace, tranquillity and harmony in this beautiful world.

CHAPTER V

LAWS FOR CYBER SURFING

Cyber technology has occupied youth mind and soul in their quest for social exploits and emotional adventures with unrestricted 24/7 access to fascinating escapades shaping unhampered affairs. Thrill and excitement seeker youngsters possess limited knowledge of cyber traps awaiting in disguise to take advantage of their vulnerability and openness.

Realistically, all laws are devised, promulgated and implemented to protect the feeble and weak from the mighty and arrogant; inferior from the superior; victim from the aggressor and innocent from the wicked. The vile individual causes upheaval, the nasty brings turmoil and the immoral triggers commotion into the lives of ordinary human souls in the society. Without appropriate rules, a civilisation degenerates into chaos, anarchy and unrest, thus paving the way for rascals and devils to dominate and dehumanise the humane values, deprive them of essential freedom and fundamental rights. Believably, the rulebooks restrain the Obnoxious committing excesses and usurping the legitimate rights of defenceless and shabby souls. The laws are in place to protect the unprotected and safeguard the unguarded and relatively helpless members of the society. Bylaws are made to control the conduct of misbehaved teenagers, as to what is acceptable in the environment. In the process of social transformation, the laws facilitate youth interaction, socialisation and positive outcomes, albeit upholding the values and norms for the protection of vulnerable adolescents, the well-being of innocent kids, safety of decency and prevention of cyber-related violence.

We are living in a digital society, unconsciously encountering network threats, and cyberbullying incidents, particularly involving kids and cyber sexual pestering and provocative erotic manners. As the social media network, has reached across the globe, every nation needs to formulate laws to prevent cyber-attacks, track down perpetrators, and administer appropriate punishment as a deterrent. The undesirable child abuse, porn dissemination, verbal harassment, cyber-stalking annoyance and teenager psycho-emotional frustration have severe repercussions for youth well-being and health. Many states lack tactical framework, analytical infrastructure, adequate resources for research and planning and proficient workforce in the law enforcement agencies. Most cyberbullying attacks remain undetected due to flawed rules and mechanism, intricate bureaucratic involvement and sedentary cyber technology expertise. In many less developed countries, electronic communication operators are not fully aware of the irresistible risks posed by precarious types of cyber aggression. They cannot anticipate seductive behaviour of the wicked individuals, nor they can foresee fraudulent cyber activities intermittently conducted by criminally minded folks.

Bullying stems from the schoolyard interaction between kids, taunting in the classrooms, mocking in the playground, jeering in the hallways and joking on the buses, markets, corner shops and school canteens. It advances in the comfort of a pleasant home atmosphere where handheld mobiles do the rest, damaging morals— manners, habits and behaviour of innocent boys and girls. Cyberbullying can be immensely emotive and psychologically complex, and it may impose a challenge for the law enforcement officials who had to be thoughtful about the societal norms and relationship patterns to investigate individual cases with insightful perceptions. Equally, the sensitive issue is online harassment of young female teenagers. They may reluctantly agree to meet up the new-found cyber acquaintance without any credible clue of social limitations and personal boundaries. How do we protect innocent, vulnerable youth who unintentionally expose themselves to be overtly abused and emotionally demoralised through popular social media sites? Currently, several websites such as Facebook, Twitter, Tumblr, Instagram, WhatsApp, LinkedIn and Snapchat are investing in introducing technological innovations for the prevention of misuse, abuse and exploitation of young website users. Predictably, innocent victims of cyberbullying hesitated to inform parents and refrain from sharing deplorable inner hurt with close friends to avoid disappointment and uneasiness. Lately, the kids' attitude has changed, and teen girls break their silence, convey the personal feeling to parents and seek advice. The mothers warn their daughters about fake accounts and fabricated characters and how to confront the perpetrators on the social network forums.

Reformation of British Cyber Laws

Western countries are conscious of the social media internet challenges and implications for societies. In England, over 90 per cent of teenagers use the websites mainly for instant messaging and photo-sharing in excess of three times a day. The school-going girls obstinately use networking facilities and confront cyberbullying more than boys, and that has an impact on their sleeping schedule. The British Members of Parliament have expressed viewpoint on these sites and opined that addiction to media websites should be treated as a 'Disease'. Professor Russell Viner of the University College London has advised parents to keep screens (iPad, iPhone, etc.) out of their kids' bedrooms to ensure their progeny have a goodnight sleep. It is not easy to restrain the endless streamed entertainment at kids' fingertips, and cyber screens have diverted family connectivity to enjoying alone. Young girls are greatly affected by what appears online such as digitally altered images of charming and beautiful cohorts, inciting jealousy and greed that undermine the self-worth of others. Some teenagers feel dejected due to unappealing and uninviting physical features. Being unaware of cyber technological manipulation by scrupulous kids who habitually boost self-photographic images, the naïve teenagers get anxious and tend to seek solace in isolation and solitude. These are the preliminary signs of stress leading to depression, ultimately affecting mental and physical health.

'The Protection of Children Act 1978, U.K., made kids sexual abuse images illegal and then in 1988, the British Parliament passed Malicious Communication Act followed by School Standards and Framework Act 1998 and Commissions Act 2003 for tackling bullying in primary and secondary schools. Under the 1988 Act, it is an offence to communicate with another person with the resolve to cause distress or anxiety, or the message is grossly indecent and offensive. The Children Act 1989 and The Computer Misuse Act 1990 covered several areas to criminalise certain forms of adolescent bullying. The Protection from Harassment Act 1997 made it a felony to cause harassment. Similarly, Act 2003 made it transgression to send an electronic message that is offensive or indecent or obscene. The Education and Inspections Act 2006 section 89 (1) makes it obligatory for maintained schools to have a behaviour policy to regulate the conduct of students and introduce essential steps for the sole purpose of developing self-control, discipline and respect. The headteachers are empowered to carry out screening and search of pupils to ensure no harmful items sneak into the school. If teachers find any kind of sharp instruments, the school management confiscates such items giving initial warning, enforcing detention or exclusion for a short period from school. The acts mentioned above emphasise indecency, obscenity and harassment which are obnoxious in British Society. It is also unlawful to publicise libellous communication on the internet. A few years ago, Welsh Government promulgated Social Services and Well-Being Act, an extension of U.K. Children and Social Work Act 2017 for the protection of adolescents placed in foster care, children's homes and secure units to ensure their safety from abuse and neglect. (www.cymru.gov.uk). Attempts are being made at council levels to root out by trailing potential child predators throughout the United Kingdom. The paedophile hunters in Cornwall are pursuing stalkers under the banner of "Safeguarding the Innocent". In October 2019, they set up a fake online profile to catch cyber-criminal, a 44-years old man- a former convict who then made contact assuming that he was communicating with a 14-year old girl. The man posted his topless photo of himself and in return, asked for the picture of an innocent girl. He also sent pictures of his private parts on WhatsApp. As soon as he arranged to meet her in person, the law enforcement officials got involved, apprehended him and brought before the court for conviction.

British schools are 'worst for cyber-bullying' reported Sean Coughlan on 19 June 2019 [http://www.bbc.co.uk/news/education-48692953]. Paedophiles have cleverly utilised Social media exhibiting shameful contents for kids viewing, setting a trap and inflicting emotional harm. The school lack teachers because this profession is not intellectually and financially attractive, their workload is substantial impacting classroom quality time. Several teachers hold postgraduate qualifications and a shortage of incentives drive them to join other rewarding occupations.

The Roman Catholic schools and Sixth-form colleges are particularly concerned about kids' bullying experiences that adversely affect quality learning. They are attempting to create a safe and happy environment for students to learn while nurturing an outlook of accountable behaviour. They base their policy on 'Preventing and Tackling Bullying', [Department for Education, U.K., July 2017] and deriving support from DFE Statutory Guidance 'Keeping Children Safe in Education' 2018. One of the significant trepidations is the peer on peer abuse explicitly sexual violence, cyberbullying and physical ferocity such as shaking, hitting, biting, hair pulling, hazing and rituals. Manipulative students use racist and homophobic language and make teenage girls feel subordinate, subservient and inferior. If a gullible girl shares online her naked or semi-naked images and sends sexually explicit messages, the boys think excited in responding equitably with sexting text that can be offensive and degrading for the female recipient. The Catholic schools aim to provide the victim's reassurance, offer counselling support and restore self-esteem and confidence. They help kids remove vulgar and belligerent online material and ask the parents of bullies to address the issues at home and cooperate with the school administration to eliminate this endemic. It is a standard practice to keep a record of all minor and significant bullying incidents occurring on school premises. They detain culprits, question them and if necessary, debar from some areas of the school. Those causing severe bodily harm have to face expulsion from the school for a limited period. In specific scenarios, the class teacher may confiscate the mobile phone. Shy reticent and introvert students do not disclose their condition of being bullied. The staff, parents and counsellors receive instructions to look for strange signs in children. They might avoid attending school, frightened of walking to and from school, starts to be truant, feels withdrawn, morning sickness, poor educational performance, arrives home with books torn and clothes damaged, bruises face, cuts on the hand. Parents can take action by contacting the teacher, counsellor or even the police depending on the situation.

Despite several measures in place to tackle school-based and cyberspace bullying across Britain, the violence at schools involving weapons has not subsided. On the contrary, knife crime in the classroom has considerably increased. Until recently, police have seized from teenagers not only knives but more lethal weapons like sword, meat cleaver, knuckle dusters, Tasers and guns. Surprisingly, 49 acts of weapon-related violence, unfortunately, was related to less than 10-years old kids. Law does not apply to underage children in the United Kingdom. In Wales, one such incident involved just a 4-year old kid, and in Greater, Manchester knife was used by a six-year-old and in another brawl, the kid was seven-year-old while in the third occurrence, two boys were eight-year-old who possessed weapons. In Hertfordshire, a seven-year-old boy had a 6inch kitchen knife whereas, in Bedfordshire, the authorities found meat cleaver, machete and fatal firearms in schools. Likewise, a zombie knife and an axe were found in a West Midland school. (Mark Ellis, 2019). In February 2019, a deplorable incident occurred in Chester where a fellow teenager physically hurt a 14-year girl while she was going home after school. A wicked girl had pounced upon her pulling down on the floor, hitting and demeaning her. The victim received wounds and bruises on hands and face feeling disgraced as other girls not only watched the episode but made a video film for circulation. Her parents boldly shared the video online to raise awareness of the bullying scenario in an all-girls school.

Individually, local authorities are devising children safety programmes for implementation in schools. Last year, Worcestershire Schools Improvement Team prepared an E-Safety Policy template which should be applied across all schools to combat cyber-technology risks and restrain the disturbing images posted on the net without permission of the susceptible child. In Worcester schools, the children are not allowed to bring their mobile phones, iPad and tablets into the classroom and school buildings. Although schools have vast computer labs where students spend a considerable amount of time for learning activities, pupils are not permitted to access non-academic networking sites, chat rooms, social messaging and non-educational blogs. Many schools are using Forensic Monitoring Software to enhance the security and safety of the system.

Because of the rapidly increasing bullying, harassment and youth violence within the schools' premises and beyond, the British Government has issued an 'Online Harms White Paper' entitled world-first "online Safety Laws". (DDCMS April 2019). Under new laws, the onus is placed on the social media platforms and internet service providers to undertake the binding obligation of alertness to shield kids and teenagers and users from harmful contents. The government would appoint regulators to oversee the performance of websites and authorised to impose hefty fines and block access to media sites. The Internet corporations, including social media sites, chat rooms, search engines and similar online platforms, have the legal and moral duty to rebuild users' confidence in newly emerging cyber technologies. For the sake of child safety, the concerned organisation should swiftly confront kids' sexual exploitation, removing harmful contents and building trust and instantly reacting to users' grievances. These sites must have built-in online wellbeing topographies to deal with catfishing, child grooming and evil behaviour effectively. The child mind bends easily into a new shape without the shred of a doubt about disinformation. The plausible innocent brain adjusts readily to change. The thoughtful measure can make the youth more confident in controlling their impulse because they unwittingly share feelings and emotions due to perplexing and inaccurate information on the net. There is a need to build capabilities to check the accuracy of the contents that provoke unlawful behaviour so that the vulnerable youth can respond accordingly. They can stay in the safe zone by immediately blocking the inducer. Manipulation aims to control by demoralising an innocent teenager for heeding to the immoral demands of online bullies. The British government has introduced Digital Charter as well as Code of Practice for Providers of online media platforms. Regional and local partnerships exist for strengthening cooperation for the exchange of cyber-attacks' information, obnoxious activities of bullies and support mechanism for the cyber victims and to halt harmful impact on innocent lives.

The following websites are remarkable avenues of learning to face cyber challenges, electronic safety, digital security and safe networking for parents, teachers, pupils, counsellors, carers, cyber-safety coordinators and bullying preys.

Anti-Bullying Network:
http://antibullying.net/cyberbullying/htm

Byron Reviews: Safer Children in a Digital World:
http://www.education.gov.uk/ukccis/about/a0076277/the-byron-reviews

Internet Watch Foundation:
http://www.iwf.org.uk/media/literature.htm

London Grid for Learning:
http://lgfl.net/esafety/pages/education.aspx?

Parents' Guide to New Technologies & Social Networking: http://www.iab.ie

South West Grid for Learning:
http://www.swgfl.org.uk/staying-safe

ThinkUknow: http://www.thinkuknow.co.uk

WES Worcestershire E-safety Site:
http://www.wes.networks.net

WMNET: West Midland Regional Broadband Consortium set up under the National Grid for Learning
http://www.wmnet.org.uk

New Zealand Cyber Laws

According to a recent survey, an increasing number of kids face bullying at schools despite having a zero-tolerance policy, and it costs nearly $444 million a year claims Netsafe. There has been a long list of laws relating to child wellbeing beginning with 1961 Crime Act followed by several other acts, e.g. Education Act 1989; Broadcasting Act 1989; Children, Young Persons and Their Families Act 1989; New Zealand Bill of Rights Act 1990; Defamation Act 1992; Films, Videos and Publications Classification Act 1993; Privacy Act 1993; Harmful Digital Communication Act 2015. The Digital Act 2015 covers protection against cyber aggression involving the posting of offensive material, photos and videos. It has created Netsafe, an internet safety organisation which can assess, scrutinise and deal with all forms of cyberbullying complaints and bring the perpetrators to justice. [www.netsafe.org.nz] Netsafe have the power to analyse and probe each case and decide on merit, which steps are appropriate to stem the tide of bullying in schools and on the internet. Netsafe cooperates with public and education sector, parents, industry, lawyers, and law courts to promote cyber safety by educating and supporting individuals. It also offers teenagers, teachers and parents, expert advice on identifying signs of cyberbullying and ensure early intervene to safeguard vulnerable kids.

This bullying menace is widespread throughout USA, Europe and New Zealand schools as the laws are not strictly applied owing to the delicate age of minors who make fun of each other and create humour, hilarity and wittiness in the school environment. Most of them are cultured, civilised and decent but innocently get caught in the unpleasant cycle of intimidation and extortion. They are not mature enough to foresee the consequences of peer coercion, dominance and resentful conduct. The kids learn to be tolerant, forbearing and unresponsive to abusive language, rude remarks and foul play. They should demonstrate a sympathetic attitude towards classmates and school friends. The parents of bullies need to take more interest in etiquettes of their kids to explore the reasons for such conduct and take necessary steps to circumvent unkind behaviour but form strong bonds of love and keep open channels of communication in the evenings and weekends. The teenagers deserve parental affection, maternal fondness and even grandparents' loving connection and warmth. The kids deserve nurturing and caring affectionately in a friendly and amicable atmosphere because the harmonious and cordial relationship with sons and daughters boost confidence, reinforces educational focus, improves self-assurance, enhances self-control, inculcates thoughtfulness and builds respectful behaviour.

European Union Cyber Laws

All EU countries are signatories to the Council of Europe Treaty 2007, which mandates EU states to outlaw conduct accessing and retrieving child pornography on the internet. The Council of Europe Convention on the Protection of Children Against Sexual Exploitation and Sexual Abuse (CETS201) is well known as the Lanzarote Convention that has been ratified by 40 states, including Western Balkan states. Cyberspace is a vital constituent of contemporary European society that equally entails perils and harms, sensitive predicaments and health exposures. Cyber platforms offer relationship opportunities and new avenues of companionships, attachments and rapports. On the contrary, such connectivity may transfigure into jealousy, bitterness and despair resulting in blackmail, sexual abuse and emotional bullying. In general, youngsters are unaware of the potential risks masked in the utilisation of online social media hubs. On 1 January 2018, Germany passed Network Enforcement Act making Twitter, Google, and Facebook websites, responsible for instantly removing offensive and disgusting materials from their online platforms. Otherwise, they could face up to 50 million euros fine.

The Anti-Bullying laws in Ukraine have the onus on teachers, principals and parents rather than the perpetrators of bullying. In the past, some schools did not report bullying incidents to government bodies for the sake of protecting their reputation. This stance had an adverse influence on the educational achievement of well-disciplined pupils. The Ukraine Parliament has promulgated strict laws covering physical, psychological and sexual violence in schools and on the electronic networks. The new legislation will punish principals of schools who fail to report bullying occurrences to the police. The parents of a bully will have to pay fines imposed by the principal of the school. Each school will employ social teachers who shall be responsible for the prevention of bullying and the creation of a pleasant educational environment for the promotion of teaching and learning at school.

Cyber Laws in Indonesia, Malaysia & Singapore

Indonesian Electronic Information and Translation Law 2008 ensured child protection and bullying prevention. The teachers are required to monitor the use of smartphones and lab computers in their schools because pupils seize the opportunity in spare time to access Facebook, Twitter and other gaming sites. In the process, cyber-attacks occur, and often the perpetrators are classmates. The government has incorporated the UN Convention on the Rights of the Child and Child Protection to strengthen existing anti-bullying laws. The teachers advise the parents to uphold ethical values at home. In Malaysia, the school discipline has been much better than many developing states. The Communications and Multimedia Act 1998 did not extend to cyberbullying activities, so in 2017, cyberbullying law guaranteed child cyber safety, offering assistance to parents on website activities. The law made it compulsory for all Malaysian schools to teach social media as one of the subjects in the curriculum. Similarly, in Singapore, the government in the absence of formal regulations has launched anti-bullying programmes for schools linking civic subjects and languages. The kids in primary and secondary schools learn to improve decision-making abilities in the use of cyber platforms. They learn to be respectful to others and safeguard personal security. An online Gaming site called C-Quest encourages parents to share online experiences and instruct their kids to be judgemental on social websites. If teenagers detect cyberbullying, they should connect with their parents for seeking advice and help to combat online aggression. They are encouraged to create new email address, change phone number, block online messages and reduce the use of social media stations. The government has created (www.cyberwellness.org.sg) propagating Protection from Harassment Act 2014, which evolves the cyber wellness education assertiveness programme. It is a compulsory part of the school curriculum. The children habitually use chatrooms, emails blogs, SMS text communication and internet gaming. The bullies use the electronic means to impress peers, show dominance and send hurtful and manipulative messages. The Singapore government recognises the foremost duty of schools to formulate physical, oral and online bullying regulations, disseminate the rules, develop awareness and create robust parental-teacher rapport.

Unfortunately, school-based face-to-face bullying, cyber-teasing and cyber-abuse impact negatively youth health, social relations, and impede educational progress.

Alcohol consumption, substance use or domestic disputes certainly influence cyber-bullies' behaviour. The society has the responsibility to look after both the victims and the bullies since teenagers are susceptible captives of the prevailing circumstances.

Cyber Laws & Kids Violence in U.S.A.

Researchers, scholars and professors of sociology, psychology, criminology and human biology unanimously underpin the conveniently available weapons as the uppermost cause of unfortunate killings of young boys and girls in schools. On the contrary, the manufacturers, dealers and supplies firmly believe that the purchasing restraint and blocked access to weapons at home can drastically reduce the school-based lethal skirmishes. They forcefully advance the arguments in their favour with numerous examples of road accidents, forest fire calamities, natural catastrophes, flood disasters and other manifestations that consume more lives than the school mishaps. Out of school confrontations plant the seeds of fantasy and contrivance in the bullies to execute identical acts. When catastrophes occur in a marketplace or a shopping centre, the negative sway spreads in the neighbourhoods instigating vulnerable youth to emulate similar scenarios in their school settings. Despite comprehensive controls, the disgruntled boys manage to sneak in weapons of violence and open the fire on innocent classmates, teachers and principals of their schools. Easily available rifles, pistols or guns are brought through delivery trucks or kitchen doors into the main building. After buying from the open market or nicking from home, the firearms in the hands of an offender, empower him for ghastly action in an unarmed and helpless school environment. In schools across the USA, gruesome acts have sporadically taken place for numerous unfathomable reasons. Although shootings for vengeance are not uncommon, albeit violent egotistic attacks less frequently. It is incomprehensible to think of a primary school kid swinging a pistol in the classroom either to frighten or physically harm another toddler. The factors that contribute to odious and wicket episodes may include mental health issues, e.g. academic stress, study workload, exam worries, family tensions, peer pressure, relationship anxiety, and emotional turmoil. Amongst teenage boys and girls, animosity develops due to jealousy and enviousness stems from abrupt romantic breakups leading to resentment, anger and depression.

The turbulent history of school-based bullying and teacher-administered punishment in the classroom goes back to 1848 as we read through the harsh disciplinary rules of a secondary school in Stokes County, North Carolina. It seems each school was entitled to introduce and implement necessary laws to penalise students for naughtiness. There was a long list of 47 mischiefs designated for physical punishment in the school. If male and female pupils play together, each one may receive a cane four times, any kids telling tales out of school, would be struck with a cane eight times. However, deceitfulness is intolerable, and a teenager who conceals the truth and tells lies would receive seven lashes. Notwithstanding that, a boy teasing, touching or joking with a girl would be awarded ten lashes. If a child makes swing and swings on it would get seven lashes. Also, minor brawls among kids and making gestures with hands or stretching legs and arms in the classroom amounted to disruption, and it was punishable with some lashes decided by the teacher. In case children play cards during recess time or conduct gambling or batting, they would be considered scamps. The teacher has the authority to use strong bamboo for hitting the rascals several times on their back to teach an unforgettable lesson. In many other schools across the USA, school-going children received tougher punishment for misconduct. These harsh and cruel methods of physical punishment had created an atmosphere of resentment between teachers and parents developing a hatred for schools and educators.

However, from 1865 onwards, the use or misuse of iron rods and wooden sticks at all school levels was outlawed. Decades of pupil bitterness and hatred towards punitive teachers had made the new generation of youth more fearless as they courageously started to confront teachers, frequently challenging their old style of imposing discipline and commanding total obedience. The earliest episode widely reported in the US press occurred in 1880 when a group of students surrounded an insensitive and tyrannical teacher who was callously hitting their classmate with an 18-inch ruler. The boys daringly pounced upon the teacher, kicking him out of the classroom, and then rolled him over and over in the heavy winter snow. This incident led to a spirit of youth boldness and courage that pushed the educators on the back foot. It equally undermined the authority of compassionate teachers who were committed to imparting knowledge to the cultured youngsters. The availability of weapons made the disgruntled teenagers more powerful, and some of them demonstrated their anger and frustration by killing honourable teachers. Between 1880 and 1920, the state schools discipline deteriorated with a slow pace allowing pupils to be more assertive and the teachers to be overmodest and bashful.

The first recorded terrorist attack happened at Bath Consolidated Schoolhouse, Michigan where on May 18, 1927, Andrew Kehoe detonated two bombs killing six teachers, school staff and 38 children. During 1950s youth gang culture was on the rise, especially in urban areas. 'Social disorganisation was to blame', says psychology professor Martin Neumeyer. On September 15, 1959, Paul Orgeron, ignited dynamite in a playground of Edgar Allen Poe Elementary School, killing three kids, two teachers. On October 5, 1966, 15-year old David Black killed his teacher Forrest Willey at Grand Rapids High School, Minnesota.

Racial tensions and fights were common in the 1960s as in 1964, 15 kids got killed, and in 1968 26 youth lost their lives in school-based violence. Initially "School Violence" appeared in the press in April 1968 when Los Angeles Times published an article drawing the public attention to this endemic. A year later, in March 1969, circulated a piece on "School Violence" in response to

Mayor John Lindsay's reaction to escalating 'School disorder'. Owing to the assassination of Martin Luther King, racial tensions were pretty high. In January 1969, Washington Post reported the killing of an Assistant Principal at Cardozo High School by three teenage boys. In April 1975, the U.S. Senate Judiciary Committee commenced work on "Our Nation's Schools- a report card-school violence and vandalism, and in 1979, a research article by Zimring provided a detailed study of teenager brawls and fights in schools. [F.E. Zimring. American youth violence: Issues and Trends. : Crime & Justice,1 (1979).

An innocent victim of bullying sometimes gets annoyed and turns to seek revenge, It so happened on February 22, 1978, when 15-year old Roger Needham shot and killed his classmate who had perpetually bullied him at Everett High School, Lansing, Michigan. Needham was released after four years in the Juvenile detention, but he continued studying until earning a PhD in mathematics and subsequently becoming a professor at Missouri. However, the student-teacher acrimony had never decreased in US schools as the teaching staff and heads remained the ultimate target for crazy pupils. Wilbur Grayson, an English teacher at Murchison Junior High School, Austin, Texas, was shot dead by 13-year old John Christian. The incident occurred on May 18, 1978, and the underage teenager went to a psychiatric hospital. The first killing by a 16-year old girl Brenda Spencer happened on January 29, 1979, at Grover Cleveland Elementary, San Diego. She lived across the road as she fired her gun from the front window aimed at the principal who instantly lost her life. Likewise, a Female psychology teacher Clarence Piggott while delivering a lecture on 19 March 1982, was shot dead by a 17-year old girl Pat Lizotte at Valley High School, Las Vegas.

The relentless targeted killing of teachers continued unabated even though the federal government had established the National School Safety Centre in 1984 under the patronage of Attorney General Edwin Messe. Even the arrogant boys did not spare innocent female teachers as was the case when on December 4, 1986, just a 14-year old Kristofer Hans mercilessly shot his teacher Henrietta Smith at Fergus High School, Lewistown, Montana. On February 11, 1988, two boys of 15 Jason McCoy and Jason Harless unleashed their anger by killing Richard Allen, an Assistant Principal of Pinellas Park High School, Largo, Florida. In the same year on December 16, a teenager Nicholas Elliot shot dead class teacher Karen Farley at Atlantic Shores Christian School, Virginia Beach. A school dropout Eric Houston also killed his teacher on May 1, 1992, at Lindhurst High School, Brooklyn New York and then, on January 18, 1993, Scott Pennington shot to death his teacher at East Carter High School, Grayson, Kentucky. An Associate Principal Dale Breitlow of Wauwatosa West High School, Wisconsin was brutally killed by Leonard McDowell on December 1, 1993, while preparations for the forthcoming Christmas celebrations were in progress. One of the youngest victims of bullying was a 12-year old Nathan Faris, an obese boy consistently provoked by a 13-year old school fellow Timothy Perrin at Dekalb High School, Missouri. To avenge his torment,

Nathan shot and killed Timothy on March 2, 1987. A similar incident occurred on November 25, 1991, when an argument developed into fatal revenge that witnessed the killing of an innocent teenager at Thomas Jefferson High School, Brooklyn New York. A bully pesters the victim through intimidation, verbal abuse and emotional taunts. The recipient feels demoralised and decides to take revenge. The faultless victim becomes violent, picks a revolver or gun from the parental home, walks into the school and performs a destructive act. Jason Smith just turned 15, pulled up the weapon and killed his bully on May 24, 1993, at Upper Perkiomen High School, Pennsburg, Pennsylvania.

The unfortunate murder of school teachers continued throughout the last decade of the last century and well into the first decade of the present century. As is evident from the following figures:

October 12, 1995- 15- year old Toby Sincino killed his teacher at Blackville Hilda High School, South Carolina.

November 15, 1995- 17-year old Jamie Rouse killed his Business teacher at Richland High School, Lynnville, Tennessee.

February 2, 1996- 14-year old Barry Loukaitis used a rifle to kill two classmates and his teacher at Frontier Junior High School, Moses Lake, Washington.

September 25, 1996- 16-year old David Dubose died his English teacher Horace Morgan on the premises at Dekalb Alternative School, Decatur, Georgia.

February 19, 1997- 16-year old Evan Ramsey killed with a shotgun the Principal of Bethel High School, Bethel Alaska.

October 1, 1997- 16-year old Luke Woodham from Pearl Mississippi stabbed his mother to death and headed straight to Pearl High, using a rifle to killing two and seriously injuring seven pupils.

December 1, 1997- 14-year old Michael Carneal murdered three and wounded five students at Heath High School, Kentucky.

March 24, 1998- 11-year old Andrew Golden & 13-year old Mitchell Johnson jointly trapped and killed a group of five students and teachers at Westside Middle School, Jonesboro, Arkansas. Golden had nicked a gun from his grandfather's house and hid it in the bushes.

April 24, 1998- 14-year old Andrew Wurst shot dead his science teacher John Gillette in the dance hall of James Parker Middle School, Edinboro, Pennsylvania.

May 21, 1998- 15-yar old Kipland Kinkle first shot and killed his parents in Springfield, Oregon and afterwards, he entered Thurston High School where he killed two and wounded 21 students.

As some teachers were shot dead during 1998, the teaching profession was in disgrace due to increased drug abuse and violence across the states. Although the Drug-Free School and Communities Act 1986 and Gun-Free Schools Act 1994 were in place, there was no end in sight of enhanced physical violence. This act had made it clear that any teenager in possession of a gun, weapon or knife on school premises would face exclusion for a year. President Bill Clinton convened the first White House Conference on School Safety on October 15, 1998. The students, parents and teachers received invitations who contributed ideas for the safety of pupils and teachers. President Clinton ordered the hiring and training of school resource officers for the community-based violence prevention programmes and behavioural health programme for youth as well as the introduction of community-oriented policies in schools. Congressman Bill McCollum had reinforced the stand on violence while he sated on October 9, 1998, that

"It is a sad reality that many of today's schools are becoming increasingly dangerous places to be. Schoolyard brawls have become lethal confrontations involving knives, guns, or drugs. Recent school-related shootings serve as a sobering example of just how urgent the situation has become. Rather than providing our children with a safe place to learn, many of our schools have become combat zones, and the schoolyard murder rate has almost doubled in the last two years. Mr Speaker, 25 students have been killed in U.S. schools since January 1998". The House Representative Bob Etheridge reiterated this fact by saying that "This recent incident must serve as a call to action. Congress must respond with effective means to prevent and combat school violence". However, no Congressman ever used the word terrorist act or school terrorism within the United States.

April 20, 1999- 18-year old Eric Harris & 17-year old Dylan Klebold executed a savage act of terrorism by killing indiscriminate killing of 14 school fellows and a teacher at Columbine High School, Littleton, Colorado. This vicious teenager's terrorist inventiveness prompted the US government to unveil the "Safe School Initiative" 1999 to investigate the philosophy, projection and related pre-attacked behaviours of school shooters. Also, presented was the "School Emergency Response to Violence" as well as the Congress created "Secure Our Schools Programme" in 2001. It was the same year when thoughtfully conceived 9/11 twin-tower attacks dominated the media and all Muslims all over the world labelled as terrorists. Although no Afghan was named in the attacks, the US bombardment over Afghanistan and parts of Baluchistan commenced in 2001, killing thousands of civilians including women and school children.

Surprisingly, a mere 6-year old boy killed a 6-year old playmate Kayla Rolland at Buell Elementary School, Mount Morris Township, Michigan on February 29, 2000. On May 26 a boy aged thirteen Nathaniel Brazill excluded for a day from school, returned with a weapon and killed his teacher Barry Grunow at Lake Worth Community Middle School, Florida.

March 21, 2005- a 16-year old Jeff Weise killed nine people including his grandfather, five students, a staff, a security guard and a teacher at Red Lake High School, Chippewa, Minnesota.

November 8, 2005- a 15-year old Kenneth Bartley Jr aimed his gun at a Principal, and two Assistant Principals standing alongside, managed to kill one instantly and seriously wounded another at Campbell County Comprehensive High School, Jacksboro, Tennessee.

September 29, 2006- a 15-year old Eric Hainstock equipped with a shotgun and a handgun entered Weston High School, Cazenovia, Wisconsin. He went straight to the Principal's office and killed him. On 2nd October 2006, fatal shooting of 5 decent girls at West Nickel Mines Amish School, Pennsylvania, again invited the national attention to school safety. The worst was yet to come as the country embraced another mishap in April 2007 when a mass shooting occurred at Virginia Tech claiming 33 innocent lives- a colossal terrorist attack in the present century. Further terrorist attacks aimed at harmless and defenceless teenage school kids continued. The perpetrators were white American Christians who have traditionally been considered lone gunman, frustrated boy, broken family youth, and drug addict. Psychologist Richard McCann has wisely posited "The missing mother and father were to blame". A week before Christmas on December 14, 2012, a heinous act of terrorism at Sandy Hook Elementary School, Newtown, Connecticut, took 26 lives of 6 to 7- year old toddlers and six teaching and other staff members. This dreadful terrorist act led President Obama to create "Now is the Time Initiative" to minimise gun-related violence across nation's schools. On September 23, 2009, a teacher Todd Henry was killed by 16-year old Byron Truvia at John Tyler High School, Texas.

Cyberbullying is a fact of life, and a serious concern for all stakeholders, but school-based fatal bullying and killings have not receded. Parental and teacher killings did not stop by any means, which indicates the instable domestic situation that predominates in thousands of socially disturbing scenarios. On October 21, 2013, a boy Jose Reyes aged 12, killed his teacher Mike Landsberry and two 12-year old classmates at Sparks Middle School, Nevada with a handgun and then committed suicide. It is certainly disturbing to view the suicidal tendencies of children as young as 12 years of age. Then on September 16, 2016, Jesse Osborne just 14 years' age opened fire in the playground of Townville Elementary School, Greenville, South Carolina and killed a teacher Jacob Hall and two teenage children. Surprisingly, a merely 8-year old kid Jonathan Martinez and his teacher Kaen Smith was shot dead on April 10, 2017, at the North Park Elementary School, San Bernardino, California. The federal government have been promoting and supporting several state-run independent programmes throughout the country.

One of the far-reaching inventiveness was the "Comprehensive School Safety Initiative", a discretionary grant fund overseen by the National Institute of Justice. It aimed to pinpoint and recognise the likely causes and magnitudes of school violence and its bearing on school wellbeing. The school shootings occurred sporadically at Freeman High School, Spokane, Washington in September 2017 and then in December at Aztec High School New Mexico. On January 23, 2018, Gabriel Parker, 15, killed two and injured 18 pupils at Marshall County Hall High School, Benton, Kentucky. A month late an act of terrorism was committed on February 14, by Nikolas Cruz, killing with AR-15 rifle 17 students and injuring the same number of innocent kids at Marjory Stoneman Douglas High School, Parkland, Florida. These brutal mass killings prompted the congressmen and women to take further action and formulate strong laws. On 14 March 2018, the students organised a nationwide protest to commemorate the one-month anniversary of the shootings at Marjory Stoneman. They chanted slogans pressuring Congress to ensure school safety and formulate gun control laws. The House was in motion the same day that passed "School Safety Bill" called 'STOP School Violence Act 2018'. On this very bill, 407 senators voted in favour, and 10 voted against it (only five Democrats and five Republicans showed resistance to the bill). Republican John Rutherford, with the support of 94 members, had presented the bill many weeks before the Marjory Stoneman incident, Parkland, Florida. In the new bill, there is no mention of gun control, although funds will not be available for arming school teachers. Eccentrically, they simply wish to set up and activate a shadowy structure of reporting school-based antagonism, expand security arrangement and give training to both pupils and teachers. Congressman Jerrold Nadler sported the bill but underlined his concern for lack of gun mechanism.

Many states have individually taken exclusive initiatives to articulate and apply cyber laws for safeguarding youngsters against potential online social media aggression. On May 20, 2009, Alabama State passed the Student Harassment Prevention Act. In August 2010, Louisiana Cyberbullying Legislation banned 'Sexting' to under 17, as a crime that would carry $500 fine and ten days in prison for retaining or diffusing an improper visual portrayal. Illinois and Kentucky implemented cyber laws involving sexually explicit videos. In contrast, Alaska Anti-Harassment Statue 2011, Colorado Comprehensive Bullying Statue 2011, Connecticut Public Act 2011 and Delaware Bullying Prevention Law strictly prohibit electronic emotional harassment and cyberbullying. Likewise, New Jersey Bullying Bill of Rights, September 2011, directs the schools to employ well-trained anti-bullying staff members and each district within the state to recruit anti-bullying coordinators. Also, schools should develop intervention programmes to prevent bullying and hazing. Other unlawful practices in the cybercrime category include Impersonating a teenager on the internet, creating a fake webpage or a blog under fictitious names. Also illegal are the posting of a demoralising text message with profane, intimidating and coarse language. In Mississippi, Cyber Stalking Laws and Obscene Electronic Communication Laws are vigorously implemented to prosecute cyberbullying perpetrators.

Australian Cyber Safety Mechanism

Instead of parliamentary-approved laws, individual states in Australia have devised policies appropriate to the requirements and demands of both school-based and cyberspace commotions, incidents and coercions. In 2011, the Department of Education, Employment and Workplace Relations put forward National Safe Schools Framework that stressed the need for adequate student wellbeing relative to the use of social media platforms, mobile phones and other electronic devices. For instance, the Code of School Behaviour (Queensland), is about preventing and responding to Student Bullying in Schools Policy (New South Wales). Building Respectful and Safe Schools (Victoria), have in place comprehensive strategies to combat bullying on school premises. You should identify cyberbullying occurrences and instigating new intervention measures for developing collaboration among teachers, pupils and parents. These acts are in place to promote a shared understanding of bullying behaviour and enunciate reactions for improper conduct both at school and on the cyberspace. These non-legislative cyber-safety procedures act as unified plans for addressing grievances on social media websites. Considering online safety, Government has made agreements with some notable websites such as Yahoo 7, Facebook, Google and Microsoft for effectively dealing with complaints and educating teenagers to tackle social, emotional and oral bullying issues. The Australian Communication and Media Authority not only take action on the receipt of complaints concerning harmful, sinister and hurtful online content but also informs the relevant websites to either delete the vindictive material or thwart access to these contents. So far a significant step has been a Victoria Government initiative 'Building Respectful and Safe Schools' as reported by 9News on June 26, 2019, that completely forbids mobile phones in all schools to purge classroom learning disruptions and commotions. One in five children have encountered cyberbullying says Julie Inman Grant as bullies pressure kids into producing porn self-images and then asked to post it on the internet. Now online monsters in New South Wales can be convicted and sent to prison for five years. Since January 2020, both New South Wales and Victoria have made it compulsory for all kids under 12 to place their mobile phones in personal lockers during school time. This practice prevails in McKinnon Secondary College, Melbourne, where the mobile-phone restriction has visibly enhanced learning focus leading to highly improved academic performance.

The Australian Government organised the first Anti-Bullying National Day across Australia in 2010. However, it had to be postponed due to CoronaVirus-19. It would have been the tenth country-wide National Day on 20 March 2020 which could not be observed by students, parents, teachers, educationists and care-givers. They had developed Awareness Raising Materials to help kindle the constructive dialogue within the communities. Despite all the necessary measures, bullying continues to take away innocent lives of boys and girls in Australia. A 14-year old Amy Jayne Everett, a former student of Scots PGC College, Warwick, Queensland was subjected to repeated bullying and intimidation, and she took her own life to stop further torment. She was the face of an iconic Akubra hat, and her parents created hashtag DoltforDolly to raise awareness of the negative impact of bullying. (The Daily Telegraph, January 10, 2018). Aboriginal girls in Western Australia are regularly facing sexual assaults, verbal bullying and racial slurs from school mates. There have been five suicides committed by teenage Aboriginal kids between January 3 and January 11, 2019. One of the 14-year old girl Rochelle Pryor posted her last message 'Once I am gone the bullying will stop'. (Mail Online, 20 January 2019).

Websites commonly used as social linkage platforms are investing heavily in research and child-safety innovations since teenagers are the backbone of their attractiveness, standing, reputation and economic success. They have become conscious of the need to combat viruses and curb Trojan horses, halt phishing and stop unauthorised access. Network hacks are not unusual. Quite often, it happens when an innocent kid opens the email, a spam message flickers that lures the user to a different site containing malware or infected files. It is an innocent trap to steal all your photos, messages and socially sensitive images and then blackmail the teenage boys and girls into participating in vulgar activities. All famous online hubs condemn cyber bullying and allow the victims to contact them for help instantly. The kids should not contact the strangers or accept an invitation to meet in person. Preferably, save the communication as bullying proof to the law enforcement officials, avoid retaliation and offer no response to the cyber provocation and incitement. Smartphones are spiteful instruments of bullying among girls who display signs depicting 'bird', 'highway salute', 'rolling eyes', 'crossing arms', gesturing 'flip-off', glaring and calling each other slut or whore to inflict emotional agony. These are strange ways for teen-girls to validate and demonstrate the feelings of personal power surreptitiously. We must remember that emotional scars stay for a long time, the pain lingers on indefinitely. The scabs are not heeled that leave a perpetual and everlasting impact on the future wellbeing of the sufferer. Electronic bullying gives rise to psychiatric complications and acute depression ailments that undermine the intellectual, ethical and social development of youngsters.

Brief History of Ancient Decrees & Regulations

Mesopotamia is the earliest civilisation to emerge in the history of humanity in around 6500 -5390 BC (present-day Iraq). The first King of Babylon was Hammurabi who subjugated Mesopotamia and established the Babylonian Empire. The laws were formulated and carved on clay tablets and engraved into stone. The Code of Hammurabi is imprinted on the "Diorite Stele", a rock shaped figure 7 feet tall and 2 feet wide consisting of 4000 lines of text presenting 282 different laws. On the top of the statue is a chiselled photo of King Hammurabi. These laws pertain to family, slavery, trade, religion, crime and domestic problems. In the preamble, it is itemised that 'bring about the rule of righteousness in the land, destroy the wicked so the strong must not harm the weak. In conclusion, King Hammurabi articulated his desire for justice for all so that the oppressed man can stand before his image as the King of uprightness. Penalties were severe for the unjust, high-handed and cruel persons to maintain peace and safety in the Mesopotamian society. For instance, if a person causes bodily harm to another citizen, he would receive sixty lashes. If a son hits his father, his hand would be decapitated. The conurbation Babylon is now in ruins, located some 50 miles south of Baghdad which was also partially destroyed by Western-allied bombardment at the beginning of the present century. However, the "Diorite Stele" statue is on display in the Louvre Museum in Paris, France.

Egypt is said to be one of the Primordial societies in which laws based on social equality and impartiality date back to 3000-2686 BC. In the same land, Prophet Moses introduced Divine Laws in 1280 BC in the form of Old Testament for his people who were emancipated from Egyptian emperors (Pharaoh) as the King along with his hundreds of thousands of followers lost their lives in the Red Sea. The Egyptian laws date back to 3000 BC, based on equality and impartiality. Pharaoh, the Rameses II, was an oppressive ruler who brutally persecuted people. Prophet Moses (peace be upon him) led the Bani Israel out of Egypt along with his brother Prophet Aaron. Then the Ten Commandments written on Tablets were given to Prophet Moses by Almighty God on Mount Sinai as mentioned in both Exodus 20:2-17 and Deuteronomy 5: 6-21. These were Divine laws for the Israeli people. Also, in the Holy Qur'an, Allah says, "We brought the tribe of Israel across the sea, and Pharaoh and his troops pursued them out of tyranny and enmity. Then, when he was on the point of drowning, he [Pharaoh] said, "I believe that there is no god but Him in Whom the tribe of Israel believes. I am one of the Muslims" [Chapter Yunus 10: 90] and further Allah says, "previously you rebelled and were one of the corrupters? Today we will preserve your body so you can be a sign for people who come after you. Surely, many people are heedless of Our Signs" [Holy Qur'an, Chapter Yunus 10: 91-92.], in the Bible Exodus 14: 21-30 and Exodus 15: 19-21, it is stated that Pharaoh was drowned in the sea, but the Holy Qur'an, mentions, his body has survived. In 1881, his mummified body was found among a group of Royal Egyptian bodies which has now been placed in the Royal Mummies Chamber in Cairo Museum.

The Persian nation is another significantly ancient civilisation in the world and the first king of Persia Cyrus who captured Babylon in 539 BC, introduced and instantly implemented laws that foresaw the elimination of slavery, freedom of religion and racial equality. The Cyrus laws were inscribed on a baked-clay cylinder in Akkadian language in Cuneiform script. The First charter of Human Rights laws enacted in the Achaemenid Empire. These laws appear in the Western official charters such as Magna Carta (1215), Retention of Rights (1628), US Constitution (1787) and French Declaration of Rights of the Man and Citizens (1789) and the US Bill of Rights (1791) Achaemenid Empire founded by Cyrus (550-330 BC) became defunct after the death of Darius III. Later on, Sassanid Empire prospered and followed Zoroastrian religion in about 225 A.D. In their reign, Christians, Jews and Turks with native Persians lived in harmony and coherence. The women had a privileged position in the society especially when Queen Boran (630 AD- 631 AD) daughter of Husrav briefly ruled over the empire. She was succeeded by her sister Azarmedukht. In Zoroastrian faith, marriages were approved within the family as the Priests believed that incestuous nuptials gave birth to stronger males and virtuous females. Many of the laws were related to inheritance to keep the land ownership system intact and the extended families unified, for taking care of stepchildren, orphans and kids from multiple marriages. The Sassanian empire was getting weak due to war with the Byzantines as Khosrau II had been defeated in 627 AD at the battle of Nineveh that further debilitated the Persian rule over neighbouring territories. In 628 AD, the Prophet Muhammad (peace be upon him) sent letters to the Kings and rulers of Persia, Yemen, Ethiopia, Egypt, Hira (Iraq) and Byzantine inviting them to embrace Islam. The Sassanian King Khosrau II ripped the letter in defiance. In the same year, he was executed as a result of the civil war in his regions. The Arab battles against Iran started in 633 AD when the Muslim armies under the command of general Khalid ibn Walid fought and inflicted the first defeat, followed by a significant clash in 636 AD at Qadisiyya under the leadership of Sad Ibn Abi Waqas. Further battles took place between 642 and 651 AD upon the orders of the second Caliph Umer ibn Al-Khattab. But the conversion to Islam was very slow, gradual and spread over a long time.

Greek is equally an ancient civilisation of the world, but there were no formal laws between 1200-900 BC. Draco appears to be the first person to formulate and write down the codes in 620BC that were upheld by his compatriot Solon in 594 BC, adding family and public laws and altering some of the Draco's punitive and strict ones. In those days, the policymakers were middle-class members of the nobility. They used to remain neutral and open-minded, playing little part in government affairs.

Turk's historical evidence can be extracted from archaeological discoveries, Orkhon Engravings and Tore, i.e. traditional law that credibly reflects community life, steppe culture and tribal customs. There are drawings, engravings and inscriptions on pots, vessels and tombstones depicting the cultural, social, moral and ethical dealings and behaviours of Turkish rural inhabitants Oghuz Epic reigned between 209 and 174 BC when the Turks were settled around a sacred mountainous Ergenekon. However, the Ottoman Empire is the shining illustration of Turkish laws solely derived from the Divine Revelation, the Holy Qur'an, the Eternal and True World of God conveyed to humanity through the Holy Prophet Muhammad (Allah's blessings & peace be upon him). It is the final Sacred Testament after the Tura; the Old Testament and the Injeel-Bible; the New Testament. The Turkish reign started in 1299 AD with the establishment of a state founded by Usman, son of Ertugrul, the celebrated son of KAYI tribal chief Salman Shah was an Oghuz Turk. Ertugrul had, laid down the foundations of the Turkish state through decades of daring skirmishes, combats and battles with Mongols and Byzantine invaders and eventually succeeded in uniting dispersed Turkish tribes from Istanbul, Bilecik, Soghut, Bursa to Anatolia. His youngest son Usman Gazi (1258-1323 AD) possessed the vision and farsightedness to further the cause of his celebrated father. Usman Gazi assumed the leadership of Oghuz and several prominent Turkish tribes in 1280 AD upon the death of his father, Ertugrul.

In the reign of Sultan Murad II (1413-1451 AD) and Muhammad II (1451-1481 AD), Constantinople, Moldavia, Crimea and Trebizond came under Turkey. Then Sultan Suleiman the Magnificent (1520-1566 AD) annexed Hungary and besieged Vienna (1529), making the Turks the most significant power in the world. The just Caliphs ruled over Balkan states, Arabian territories and some European countries, but never attempted to impose Islamic religion or Islamic laws over the populations. Instead, the inhabitants were free to set up their courts to administer justice within their communities, build churches, synagogues and chosen places of worship without any restrictions. The Ottoman Empire began to decline owing to wars with Russia and the French army under Napoleon Bonaparte, invasion of Egypt and Syria, the annexation of Algeria and Tunis, exacerbated by Arab revolts in Hijaz and Balkans independence followed by the loss of Albania, Macedonia, Serbia, Bulgaria, Romania and Montenegro.

The Turkish state was in massive debt since Sultan Abdul-Aziz (1861-1876 AD) could not even pay any instalment of interest and in 1881, complied the treasury supervision by European Bankers. Under precarious economic conditions, Sultan Abdul Hamid (1876-1909 AD) became Caliph facing internal discord and foreign threats.

He abdicated in 1909 when young Turks and army units exercised full control over the government affairs. He was replaced by Mehmed V (1909-1918 AD), Sultan Mehmed VI (1918-1922 AD), and finally Sultan Abdul Majid II (1922-1924 AD). During the Turkish nationalist movement, General Kamal Ataturk emerged as the saviour of the nation who negotiated with the British and a treaty was signed to save the remaining territories from foreign occupation. The honourable Turk Caliphs reigned with dignity promulgating Divine laws for the betterment of all subjects irrespective of religion, sect, tribal roots or ethnicity. Throughout the sovereignty, the Caliphs faced internal and external treacheries, conspiracies and seditions. As yet, after two World Wars, Balkan and Armenian insurgencies, the Turks emerged as a unified and cohesive nation. In the Ottoman system of administration, the secular and religious laws coexisted aimed at justifiably accommodating culturally and religiously diverse communities. Turkey had three independent court systems to ensure justice, impartiality, and fairness. First the Sharia Muslim Courts for dealing with legal problems about Arab-Muslim people. Second, the Jewish Courts and third the Christian Courts in which the Jewish and Christian judges occupied the bench to give ruling related to their communities. The Muslim Courts were not permitted to hearing or settling any trade disputes or social litigations concerning Christian or Jewish population.

CHAPTER VI

YOUTH IDENTITY DEVELOPMENT

Parents strive for decent upbringing, good moral growth and virtuous attributes that enable youngsters to lead their lives with dignity, integrity and fidelity. Kids learn to be just, honest and truthful and realise never to betray others for the acquisition of material benefit, quantifiable advantages and gratuitous subjective gains. The personality of a teenager develops in segments viewing surroundings, observing ambiences and absorbing information. Preschool training in kindergarten or nursery lays the foundations of traits required for pleasant disposition and worthy moral character. Kids learnt manners and etiquettes, righteousness and ethical beliefs that assist them in distinguishing between truth and falsehood. If a child has credible qualities and positive virtues, the actions would be upbeat and affirmative. Parents teach children well-intentioned conventions, ignite confidence and promote emotional strength. They endorse social virtues, foster helpfulness, incite kindness and kindle mildness of temper. Youth personality possesses both positive and negative features impacting their teenage upbringing. Refined acuities in a harmonious household strengthen decision-making capabilities. Youth in general, value freedom of thought and deeds, dislike parental control and shape their traits to promote the conditions under which they comfortably lead a happy, satisfactory and thriving life. Youth imitate parents as role models and follow their instructions in making ethical improvements and forming social networks.

Do domestic conditions have a significant influence on youth character in making them who they are rather than who they want to be? External factors act as a stimulus to shape their personalities in terms of career choice during school years. Networks such as social media, websites, cyber connectivity, internet use, chatrooms, movies and Television programmes affect youth directions, actions and activities. Some are inspired by world-class musicians, film actors and showbiz personnel while others are impressed by sportsmen, designers, beauticians and models. In industrialised countries, most kids choose a career path according to their desires and personal interest. The kids in Europe, USA, Australia and Canada, are not under kinfolk pressure to pursue a particular field of study. The intellectual freedom makes them creative, inventive, imaginative and reflective. Moral character plays a part in the selection of occupations entailing tremendous effort, tenacity and resilience. For instance, admission to universities requires the achievement of higher grades in final school exams. A small minority of students receiving personalised tuition and coaching at home secure excellent marks. Without determination and perseverance, it is virtually impossible to get a university place in a demanding academic profession.

In dictatorial states, they destroy the personality of young citizens by the imposition of punishment and atrocities. They use massive brainwashing scheme to transform detainees' thinking, obliterate religious ideas and turn them into atheists. China has detained countless youth in detention centres. Xinjiang re-education camps in the Uyghur region holds over million Turkic Muslims of Kazakhs, Kyrgyz and Uyghur origin as reported by Randall Schriver of the United States Department of Defence (May 2018). In 2019, the U.N. ambassadors from 23 nations including Australia, Canada, France, Germany, U.S.A. and Japan co-jointly raised severe concern about the plight of innocent people from ethnic minorities imprisoned in Chinese concentration camps. The letter was sent to the Chinese government to close down inhuman facilities. In early December 2019, when a Panorama journalist asked Chinese ambassador to London in a press conference to comment on this issue, he flatly rejected the allegation to be false and fabricated. Millions of innocent souls whether in Burma, Indian held Kashmir, and occupied Palestine face bleak future under deplorable living conditions. These humanities are helpless, demoralised and dispirited.

During the last two decades, E.U. and Turkey have welcomed thousands of refugees from Syria, Iraq and Libya. European governments have influenced public opinion in favour of immigrants from war-torn countries. Migrant youths' adaptation to a new culture and values creates multicultural societies. Social freedom and openness in the West have produced all-inclusive communities since governmental policies are unbiased and tend to promote equal rights for citizens. Western traditions, values and education system are standard norms even for non-European. These strategies reflect supremacy in economic, technological, industrial and military power. It has no spiritual backing from the Christian Church, but intellectual tradition has survived and supports the Western civilisation. Ironically, Arabs and Muslim countries have lagged in keeping up with the pace of technological and industrial progress. These developments are indispensable and crucial for the economic, social and communal welfare of people.

The education system of many developing countries is a replication of Western academic standards. Notwithstanding that the governments of developing countries are partially dependent on economic aid and reliant on the import of medical equipment, energy plants, engineering apparatus and knowledge. The culture of the real Islamic world is infinitely pure. Still, their banking system is similar to the West, where billionaire money lenders and financial institutions charge interest on home mortgages. Even university graduates in the Western world find it increasingly difficult to raise a deposit to buy a small house. Compassionate parents gift basic 10 to 20 per cent down payment. First-time young home buyers have to pay a big chunk of monthly salary towards the mortgage repayments. The economic inequality is much worst in third world countries where educated youth face massive unemployment and bleak future. Ironically, destitution, poverty and hopelessness drive the child towards unlawful and illegitimate activities.

Creating Virtuous Character

Generating noble qualities, eradication hurtful characteristics and inculcating kindly feelings in the youth are the shared responsibility of the immediate family, schools and the communities. Parental guidance, learning directions. Proper parameters and instrumental schooling yield virtuous and caring teens. When ethical and decency standards change, immoralities become acceptable in a liberal free world, allowing youths to seek thrill and satisfaction through socialisation practices. The thinkers, scholars, visionaries and intellectuals express their concern and put forward workable ideas. A new breed of covetous moralists pays little attention to words of wisdom. The current century has already seen the rise of typical self-centred personalities who are admittedly 'a bit of a character' in a civilised world.

The word **character** comes from the Greek term 'Kharakter' denoting engraved mark that shapes youth character. Youth Practical conduct in deeds and performances is an admirable attribute impacting others. Some examples are, for instance, telling the truth in the face of temptation, lying to save face and showing patience upon witnessing adversity: the choices we make and the actions we take to strengthen youth character. Constructive and productive engagements reinforce the role and boost its appeal. Conversely, sceptical, distrustful and dubious actions devalue and degrade youth character. Wealthy men in the developing world are known to be arrogant and snooty because they usually have little regard for the lower classes. The ruling elite most often misuses power by conducting unjust business and significant influence to gain political strength. Once former U.S. President Abraham Lincoln avowed that 'Nearly all men can stand adversity, but if you want to test a man's character, give him power'. They feel the fate of people is in their hands, and therefore, they misuse power to belittle others. The supremacy and domineering insolence is a familiar phenomenon passed on from generation to generation. Mistreatment is an awful character trait peculiarly associated with arrogant and unruly children who inherit scornful and selfish characteristics and feelings of superiority from overconfident families.

Moral courage is more important than physical strength. Formation of an ideal character requires overpowering superfluous desire, castigating immoral habits and overcoming indecent thoughts. How we treat and understand others depends on our intellect and brainpower that adds to the potency of character. 'Every person has a different view of another person's image. The nature of a man, the integrity, that's who you are? Good character is a hidden treasure, and it is about doing the right thing when nobody else is watching. Youngsters erroneously think it is fine to get away with anything, and the only wrong something is to get caught. We can build Virtuous character in children empowering them to dream for a bright future and to make a difference in the lives of others.

Developing a virtuous character requires freedom of thought, speech and action in an amicable setting. In democratic societies, Teenagers enjoy the friendly atmosphere in modern democratic societies where genuine opportunities exist for shaping admirable character. Youths' thoughts, beliefs and judgements reflect their true nature. Although every kid is the originator of his/her personality, external factors play a significant part in transforming acuities, values and morals. Youngsters are hopeful of leading comfortable and blissful lives, but a happy youth must have moral qualities of character such as fairness, sobriety, courage and prudence. He/she must believe in equality and justice, abstinence and soberness, and be capable of standing against the odds, tyranny and oppression. During high school years, the youths in an open dialogue and interaction with fellow pupils, build up understanding and feelings for others and develop farsightedness to act judiciously. He/she learns to solve in-school disputes with thoughtfulness and discernment, acquires decision-making skills and expands knowledge about human values. In predictable situations, most youth actions are performed for other's sake to seek moral satisfaction.

Virtue arises from our stances and yearnings as we feel to be just in matters of vital importance and feel good to abide by our commitments and keep promises. Individuals are either habitual cheapskate or customarily generous. In the former category are those who seek pleasure in accumulating wealth and material possessions for personal pride and comfort but in the latter category are those who seek solace and consolation in giving away in charitable causes. Altruistic youngsters perform noble deeds and feel happy in giving donations to the less fortunate. Likewise, fidelity is a virtue possessed by reliable and trustworthy individuals. Honest and dependable youth gain respect and praise from parents and teachers. An expression of rational power is the quality of a virtuous person who enjoys self-confidence. The miser is self-centred, displays stinginess and meanness towards the needy, the destitute and the deprived people. Unjust self-preference is a deplorable trait and an awful characteristic that is not supported by rightminded people.

Self-satisfaction is achieved by disabling immodest propensity and controlling resentment and anger when challenged by others. The moral character of youth comprises dynamics such as infant experience, the influence of surrounding ethos and genetic legacy. Well brought up and inborn talent directs the kids towards different occupations, whereas **culture clout** shapes our conduct and outlook. Sound initial grooming and education tend to morally equip the youth to resist the negative power of culture. The relationships youth forms at school do influence moral traits, and antecedent circumstances shape the character. Domestically, problematic brought up in a broken family does not have a positive impact on the individual. The individuality can be malformed due to unfitting social, economic, and family conditions.

Nonetheless, the positive transformation would require appropriate environment for building virtues, values, and attributes Virtues are robust traits. Still, such characteristics are equally unstable when the personal mood comes in the way of dealing with others. The virtue of being helpful and accommodating is a positive attribute. Morality is a condition that makes an adolescent morally right to fulfil the desired task well. A mission is a logical activity undertaken to prove virtuous quality. Common sense development is imperative for the youngster to judge better the validity of his actions in a particular situation. A young boy or girl equipped with general edification and training can wisely exercise judgement and make timely decisions.

Moreover, virtue necessitates coherence between mental and emotional elements of a character. Good emotional habits support the right action and sound judgement. Moral character prompts an individual to act in a way that would be for the benefit of others. Our intuitions and inherent impulses make us feel sympathetic towards fellow human beings. A morally noble and decent teenager never participates in any unlawful activity for personal gains and does not take advantage of others' weaknesses. For example, any youth who wish to be successful needs a suitable environment or maybe, he/she needs a particular context to succeed or that he would not flourish without a specific situation. A morally deceitful person can be immoral, unjust or untruthful, but we cannot label him devious instead we say that his actions are incompatible.

Unblemished and flawless child nurturing is challenging without a morally friendly social atmosphere. The culture of schools developed around a moral vision based on divine laws can better train and educate the youngsters. There is an overwhelming influence of literature on the development of youth character. We follow human-made precepts to solve our problems, and yet, find flaws in our understanding and application of those regulations. We have not succeeded in establishing equality, justice and fairness in almost all societies around the globe. The Christian cultures have long abandoned belief in divine law. The Protestants do not deny the existence of religious doctrine. Still, they believe that it was given, not to be obeyed, but to show man's incapacity to follow it even by grace. The Muslim divine law is derived from the Holy Qur'an but implemented in a handful of countries around the world. Realistically, the divine law is God-given commandment incorporating all aspects of life, whereas humanly devised regulations and protocols embody shortcomings. Although truly democratic societies have made genuine efforts and introduced legal systems for the wellbeing of all subjects, there are still disparities, injustices and inequalities in the conduct of state affairs. All modes of governments, whether communism, capitalism, autocratic and dictatorial, have deficiencies, inadequacies and imperfections.

Imitating Role Models

Ethical mellowness is a stage where pre-teen kids explore peculiarities, experiment with socially enthused excitements and experience virtually innocuous activities. While the teenagers enter the process of intellectual nourishment, they begin to use common sense, show decency in manners, affability in attitudes and pleasantness in etiquettes. Their expressions are thoughtful, dispositions admirable and sensibilities nurtured. Capable of assertiveness equipped with doctrines and beliefs, they are likely to be decisive in principled postures and forthright in moral judgement. Builders of national character and custodians of human values such as Turkish President Recep Tayyip Erdogan; thoughtful instigator of all-embracing multiracial coexistence like Nelson Mandela of South Africa or an advocate of mutually respectful multi-ethnic cultures like Malaysian leader Dr Mahathir Muhammad, are some of the vibrant role models for our youth. The politics of right-wing or the left-wing must not infest, impede and indulge in the smooth journey of moral maturity that would otherwise have undesirable corollaries for any society. It would be difficult to curb the ramifications of misinformation that might well negatively affect innocent perceptions. Morally matured youngsters can resist the dehumanisation of other human beings through dialogue and assertiveness. In the course of growing up, children in a multicultural society encounter a multitude of cultural expressions, edifying and enlightening youthful cognisance. This observance develops concentration, improves focus and ripens understanding.

Every school's educational environment and meaningful instructions are facilitating tools for kids to comprehend guidelines and follow directions for moral strength and ethical power. This much power of school ethos plays an enormous role in shaping the teenager's outlook and stance towards other compatriots. Diversified voices in the society surround the young who must withstand the counterproductive power of moral code. If kids have received sound and comprehensive primary education at school, they are in a better cognitive form to tolerate and endure provocative scenarios. The school and junior college atmosphere can in many ways, offer a fertile knowledge-driven venue for the teenagers to grow, relish and prosper without constraints and limitations.

Fabrics of Character Decline

Before we discuss the resources and frameworks for our kids' moral improvement, it would be pertinent to pay attention to the ingredients of character decline related to youth activities in educational settings. There is no denying fact that third world countries are not better off than the industrialised nations in terms of morality issues. Rampant cheating ranging from school, college, university to public service written competitive exams is prevalent all over the world. Atlanta Public Schools Cheating scandal is notoriously disgraceful in which students showed no remorse, and they did not feel ashamed of cheating in the examination. The notorious scandal involved 11 educators who acted as facilitators in the test cheating embarrassment that had markedly upgraded students' test scores on the Criterion-Referenced Competency Test. (The New York Times, April 1, 2015). Over the last five years, the exam pattern throughout the United States has undergone far-reaching technologically oriented modifications, eliminating any possibility of cheating and deceitful practices in the academic institutions. There are many South Asian and African countries where public employ devious methods for manipulating exams, fiddling with test results and even obtaining fictitious certificates and professional degrees. Examination bodies and institutes of higher learning have turned into factories of fake degrees leading to the production of incompetent youngsters for competitive job markets.

In Africa for example, over 52 high schools in the Republic of Benin have been declared substandard by the Nigerian Ministry of Higher Education because a large number of their dropouts and failed students had obtained a qualification from Benin. In the United Kingdom, 40 websites awarding counterfeit and hollow degrees were closed down by the Higher Education Degree Data check, claims Thomas Lancaster, Associate Dean, Digital Technologies, Staffordshire University. Almost all international students pay hefty sums to acquire bogus degrees, return to their respective countries and get involved in corruption, malpractice and perversion. The phoney universities also operate in the Unite, the d States and some of these have in the past appeared in media such as Collins University, Columbus University, Baytown University, Kingsbridge University, South Creek University, University of Atlanta and the American University of Hawaii. Higher education has become a hothouse of sleaze, especially for wealthy international students from either prosperous families or sponsored by their governments. They wilfully use various tactics, e.g. bribing professors for good grades, collusion in exams, plagiarism and paying cash for research and writing. The school or university culture is an institutional character that offers students qualitative education and training beyond its structures and resources. All such practices amount to moral decline comprising habits of falsehood, deceit and lies. It is an undeniable fact that character vacillates in happy and affluent times. In some developing countries, unfortunately, the deep-rooted culture of dishonesty and corrupt practices are supported by unfounded motives. Ostensibly, children's determination to succeed by unfair means make them manipulate and deploy all tricks to attain higher grades. There are numerous instances of dishonesty prevalent in many countries. Acquisition of fake qualifications for gaining posh jobs is a just proof of youth character decline and ethical regression.

In Bangladesh, for example, examination question papers are leaked well before the exam date for students to prepare notes and then, sit in the designated centre to copy the answers. In some centres, exam supervisors are the collaborators, and the invigilators allow cheating in return for cash. (Dhaka Tribune, December 10, 2019). In many instances, family members, friends or paid -for agents take the exam instead of the original candidate by faking identification with the cooperation of monitors. The girls with headscarf hide earphones for transmitting questions to someone outside the exam hall and then receive replies. Upon completion of higher secondary education, the medical and engineering colleges entrance test triggers the application of deceitful methods to qualify and gain admission to the demanding career. In the past, students have been caught red-handed in Thailand cheating in Rang sit University. The supervisors confiscated several glasses worn by students who had concealed a tiny camera inside the frame while others had electronic wristwatch with message devices. In Pennsylvania, the USA, international students sitting SAT (Scholastic Aptitude Test) used high-tech tools which included, a hidden loop in a shirt, small batteries, a smartphone, and a receiver. The students who qualify SAT by devious means, enter the universities and continue malpractices in graduate studies. Ambiguous websites are offering academic writing, research and editing services to inept international students. They do not wish to learn and gain knowledge but search for stress-free methods to complete their degrees. The course work and term papers, assignments and reports are written by professional agents who offer academic services online and make hefty money from affluent students.

In Australia, a big cheating scandal came to light when the controllers caught 70 students appearing in a year-12 final exam, using mobile phones and electronic calculators. (The Western Australian, Digital Edition, December 9, 2019). Dan Tehan, Australian Minister of Education, declared that university exam cheaters could be imprisoned for up to 2-years and fined 210,000 dollars. He admitted that contract cheating was widespread in

Australia because many students outsource assuagements. (The Guardian, U.K. Edition, April 7, 2019).

Moral decline is not limited to exam cheating alone, but it has perturbed family life. For over a century the Western countries have embraced marriage being companionship and embedded in the romantic adoration and personal commitment of the spouses (husband and wife without legally married); both male and female living together as partners. Non-marital intimacies had never been discouraged ether by the state machinery or the social and cultural organisations. Until World War II, the fundamental purpose of marriage was encouraging procreation to transpire within marriage. Naturally, human survival depends on the conception and also, it stabilises family life for adolescents. Moreover, it is a religious obligation and crucially important for the continuity of the human race.

Moral values continued to decline due to youth rejection of any legal and principled constraints that undermined their dissipated illicit adventures and social habits. The pleasure became paramount over socio-moral responsibility paving the way for civil partnerships that shattered the original concept of marriage, kids and family values. A renowned U.S. intellectual Kohlberg asserted that there was no need to imposed values on students. The youngsters could freely choose the ideals most suited to their social and biological needs without interference from authorities. The youngsters do not like their autonomy to be compromised and subjectivity challenged, but those coming from single-parent perturbed families find it problematic to focus on their studies. They divert energies towards unpleasant and sometimes evil activities that equally cause disturbances and teenage conflicts. Many youths are unaware of moral values, moral dimensions and ethical limitations in interpersonal relationships. In the absence of adequate moral maturity and self-control, the boys, in particular, exert themselves without due regard to the feelings of intimate friends. For want of knowledge about moral values, they cannot personally handle social issues which arise in the course of forming new friendships. Merrill Harmin (1993) in her esteemed publication 'How to Plan a Program for Moral Education' emphasises the need for proper awareness of moral issues among youngsters. There are many troubling ethical issues which include family instability, parental disputes, school violence, theft, lies and deception. Peer chauvinism, spitefulness, violence, sexual harassment on school premises are not uncommon in many industrialised countries. The pupils generally seem more inclined towards a matter of choice rather than a matter of moral obligation in making a judgement of right and wrong, good and bad, appropriate and inappropriate. Globally, as the school authorities relaxed the rules of discipline due to students-led social-mixing pressures, moral reasoning began to gain ground in favour of social autonomy. In effect, a wave of secular thinking penetrated the liberal minds of youth, even in developing countries. The intellectuals in support of age-old practices produced books, and free media promoted liberal social values that deluded and beguiled the teenagers and captivated their perceptions.

Character Building Curriculum

Western countries are much concerned about youth character development. Based on authenticated research findings, several European states have taken comprehensive initiatives towards the promotion of youth character. They are considered an invaluable human resource for nation-building. For example, a movement called CHARACTER COUNTS is an alliance of 500 non-governmental groups committed to instilling great features in youth across the USA. The partners include reputable names such as Association of School Administrators, YMCA, American Federation of Teachers, Big Brothers/Big Sisters, ACA, NFA, United Way and the Points of Light Foundation. Since 1995, Josephson Institute of Ethics has been playing an active part in promoting fundamental human values in school-going children. These include Fairness; Caring; Citizenship; Respect; Responsibility, and Trustworthiness.

Hundreds of schools have already incorporated these tenets into the curriculum. Constructive youth development evolves learning to exercise fairmindedness, compassionate attitude, and reverence for others. The present writer proclaims that our choice of words, the tenderness of voice, albeit clear but not loud, facial parodies and physical gestures communicate values. The secularism and social media networks do more harm than good and contribute little in advancing any moral development initiative. Also, the impact of social inequalities on mental wellbeing across diverse communities impedes the transmission of value-based instructions to youngsters. There must be social accountability within the schools and beyond for smooth application of ethical principles. Before 1800 A.D., moral and religious values formed a significant part of the standard academic subjects such as pure sciences, Engineering and even humanities. Today's youth takes a negligible interest in STEM (Kiemer et al., 2015) but happily chooses drama, music, acting, and sports-related subjects in the school curriculum. Now social life complexities have downgraded traditional values and promoted liberalism in all walks of youth life. "A wide range of misunderstandings and misconceptions surround morals, values and ethics" (Churchill, 1982). The classroom instructions should develop "shared feelings and make one committed to one's responsibilities" (Campbell, 2008). In real life, we make choices that reflect moral thinking and our moral actions impact society. Morals are a way of life which invigorate and revitalise character foundation. Halstead (2007) emphasises "Moral education is about an inner change, which is a spiritual matter and comes through the internationalisation of universal Islamic values". As stated above, faith and theology are insignificant because Western societies are socially progressive and nonspiritual. (Arthur & Carr, 2013). Islamic faith castoffs the view of personal and moral autonomy and encourages good behaviour. The school culture must be responsive to character development.

The code of moral values should be applied to achieve moral excellence (Anderson, 2000). Three stakeholders, families, society and religious bodies can coordinate in teaching character. (Berkowitz, 1999). Predominantly, four values Honesty, Discipline, Wisdom and Kindness lay the foundations of good character. One of the distinguished religious scholars was Al-Ghazali (1058-1111 A.D.) who accentuated the inevitability of teaching character and virtues so that the individuals perform noble deeds that benefit the society and the community at large. Equally crucial for university students is the acquisition of knowledge that reforms their perspectives about morality and values in a multicultural, multi-faith and multiracial society.

Why do youth make morally incorrect decisions that adversely affect others? It is presumably a social intuition comment Haidt (2007) because morals "excite passions and produce or prevent actions". (Hume, 1978/1739). In many cultures, the rules of morality are not consistent as some believe in one act ethically justified while others consider the same exploit indefensible. A court decision favouring the oppressor would be applauded, but his conviction might be labelled a flawed judgement. Moral instinct and sentiments cause moral judgements'. (Haidt., 2001, p.814.). Kent disagrees with this viewpoint as he believed that personal independence and not the craving is at the heart of morality. In a pleasant family upbringing, the children learn to observe situations that make them understand what is morally legitimate and appropriate. For instance, before 1950's a baby born out of wedlock was considered an illegitimate child (born of unmarried parents), but during the last several decades' cohabitation has become an acceptable norm in the Western societies and to a considerable extent in non-Western no-white nations. Consequently, the institute of marriage has been relegated and living together without legally tidying the knot is morally justified. After parliamentary debates and approvals, the societal novelties and moral practices have turned into state laws duly recorded in their statute books.

The women are still an oppressed race in many non-Western countries. Honour slayings of young girls and exchanging daughters to compensate for killing to save a male murderer are usual practices. Moreover, marrying off 9-year-old girls to older adults for a substantial sum of money and treating wives and daughter-in-law's as slaves are prevalent in many Afro-Asian communities. Female domestic workers continue to receive bad treatment from their wealthy, powerful, and superior employers. Such parameters of national and local cultures leave traces on the tender minds and emotions of teenagers. Morally corrupt societies have been struggling to build systems based on mutual respect, understanding, tolerance and honesty. The wealthy elite thinks of affluence only while accumulating more capital and acquiring more resources. Middle and lower-middle classes are consistently and invisibly sliding down towards the poverty line and impoverishment. This unstoppable economic deprivation is the root cause of moral regression, values reversion and tenets corrosion. Under such deplorable conditions, it is difficult for adolescents to differentiate between affirmative action and cynical act. Failure to keep a promise is an immoral act, breaking a simple agreement between two individuals is equally ill-mannered and undesirable. Acquisition of luxuries when others around us are starving is a grossly unprincipled act for upper and elite classes. Leading a prosperous life and lavish spending when others might be starving is utterly disgraceful.

Similarly, drinking alcohol is morally wrong for believers of divine revelation, but perfectly permissible for secular people. One may argue that a haughty conversation is not a moral issue while the emotional effect of such discourse might well be an ethical concern. Press reports frequently mention appalling incidents of youth stabbing to death their biological parents to inherit property. Honour killings of daughters and sisters in tribal areas of South Asia have attracted some world media attention, but no end in sight to abhorrent inhuman practices. Such female abuses recurrently occur more in third world countries rather than the industrialised world. Economic disparities in Afro-Asian societies create unemployment, instigate youth rebellion and cause moral waning.

Emotional turmoil necessitates "moral evaluation" (Haidt, 2001; Greene et al., 2001) because the killing of parents is an emotional decay and mental disorder. A level-headed boy would never think of murdering mother or father for the sake of acquiring the house in which he was born, reared and looked after. It is, therefore, the worst form of a felony and moral rot that has no justification. Mentally perturbed youngsters perform immoral acts such as child abuse, theft, incest, shoplifting, pilfering neighbour's property. The perpetrators execute hurtful actions on account of adverse emotions. It is not appropriate to steal to perform an act of kindness. Piaget (1965/1932) studied young children with specific scenarios and Kohlberg (1984) researched kids' moral development focusing on the nature and validity of moral stages. For example, a boy X meets his friend Y, who is starving and has nothing to eat and asks for help. Boy X has no money to buy his friend food, so he enters a baker's shop and quietly nicks a small loaf of bread, walks out and gives it to his friend Y. In a second episode, a nine years old innocent girl goes into a shop selling goodies; she fancies a colourful ribbon.

In contrast, the shop lady serves another customer; the young girl steals the fabric and runs away. In both situations, the kids focused on motives rather than consequences of immoral theft. Should they both be punished if caught or set free as they are under the age of 10? Who should or should not be punished? Should the boy pinching bred be penalised because bred costs more than the ribbon? Which one of them is cheekiest? Since the boy stole bread for his starving friend and the girl pinched a colourful fabric for herself. In these scenarios, the kid's emotions either centre on consequences or another time on intentions. In the case of a loaf of bread, the purpose seems to be noble, but the method is ethically incorrect.

Conversely, in the framework of ribbon theft, the intention is self-satisfaction and entails no morally wrong validation. Causes are responsible for eventual outcomes because good reasons are commendable for positive moral sequels, but contemptible ignoble purposes produce immoral upshots. In effect, immature kids can distinguish between the two issues. (Frosch, Johnson-Laird and Cowley, 2007), but Mill (1843/1973) considers it capricious and unpredictable. Let us find another setup, a person while crossing the road is knocked down by a car, sustaining life-threatening injuries, when a stranger out of compassion, uses a stolen vehicle to transport him to the hospital. Upon arrival, the wounded person is admitted to the hospital while police arrest a stranger for car theft. What caused him to steal the car to perform a good deed? It is an emotional reaction to help out without thinking about the probable consequences. What should be the moral implications for the culprit? Monica Bucciarelli and her colleagues (2008) present a theory of reasoning about moral propositions related to what might be permissible and impermissible in social relations. They assert that people rely on specific knowledge of their cultures and know fully well what is and isn't a moral issue. In the West, we pay interest on a home mortgage, and this is not a moral issue, but "Under the Sharia law of Islam, however, it is immoral to pay interest, and banks make special provisions for financing the purchase of houses"

(Bucciarelli et al., 2008, p.135). The theory predicates that some scenarios trigger and evoke an emotional response and then a moral evaluation.

The latest example of violent emotional response fits the current situation in India, where ordinary Hindus are consistently killing Muslims. Hindus consider morally wrong to kill cows. In the West, however, Christians and Jews love beef, ham and pork. The cows are extremely sacred in the Hindu religion, and the Indian government has strictly banned the slaughter of cows. Diwali celebration for Hindus is linked to cow worship. Gandhi once said in a large gathering of Hindus that he worships cow and defends its worship against the whole world. Conclusively, it is immoral for any sect, religion or creed to kill a cow because 1.2 billion Hindus revere it. Although, Jews, Muslims and Christians are permitted through Divine revelations to slaughter and eat beef that is morally, spiritually and socially permissible.

Moral values have a significant bearing on the formation of our attitudes, (Corrigan et al., 2010) manners, stances and thoughts. The way benefits are understood by the youngster considerably varies from culture to culture. Several social practices are morally considered correct in European and American societies. A UNESCO report published in 1991 specifies that we can cultivate moral values by the deployment of numerous techniques such as dramas, debates, discussions, brainstorming, stories, poems and songs. Other methods include project assessments, interviews, anecdotal records and audio-visual evaluation. (Churchill et al., 2013). Growing parental concern for youngsters' demands for more autonomy and less social restrictions have made it imperative at state levels to introduce measures geared to the development of ethical values through governmental initiatives. Also, changing social dynamics and economic disparities have created frustration due to lack of job opportunities for school leavers and college graduates. They seek refuge in substance abuse, immoral activities and recreations undertakings.

Acquisition of wealth, attainment of luxury and procurement of extravagance are various forms of moral decline that keep individuals away from constructive and thoughtful undertakings. Overindulgence of any description has morally undesirable and ethically detrimental implications for vulnerable teenagers. The family decline occurred in stages due to world wars in which millions of men perished leaving widows, single mothers and young women to take care of childrearing, work in factories to earn some money, and run the household. Leading the family without a male guardian had repercussions for the adolescents. In the Western world, religiousness slowly lessened since men were not around to take kinfolk to their local Church for spiritual instructions.

While tracing the history of family decline in Greece and Roman times, Carl Wilson in his revered book "Our dance has turned to death" mentions different steps of decay which are not dissimilar to the pattern rampant in modern times. These include family desertion by men, weakening spiritual values, upsurge in material gains, falling ethical canons, emphatic sensual intimacy, increased divorce rates, and marriages frequently ending in separation. Couples split leaves kids without paternal love and tender care in an ideal household. It is an irrefutable fact that long-lasting monogamous marriage relationship is the cornerstone for contentment, constancy and social order. The social decline is a moral decline, and the negative impact of recreational games on society causes societal regression. Many human-made laws debated and approved in parliaments do not correspond to the divine teachings of Prophets Moses and Jesus (peace be upon them). A German Biblical scholar Julius Wellhausen (1844-1918) was an authority on Old Testament studies who commented that early books of Bible were not put together by Moses himself, but were collected together several centuries later. Likewise, Prophet Jesus did not hand over divine messages to his disciples, but much later, his followers wrote what they had heard or remembered.

On the contrary, Qur'an was revealed in 23 years which was simultaneously transmitted orally to the believers gathered around the Prophet Muhammad (peace be upon him). The devotees instantaneously memorised word by word and chapter after chapter, the entire Holy Book. Even today, millions of Muslims around the globe have learned the complete Holy Qur'an. It is a credible, uncorrupted Divinely Revealed Book that has survived in its original form for the last 1442 years. The

Holy Qur'an is a complete code of conduct, an all-inclusive constitution that guides humanity towards the just moral path, decent, ethical conduct and virtuous living.

Family breakdowns happen when separated couples replace obsolete relationships with remarriage or began to live with another partner. Unpredictable social change creates jealousy, bad chemistry and bitterness in kids who most often deride and ridicule stepfathers. Youth witness early stage of both social and family regression in which they seek tricks outside the household that might involve substance abuse, rape and theft. All these activities are called immoral. We can say that telling a lie is moral atrophy. Not long ago, Clergy disapproved gambling, but the dice was a popular game in Roman times. The rolling of dice was an act of gambling that promoted sinful propensity. The Divine Revelation, the Holy Qur'an equally banned all games of gambling which true Muslims believe, accept and apply in their practices. The Muslims whether Arabs or otherwise who drink alcohol, conduct gambling in New York, Paris and London Casinos and engage in prohibited immoral practices are not the practising believers but claim to be modern or moderate believers.

Character Development

YOUTH OUR HOPE, WHO HAPPILY COPE (Poem)

Youth is The Future of Humanity

Possess Hope, Wisdom & Serenity

Builders of Society, Free from Vanity

Front Line Doctors Serve with Sanity

Sacrifice Their Lives in COVID-19
Fearless Souls are Valiant Teens

Freedom They Cherish in The Cyber Space
Exhibit Understanding & Act With Grace

Socially Educate, With Little Constraint
Grant Empowerment, With Self-Restraint

Tools of Wisdom, Love and Care
Assets They are in Human Affair
Inculcate Virtues of Self-Esteem
Let Them Have Bigger Dream

In Adversity, They Do Survive
In Abundance, They Happily Thrive

Resources They Need, to Glow & Bloom
Stressful Upbringing Invites Gloom

Youths Are Gleaming Spark and Light
Let Us Offer Them Future Bright
Render Guidance With Optimum Might

So Do They Contribute With Full insight

Invest in Grooming, Rear Them Well

Reward You Reap, Rose Like Smell

[Composed by DR NAZIR AHMAD 10 June 2020]

Good habits are the backbone of strong character as virtuous conduct, and traditional components of family values implant endurance and courage from the very early stages of infant upbringing. "Character building begins in our infancy and continues until death" (Eleanor Roosevelt, 1884-1962). Parental interaction with children should focus on productive themes related to integrity, goodness, honesty and self-esteem. Integrity is the feature of exhibiting a steady and inflexible adherence to resilient moral and upright beliefs. We teach our kids integrity, decency and serenity. We pay particular attention to:

- Truthfulness and Frankness
- Endurance and Silence
- Patience and Forbearance
- Tranquillity and Calmness in unusual situations
- Composure and Quietness in odd conditions
- Rectitude and Correctness in unexpected settings

- Accountability and responsibility in matters of self-culpability

- Critical thinking for decision making and evaluation

- Peaceful Home Atmosphere

Mother is the cradle of primary training for youngsters, making them understand the reality of being truthful and frank under any circumstances. Indeed, "One word of truth outweighs the world" ((Aleksander Solzhenitsyn, 1918-2008). Accuracy and veracity overshadow falsehood and fabrications, which are actual, negative aspects of youth character. One needs courage to stand up for justice, fairness and integrity. As Spencer Johnson (1938-2017) proclaims that "Integrity is telling myself the truth and honesty is telling the truth to other people". Practising righteousness and integrity in a complex environment is a challenge for youth. However, "Rectitude is the bone that gives firmness and stature" (Rick Remender 1973-). According to Ralph Waldo Emerson, 1803-1882) "Rectitude is a perpetual victory, celebrated not by cries of joy but by serenity, which is joy fixed or habitual". For youth to grow up as morally perfect, tranquillity and serenity are salient features of an admirable character. It could only be achieved in a friendly family set up. A famous German writer Johann Wolfgang Von Goethe (1749-1832) tags just one feature of the cheeriest youth, "He is happiest, be king or peasant, who finds peace in his home". It literary means, in our teenagers, we must sow the seeds of truth, honesty, endurance and thoughtfulness, and reap the rewards afterwards.

A great Scottish writer Thomas Carlyle, 1795-1881) once said, "Endurance is patience concentrated" whereas "Egotism is the source and summary of all faults and miseries" so that our children do not grow up selfish, self-centred and arrogant. Carlyle asserts that "Silence is the element in which great things fashion themselves together" because chronicles indicate that individuals who outperformed in any significant branch of knowledge spent a considerable number of youth years in isolation and solitude. It is crucial to hold purposeful discussion with children who learn a great deal from mother and father and raise concerns. As Edward Gibbon (1737-1794) believes that "Conversation enriches the understanding, but solitude is the school of genius". Remoteness and inaccessibility are the keys to imaginative ideas and creative writing. Albert Einstein (1879-1955) thinks, "imagination is more important than knowledge; knowledge is limited, imagination encircles the world."

George Bernard Shaw (1856-1950), an Irish great playwright and novelist quite rightly stated that "Education can and should do much influence social, moral and intellectual discovery by stimulating critical attitudes of thought in the young". He also remarked that "There is no accomplishment so easy to acquire as politeness and none more profitable". Mothers explain to their kids how to address teachers, grandparents and older adults. They tell their children the vitality of good manners and respectability. Haughty and big-headed youth with innate arrogance develop feelings of superiority and supremacy. During classroom lessons, instrumental teachers spare a few moments to speak on topics of societal concerns. They instruct pupils about manners and degradation, and the ills of insufferable insolence and rudeness. For instance, never say or do things that make other pupils look small, insulted and humiliated. Human beings are born free and equal, and nobody is inferior or superior due to creed, faith, gender, race, wealth, and affluence. Treat others the way you would like to be treated; greet others the way you would like to be welcomed.

There is a secure link between self-belief and respectfulness which must be promoted by family members and allow the children to express openly their feelings, thoughts and opinions on social, personal and educational matters that relate to overall psychological health and physical wellbeing. Parents should hold a frank discussion, but ignore the inappropriate response, support the reflective feedback, encourage the engagement and complement thoughtfulness. Mother or father should build up a rapport with school teachers for monitoring the kid's academic performance and frankly discuss any emotional issues. If we ignite meaningful conversation between teachers and pupils, and between parents and children, regularly, we can articulate considerable progressive and inculcate productive features in our youth.

CHAPTER VII

DECENT VIRTUES AND VALUES

Good moral character comprises all essential virtues, qualities, and features that make a worthy youngster member of the society. In early teen years, the children are more interested in explorations and discoveries about self and others and far less concerned about morality, integrity, and truthfulness. Sincere lifestyle alternatives have substituted distasteful manners owing to swapped patterns of conduct and imitation. The teens are communally liberal rather than socially conservative, thus becoming exceedingly indulgent in intimate relationship performances. They set personal scruples dismantling social rules and traditional undertakings. Moral tenets are declining due to lack of forbearance, respect, and consideration for others. On account of weakening faith, increased licentious and impious practices have subjugated youth perceptions about morality, virtue, decency, and values.

People in diverse cultures accentuate distinctive values as in Japan, says Schwartz and Sagiv, 1995, friendship falls into security rather than benevolence. He presented a values theory based on 88 samples in 40 countries and offered yardsticks for detecting what is culture-specific in value meaning. Values are the staple dogmas about what is moral and what is immoral? Just as a child born out of wedlock is illegitimate and conceived by a lawfully married mother is legitimate.

Virtues and Virtuousness

Virtuousness is a human trait comprising decency and goodness, not transferable to anyone. It is a feature or a group of qualities nurtured by parents, cherished by teachers, and fostered by an environment in which the adolescents live, study, socialise, grow up and then become worthy adults. Virtue ascertains how a child handles calamity and endures any unexpected hardship. Attributes are unlike aptitudes that cannot be misused. One can heap propensities for indulgences and gratifications. Naturally, children learn manners at the dining table. When mum or dad tells them to sit still, use a knife and fork, eat gradually, and ask any questions gently. If a kid talks loudly, mum reminds him about politeness, civility, and graciousness. Virtues are inherited and innate, but many attributes are attainable just we can achieve wisdom can through potencies such as inquisitiveness, ingenuity, open-mindedness, craving for knowledge, and perception. Six universal virtues quoted by several authors are wisdom, courage, humanity; justice; temperance, and transcendence.

SIX UNIVERSAL VIRTUES

Courage: youth should possess valour, Audacity and Fearlessness.

Humanity: Youth must be kind-hearted, sympathetic, and Compassionate.

Justice: Youth should be upright and show fairness and impartiality in dealings.

Temperance: Youth should have sobriety, abstinence and exhibit self-restraint

Transcendence: Youth must dismiss superiority complex and supremacy.

Wisdom: Youth should seek wisdom through knowledge and perception.

In various civilisations, humanities, cultures, and beliefs, ethical values, and social structures vary, and there is no single coherent morality for the entire universe. However, there are resemblances in noble virtues which originate across all established societies. In major religions of the world supported by Divine Revelations such as Islam, Christianity, and Judaism, ordinary moral virtues do exist, which form the basis of national and individual character. These are essential for the embellishment of humanity and the maintenance of social order. Catherine McManamon (2017), in her GetFed blog, mentions ten virtues: Angelic Sweetness; Charity; Obedience; Mental Prayer; Divine Wisdom; Patience; Lively Faith; Profound Humility; Surpassing Purity; and Universal Mortification.

To begin with, she asserts be kind, gracious, articulating gratitude, and be sensitive towards others' needs. Through charity, we express genuine love for Almighty God and be obedient to Him and Him alone who has no partner, son, or daughter. In Islam, the Muslims praise Almighty God, meditate, remain silent, speak when necessary, and donate generously to the noble causes for the pleasure of Allah, the Almighty One God, the Creator of everything in the universe. We should demonstrate humility and humbleness, endure suffering, NGS, and distresses with patience and resilience. Within each family, these virtues should be practised daily and simultaneously transferred to our adolescents. Attributes are the depiction of an individual's action influenced by conventions, customs, and traditions.

One cannot claim to be a person of robust character if he/she does not possess fundamental virtues, prevalent indecent individuals. Several nations in the East and West are grappling with predicaments of youth character decline owing to morally perturbed rehearses and socially enticing practices. Character cries can be visibly heard from classrooms, school playgrounds, forecourts to sports arenas, and community venues because character traits are the substratum of youth wellbeing. Socrates, Plato, and Aristotle consider virtues as the traits of character that make someone a decent human being. Any person visiting a store selling greeting cards would not miss Hallmark's birthday or wedding anniversary cards. They also have got well soon, and Christmas cards, each containing beautiful words. Some of the jargon and poetic verses express human virtues inspirational messages, song lyrics, and breath-taking morally enlightening quotations. The tickets are tools for emotional communication since the lovely wording touches the sender's heart. (West, 2018). Truthfulness is a 'Social

Virtue,' which I have noticed in many different types of greeting cards as an expression of correlation (Guignon, 2004, p.151). All universal virtues are mentioned in either text form, poetic verses, rhymes, and stanzas. Fascinating couplets and lyrics are printed on Valentine's Day, Mother's Day cards. The meaningful and eloquent words astoundingly articulate sentiments enumerate virtues and highlight human merits and qualities.

Virtue is the ability to view things from other's perspectives and the flexibility and willingness to seek consensus or common ground. Merit can be acquired through habits imitating role models. Virtue is like a practical skill, can be refined but need motivation and coherence to learn it.

Youngsters should have the virtue of moral, physical, and mental courage to absorb fear, confront danger, and endure hardships. Likewise, the purity of justice will enable broods to accept responsibility for self-actions and treat others justly and equitably. Humanity relates to empathy, understanding, and compassion for friends and strangers to reduce the miseries of other people. Temperance is concerned with persons' sensual pleasures as prudence demands self and emotional control, albeit extending the social network. It is a human instinct to admire the natural beauty, exercise a sense of hilarity, and explore the spiritual aspect of humanity to lead a purposeful life. Wisdom is one of the essential virtues believed to be God-given. However, Western philosophers argue that it is "practical intelligence which presupposes truth but believes it to be necessary for the process of socialisation- an accurate representation of reality" (Greic, 2013).

Righteous Beliefs

In the learning context at school, whatever children contemplate, feel, and accomplish are, to a considerable extent, personality traits. Moral dogmas and instincts guide kids' conduct in day-to-day matters. Graham et al. (2011) discuss moral foundations such as care, fairness, sanctity, loyalty, and respect that can be tested in practical scenarios to identify strengths of pupils' character. Virtues are purposeful engagements leading to happiness, cheerfulness, and exhilaration. Kindness is a supreme virtue once expressed radiates joy and peace, goodwill and harmony towards others.

Religious beliefs inform us about human virtues primarily based on Divine Revelations. In contrast, philosophers present attributes from their non-religious perspective, while intellectual and scholars argue that subjective characteristics form the basis of virtues. Moreover, some virtues are unique to specific cultures such as big-heartedness, and kindness stems from French civilisation. Attributes, however, do unite or swerve in multicultural societies because human beliefs and values impact individual actions, thereby giving rise to different ethical communities. Some nations share the same virtues due to prevailing social and cultural patterns. German and Dutch people, in general, possess attributes of candidness and trustworthiness. Erikson (1959), in his study, documents eight virtues, namely, care, competence, fidelity, hope, love, purpose, will, and wisdom. On the other hand, Van Oudenhoven et al., (2012) narrates 15 virtues- courage, faith, helpfulness, hope, joy, justice, love, mercy, moderation, modesty, openness, reliability, resolution, respect, and wisdom. We have motivational virtues, says Haslam et al. (2004), that command people to act and perform tasks considered to be beneficial for others. Attributes are relatively tangible, which can be effectively transmitted. (Van Tongeren, 2003).

Virtues are decisive actions that result in personal contentment, optimism, and animation. Helpfulness is one of the admirable virtues once articulated derives bliss and amity, exhibits benevolence and concord towards others. Youth possessing such attributes are considered helpful, trustworthy, and soft-hearted. Intellectual virtues like wisdom, prudence, and intellect instigate and nurture through parental training and classroom instructions. Temperance, self-restraint, self-control, and generosity are ethical virtues gained through observations, habits, customs, and practices. Immorality does not stain human nature; a person can undoubtedly perform some noble deeds. Attributes such as courage, bravery, and fearlessness are unique, usually found in youth who become great leaders. Theodore Roosevelt got shot in the chest during a campaign speech, but he consented to treatment after an hour of the incident. The virtues we hold profoundly exist for our subjective motives, and therefore, constant evaluation of merits is necessary lest any single attribute overused backfires. Raising error-free kids who get little chance of learning from mistakes is unlikely to demonstrate courage and bravery in complex situations.

In the social correlation context, virtues of love, compassion, and adoration, women attach great importance to men because female preference is stability and durable qualities. Young girls will fall for boys who are reliable, brave, courageous, and respectful.

Personality Traits

Virtue will be ineffective if the personality traits of our youth are mediocre. If any teacher lacks the robustness of such characteristics, the influence on pupils would most probably be minimal or negligible. Unsurprisingly, children have different dispositions enshrined in traits such as carefulness, meticulousness, affability, and diligence. These attributes are consistent and stable, which form a significant part of the personality. It a teenager is covetous and egotistical at the age of 15, he would most likely be the same in 20 years, although a change in circumstances does influence the conduct of pupils at school and elsewhere. One of the universal virtues is honesty that can be conveyed by instruction and practice. But the unrighteousness is a rare phenomenon asserts Doris and Stich (2005, p.121). Though virtue is inert and unswerving, it can still be a predictable disposition in certain situations that incite a virtuous reaction. Mischel and Peake (1982) evaluated pupils' conduct based on their timely daily attendance, assignment completion schedule, and recording abstract knowledge during lectures in the classroom. The teacher aims to inculcate in students a particular virtue of conscientiousness. He/She makes them understand the desirability of punctuality and promptness in performing tasks. Being obedient and willing to follow instructions have a positive impact on work habits and academic performance.

Academic dishonesty is the result of personal failings argues Lickona (, 1996). Virtue is the quality of being morally good with excellent traits. Why do some pupils display academic dishonesty is the result of several factors? We do know children are primarily innocent, generally innocuous, and mostly blameless in their conduct, actions, and perceptions.

Academic dishonesty stems from environmental enticements, family pressures, and external social influences. Although the power of genetic control is excellent and shapes the conduct of a child, competition to achieve higher grades to ensure acceptance at a university exerts undue pressure. Both the school's settings and parental expectations and social life commitments change the teens' acuity towards exams. The strength of character is at a delicate point when inducement to be dishonest is irresistible for a child. He might possess some admirable virtues, but after all, the innocent kid vulnerable to enticement. According to Wright and Mischel (1987), the traits reliably definite themselves in situations that are suited to their expression. Even minor factors influence conduct in diverse ways and manners. Professor Walter Mischel experimented in 1970 at the Bing Nursery School of Stanford University when he offered a marshmallow, a cookie to each of a group of 4-6-year-old kids and told them to wait for 15 minutes before consuming it so that they would get two marshmallows." Attentionally exited the classroom to stay away for a while, but upon returning after a short interval, he became amazed to notice most of them had eaten it. The teacher repeated the experiment in another class but explained to them that they should pretend that cookies were not on their desk and wait for more cookies. As before, he departed and came back to the class only to observe that the kids were still waiting and did not eat anything. It was a delayed gratification and test of their patience at such a tender age. The self-control virtue which the children practiced at the age of four determined success throughout life, being happier and better academic performers. Dr Mischel, an Austrian born Psychologist in his book 'The Marshmallow test: mastering self-control' reflected that "Children who hold out longer for the bigger reward in some conditions were also likely to have higher SAT scores to function better socially and to manage temptation and stress better."

On the question of cheating in exams, Geno et al. (2009) research findings indicated that the inclination to cheat was affected by the dishonest conduct of others. If the peers and classmates use unfair methods to succeed in the exams, the virtuous kids would be at a disadvantage. They could equally indulge in such deceitful practices. Hartshorne and May (1928, p.328) studied children's conduct during exams. They noticed that the kids who cheated in mathematics class did not cheat in the geography class, and those taught by a different teacher next year showed complete honesty and decency. The new teacher was instrumental in instigating honest discussions that helped improve the character traits of pupils. (Colby, 1977). The classroom ethical dialogue with students helps promote morality, and cooperative learning enhances academic achievement. (Berkowitz et al. 2007, p.428). Classroom cheating occurs if the teacher is too lenient and soft. Also, when the opportunity to deceive is available, they would not hesitate to take advantage of the delicate situation. Once children begin the ownership of their actions, their moral perceptions and activities change for the better.

The beliefs, assumptions, and postulations that kids have acquired from families, teachers, and religious scholars are the filters through which they view the world. Then use mental powers to reflect and replicate differently about other people and situations, surroundings, and settings. Virtue is a powerful instrument to enhance cohesion providing these are reinforced regularly in the school settings, playgrounds, and sports clubs. Exposure to Divine Revelations with the sincere and unbiased approach would undoubtedly open the door to understanding the real purpose of our lives on this earth. The spiritual standards are far more superior than secular beliefs. An Irish literary personality George Bernard Shaw, (1856-1950), a Scottish scholar Thomas Carlyle (1795-1881), an English writer Muhammad

Marmaduke Pickthall. (1875-1936) and an Englishman Rowland Allanson-Winn, 5th Baron Headley (1855-1935) fully support divine truth and moral strength. Lord Headley's two notable books are "The Three Great Prophets" and "A Western Awakening to Islam." A virtuous teacher should act as a role model and help kids develop noble characteristics and magnanimous virtues. Some pupils might have genetically transferred ideal attributes and profoundly epitome qualities, while many kids might have a few attributes, but teachers committed to promoting high moral virtues can make a difference. The teachers can shape the character traits of school-going children, transform behaviour, and alter some undesirable habits.

Initially, paternal attention and maternal affection can provide decent guidance to their children in a pleasant household setting. All cultures appreciate virtues because qualities and values are an invaluable segment of human conduct, indiscriminately an implicit exposure to the outside world. More specifically, what is refreshing about the good life is 'Personality Traits' that make someone a person of exemplary character. Reasonable conduct is not merely virtue-based; it has rooted in total obedience to the Commandments of Almighty God. As Christianity faded in standing during the past few centuries, the Divine Law ultimately gave way to a secular parallel marked moral law. Still, they accentuated rubrics of acceptable behaviour in contrast to the stoutness of character. Realistically, one cannot develop personality without adherence to God-given laws. In some societies, human happiness is at the forefront of all regulations at the cost of rebellion against beliefs, norms, and spiritual insights. Real and original Visionary teachings have been distorted to suit the limitless freedom and boundless pleasures of humanity. Some of the laws in Western societies are unreservedly reprehensible. These shameful laws are against the teachings of Prophets, including Jesus, and yet, enjoy complete backing of prominent personalities and influential individuals. Strangely, media is no longer unbiased and copiously support these movements but simultaneously dampen the voices and concerns of rightminded intellectuals who dare to speak out against such undesirable and immoral practices.

Nobel men have grave fears that in these momentously developed and crucially acclaimed enlightened societies, sooner rather than later, the incest practice would be made legal under the camouflage of GSA.

Dahlsgaard et al. (2005) study of major religions of the world, including Islam, Judaism, and Christianity, provides the relevant text of various traditions and positive features. The authors assert that religious sources guide us in the choice of character traits. Dr Kohlberg (1958), in his PhD research, discuses modes of thinking and opportunities in years 10 to 16," then presents a theory of moral reasoning of children irrespective of their cultural background. Social diversity plays a part in cognitive and cerebral development. Piaget hypothesises that a child feels a sturdy, honest reverence for the adult authority.

On the contrary, Kohlberg has a divergent view that 4 to 8-year-old kids' moral judgement is based on 'hedonistic' view of right and wrong. He researched 95 children aged 4, 5, and 7 with stories in which kids demonstrating disobedience to a rule received a reward, but in other tales, obedience amounted to punishment.

European countries consider 3-6-year child grooming critically crucial for laying the foundations of good morals. The Netherlands, Republic of Ireland, and Iceland start obligatory preschool education at the age of 4, but kids as young as three are encouraged to register in nurseries. Likewise, Turkey has a splendid national education programme in which young ladies with 0-3-year-old children get an official break from work to focus on basic training. The Turkish government provides free enrolment in preschool nurseries for infants allowing professional mothers to go back to work and contribute towards the innovative development of the nation. There are correctly qualified teachers in kindergartens who are responsible for the cognitive, physical, and character development of innocent children.

As children's transition from junior school to high bring specific changes and challenges in their lives, some of them find it difficult to cope with new tasks and experiments. They do enjoy more freedom of thought and action, but new friendships impact their habits and etiquettes. For example, the distinction between moral and immoral acts gets blurred in the teenage years. They do not know whether smoking is morally wrong or permissible; neither do they discover the true meaning of morality and means to avoid immoral activities. Exam cheating is considered potentially undesirable, but it does not directly harm anybody else, and it cannot be labelled immoral action. Moral laws are accurate and irrefutable, but these could be applied to maintain equilibrium and symmetry in society. Let us suppose two teenage kids are arguing about 'fulfilling promise' and argue that breaking it would be an utterly immoral act. The other presents a counterargument by stating that immoral acts carry punishment, but breaking promises does not warrant retribution.

Similarly, smoking is morally wrong, which does not harm anyone. As such, illegal acts are mostly immoral, but all corrupt activities may not be considered illegal. In the educational context, incongruous examination in which teachers facilitate cheating is unethical and backstabbing, telling lies and misleading peers are equally immoral practices. Notwithstanding that nicking items form other classmates' bags, hitting a friend, and malicious teasing is also immoral acts.

Resilience improves peer-to-peer relationships and creates a supportive and friendly culture in schools. Niemiec (2018) has produced 70 evidence-based, step-by-step activity handouts for both teachers and parents, which help to develop in kids' character strength awareness so that they can find meaning and engagement in their lives. Dr Ryan Niemiec was an Education Director of VIA Institute on Character, Cincinnati, Ohio, who had conducted invaluable research and devised strategies for youth character building in the USA.

Hartshorne and May deal with the concept of situational integrity as their co-jointly research from 1924-1928 on the conduct of 7000 children aged 8-16 in the United States shows new horizons. They proclaimed that honesty is a resolute situational factor. Being truthful in one situation was no indication that the same kid would be candid in another location. Dysfunctional environment arising from poverty, broken homes, and the wicked neighbourhood is partly to blame for crimes such as thievery, embezzlement, and street violence. The children possessing traits of honesty, goodness, and fairness belonged to homes placing tremendous value on morality. Our surroundings have an enormous influence on our conduct in society. Honest children are unlikely to succumb to immoral and deceitful undertakings. Such kids would not think of manipulating academic exam results in dishonest means. Only sluggish and disgruntled children who believe they would not be caught red-handed do employ unfair methods of fraud and duplicity.

Hutton's (2007, p.171) CAI survey reported 32 per cent of students admitted laziness was the primary factor for cheating in exams; 29 per cent of students conceded to getting higher grades was the main reason for this act, and just 12 per cent blamed parental and external pressure to succeed. In another survey, McCabe and Trevino (1993) found that business studies students cheated more than students from another academic discipline such as sciences. Also, business students were tolerant of unethical behaviour. (Crown and Spiller, 1998). Moreover, Smyth and Davis (2004, p.106) specified in their research findings that "Business majors have a higher incidence of collegiate cheating and are more prone to consider cheating socially acceptable." When Strom and Strom (2007, p.105.) questioned teenage college students about these practices, 95 per cent of the students surveyed, unanimously replied that they had been deceitful, but never got caught.

Gehrig and Pavela (1994, p.5.) termed cheating as educational dishonesty related to forgery of documents, impeding or damaging the literary output of others and assisting students in this act. Plagiarism is also a form of cheating (Stokes & Newstead, !995) as the other's work is copied without an acknowledgement, and unfairly credit is acquired.

It is possible to curtail despicable habitual trickery through the structural exam re-evaluation, and redesigning assignment methods. This obnoxious addiction of simulation can be further reduced utilising assessment appraisal techniques, thus creating a pupil-friendly learning environment. Nonetheless, an incentive for cheating will subside if we introduce open book tests and collaborative classroom assessments. Admittedly, pupils in general, don't like memorising any complex piece of scientific information because they find it dull, tedious and dreary.

Child grooming concerning moral matters commences in the first five years of childbirth since he/she learns to obey rules in the absence of monitoring, a 'milestone in children's social and moral development' (Hoffman, 1994). It is indeed a 'covert and deliberate way to break a rule to gain an advantage' (Green, 2004). In a guessing game, Green et al. (2009) studied child motivation to cheat and found that only some kids resorted to cheating. In an experiment in the school environment, Evans et al. (2011) asked 3 to 5-year-old kids who were left alone in a room, not to lift a cup to peek at its contents. On returning to the classroom, the teacher noticed rather amazingly that 5-yeat-olds tended to glance more than three and 4-year-olds. In secondary school exams, children have reduced inhibitory control to benefit from cheating to secure higher grades. Lack of confidence in their abilities, inadequate exam preparation, and fear of failure are a few significant factors in kids' cheating practices. In the early stages of moral development stated Krahn,(1971, p.373.), the Pastor of Trinity Lutheran Church, New York, most kids considered ethical rules merely mandatory and inviolable, which was previously proven by Kohlberg's (1963, p.21) research findings. Children perceived rules which mirrored parental influence. The kids were not entitled to challenge parents' power and ask unnecessary questions. Both moral and immoral acts were clearly defined by either mum or dad so that the kids learned about right and wrong, true and false in their day-to-day activities.

Kids are supposed to improve academic skills and develop ethical conduct. They should learn to read and write and especially how to get along with classmates. In the process of mingling, they learn human values and positive aspects of cultural diversity. They learn to be quiet in the class, work well, respect teachers, stand in the queue, and listen attentively when the teacher is lecturing. They comprehend the necessity of relationships, sharing views, and forming social connections. We can robustly gauge kids' talents in an informal cordial setting. In schools, recess time brings children together for fun and giggle, relaxation, and amusement. In such an atmosphere, there is little distraction from quality education; kids learn self-restraint, problem-solving and cognitive skills. The social togetherness at school builds values and social norms. If the girls are habitually polite, the boys are supposedly oblivious. Globally, the school dropout rate of boys is more significant than girls who might enjoy teasing and bantering each other but keep calm and show enhanced attendance. In some European countries, boys perceive themselves better at math and science subjects, and girls perform in humanities and social science disciplines.

Character Strengths	Traits/Virtues
Kindness / Niceness	Love, Affection, Empathy, Soft Heartedness, Concern, Sympathy, Positive Relations, Altruism
Spirituality	Purpose, Resourceful, Divine Guidance
Courage	Perseverance, Boldness
Humility	Serenity, Meekness, Tradition (Value), Patience, Intelligence, Caring, Sharing
Self-regulation	Conformity (Value), Discipline, Scrupulousness, Reliability, Consciousness, Punctuality, Modesty
Curiosity	Anticipation, Openness, Personal Growth, Stimulation (Value), Love of Learning
Creativity	Imaginative, Integrity, Self-Direction
Generosity	Benevolence, Philanthropy, Helpfulness
Self-control	Tolerance, Prudence
Justice	Fairness, Impartiality
Persistence / Tenacity	Diligence, Will-Power, Determination
Humour	Playfulness, Light-Heartedness
Hope	Optimism
Wisdom	Critical Thinking, Judgement, Knowledge Acquisition
Wittiness	Keenness and Cleverness

Sources: Niemiec (2018); Cawley et al. (2000); Schwartz & Sagiv, (1995); Peterson & Seligman (2004)

The consensus among intellectuals, sociologists, psychologists, and social science researchers points to the unwavering fact that most virtues can be taught, applied, and formed to shape the lives of youngsters. Among the common qualities are caring and sharing, respect and responsibility, fairness and trustworthiness that illuminate the character of our teenagers. A flexible and comprehensive character education programme instituted in schools has a lasting impact on kids' discipline, behaviour, morals, and etiquette. A consciousness family initiates character building at home, which is enhanced and supported at school where social and educational venues amplify the modelling of ethical ideologies. Youth need to understand what is morally wrong in a particular culture may not be sinful in another culture. In an Arab or Muslim society whether Bahrain or Indonesia, paying interest on house loan is immoral, but in the West, interest on a home mortgage is morally correct and legally binding. Islamic laws/Sharia laws forbid usury, but the Western banking system is entirely based on moneylending and charging interest. Alcohol consumption is also prohibited in Islamic Divine laws, whereas Western culture morally commends and legally accepts pubs and night clubs as an integral part of the society. Bribery and perjury are immoral acts, and perpetrators, once caught, can be tried in the court of law and duly punished. Despite proven immorality, corruption, sleaze, and bribe are widespread in many developing countries. Almost all businesses prosper in African and South Asian nations due to the contaminations of consumable food items that act as a milestone for profiteering. Industrialists and factory owners do not lag in amassing wealth, hiking prices, and maintaining the highest standards of living within deprived majority populations. They are insensitiveness to other living conditions but continue fast track on the wrong path of greediness. We should teach our kids at school, the rights and wrongs about bribery, inducement, kickbacks, and food contaminations. In developing but corrupt economies, the children might grow up to show enough courage and question their fathers about the potential sources so much money and luxury that resultantly made their life comfortable.

Individuality & Self-Indulgence

In the 1960's global rise in individuality, independence and self-interest brought new perception to the forefront where distinctive rights and freedom took precedence over accountability. Loss of moral authority and weaker belief in ethical standards resulted in people's preferred self-indulgence, pleasure-seeking, and hedonism. The elite favoured secular modes of living, admirably appealing to the majority. Youth despised the imposition of values that impeded their socialisation. The youngsters were free to choose their pathways rather than being taught at school. Character education was considered unnecessary and irrelevant to the changing needs of a school-going kid. An individual cannot openly discuss purely personal desires and social relationships in any public forum. Although the London born Jerry

Springer show in the USA, crossed all moral limits, and emotional boundaries in televised debates, it had a great deal of real insight, ethical learning, and youth development rarely seen in media. Jerry Springer aired the dirty laundry on each tv episode for more than twenty-five years. But his emotionally inspirational concluding remarks at the end of his shows shaped the lives of hundreds of thousands of couples around the globe. In the European countries and the USA, moral education was not a debatable subject until the 1990's when they reconsidered and revised the school curriculum to incorporate values training. European influence in the US educational institutions created a distinction between facts and values. The factual syllabus would enumerate actualities of life without exaggeration.

Moral enlightenment, in the past, orbited around instructions, expecting youth conduct revolving around the Christian standards. The school communities in the West were considered ethical societies (Walker, 2015, p.83). However, in the present century, moral education emphasis changed towards delicate emotional selves and self-esteem. Moral actions form the basis of emotions, whereas moral reasoning is intentional, having personal mindfulness of any impending moral judgments. Two mental measures are at work in decision making, namely reasoning and intuitions, the latter being innate and instinctive operations upon construed moral sense. If a young man commits an immoral act, it is emotionally driven moral intuition. The same individual can withhold intuition to prevent undesirable action. There are recurring and corresponding relationships between emotions and character traits. Unconsciously, our emotions direct our feelings. It is challenging to act morally in diverse scenarios because our moral emotions influence behaviour in social situations. Our social environment has a considerable impact on kids' moral development.

Such an environment involves teachers, peers, neighbours, parents, and friends, as all of these exert a direct influence on morality. It is inapposite to impose morality on pupils, but it would be praiseworthy to inculcate ethical norms through rehearses and presentations. Teachers should act as role models and help create a social environment in which children learn by observation and reflection. The kids learn more by watching parents and peers, friends, and acquaintances. Albert Bandura (1986) presented a theory of learning by observation, advising school teachers to conceive strategies geared to the learning levels of students.

Notwithstanding that, children's socialisation with classmates has an invaluable role in the moral development within the school atmosphere. They deride the curtailment of freedom, enjoy the culture of self-indulgence, individuality, and independence. All modern societies seem reluctant to accept any kind of abstinence that might undermine secular values and ideals. Even in non-secular cultures, teachers are not equipped with intellectual tools to impart behavioural training.

Turkish Model for Values Teaching

Industrialised countries do not offer specific teacher training for accurately imparting values education to school children on account of secular societies in which people are free to choose their way of life. The state laws' implementation protects human rights, Western values, and cultural tenets. The behavioural norms are different in different multicultural and multi-ethnic societies. Likewise, teachers are not inclined to engage in moral education in Turkey. (Frey, 2010). During the Ottoman Empire (15th to 18th centuries), the authorities did not introduce culture. During the Tanzimat period (1839-1876), the European education system was prevalent in all Turkish schools. After the Second World War, Turkey followed Europe in adopting the secular order, and even the Latin script replaced the Arabic style of writing.

In 1924, John Dewey was invited by Kamal Ataturk to overhaul the education system and make concrete proposals. Owing to his tangible prepositions, the Ataturk government established Village institutions and schools in various parts of the land. (Sahin, 2017), but eventually closed in 1948 due to political and administrative reasons. The Ataturk administration was very keen on making Turkish values, a formidable part of community school programmes. The teachers were not sure what exactly should incorporate in the Values part of the syllabus. There were large number of Turkish Christians residing in all parts of the country. They did not have their private faith-related institutes of learning. In the 1950s, theologians suggested moral and educational elements that accentuated religious values. During the same decade, religious education became part of the standard curriculum. However, it was not compulsory, but optional for schools, being free to choose between the spiritual and non-religious. In 1982, education authorities formulated a unique all-inclusive curriculum embracing ethical, and general academic elements. The educationists affirmed that moral intuition was challenging to teach because it was the impulsive appearance in cognisance of "moral judgement, including an affective valence." (Haidt, 2001, p.818).

Currently, the Turkish educational curriculum includes religious culture and ethics course, which is offered to 10-17 years old kids across all schools. The topics covered in this option comprise Sunni faith morality, secularism, and Ataturk's principles, including comparative religious studies. The Turkish Ministry of Education has consolidated the academic curriculum and made it mandatory on all schools, except for Armenian, Jewish, and foreign embassy schools. Mere knowledge of morality hardly leads to admirable moral conduct. (Blasi, 1980). Moral education seeks enrichment with the application of ethical standards pragmatically applied around the world. Moral standards are justified when their popularity in society serves to restructure "the problem of sociality and our vulnerability to one another." (Hands, 2014, p.528). Peer-to-peer communication permeates all facets of school life, which affects their moral improvement. Teachers are in a better position to know their students and honest biology to transmit values and qualities. Hursthouse (2012, p. 169.) quite rightly states that nature has blessed us with the capacity to acquire virtues through habituation. Dewey (1922) believes that habits can be reformed by self-reflection and deliberation in changing circumstances, and education is vital to instil habits. Morality in Turkish society is varied because their culture snuggles in between peculiar European culture and collectivist Eastern cultures. The secondary school students in Turkey learn to apply moral standards in social interactions. It is not possible to guarantee that teenage pupils would not break moral norms in their pursuit of social and emotional needs.

Inspiration and Motivation

Approbation for a nominal achievement, praise for the small endeavour, and support for a sporting event elates the child and builds confidence, self-esteem, and self-respect. When they show enthusiasm in learning accomplishments or excel in a particular sport, give a worthy performance in school-based activities, then reward is due to encourage motivation and inspire participation in other productive chores. In doing so, the children will acquire traits such as teamwork, humility, fairness, kindness, and justice. They would begin to understand the true meaning of unfairness, injustice, arrogance, and haughtiness. The physical instructors and sports teachers have an indispensable role to play in the school by encouraging participation of all kids in various activities, supervising their behaviour with suppleness and agility. In return, kindness will resonate in the experience of children, making them feel praiseworthy. If teachers with adequate training present themselves as role models, the kids would aspire to emulate and happily adopt commendable traits enshrined in an ideal person. It is the settings and situations that lend themselves to the promotion of character traits. The educationists apply inspirational strategies in a friendly environment to shape youth lives, provoke motivate, and make them good human beings who are kind and helpful. The kids develop the habit of self-control since inhibitions are desirable for harmonious interactions. In a classroom, teachers conduct exams and tests and expect kids to be honest in answering questions. They explain the negative side of cheating before commencing any review; namely, it is morally wrong to cheat, and secondly, getting caught warrants punishment leading to expulsion from the class for ten days. The youngest children may not digest the implications of the morally wrong side of deception but would hesitate to copy or cheat due to the fear of expulsion. Conclusively, the accountability factor could be more persuasive than the morality element to prevent the dishonest practice of cheating in the exams. Some children would learn to make ethical decisions because they would have learned that it is unfair to cheat for the sake of honest and intelligent peers who habitually perform well academically. In 1928, Hartshorne and May jointly undertook a study of moral conduct among school children to discover traits of honesty and dishonesty. They established scenarios at homes, schools, and playgrounds, offering kids an opportunity to misbehave about cheating on a take-home test, lying to a teacher, and Stealing. They found moral conduct among school children was not coherent and resolved that honesty was not a general trait. The researchers determined that children "with better working memory and inhibitory control are less likely to cheat." (Hartshorne and May 1928, p.414.) In principle, "the main attention of educators should be placed not so much on devices for teaching honesty or any other trait as on the reconstruction of school practices in such a way as to provide no occasional but consistent and regular opportunities for the successful use of both teachers and pupils of such forms of conduct as to make for the common good." (Hartshorne, p.414.) The action of stealing occurs out of self-cherishing thought, and it harms other people. Intrinsically, the morally stable child would conform to moral principles performing acts of kindness rather than pilfer property or goods of others.

For many traditional families, and academic performance is of utmost importance for their broods, which are comparatively disciplined and enjoy self-regulatory learning at home. They are good at time management, allocating a fair amount of time to studies and recreational activities. We inculcate open-mindedness in adolescents who conduct scientific experiments to discover unexplored areas of knowledge and utilise critical thinking for making valued judgments. They accept vitality as a unique trait for leading an adventurous life and firmly believe in sharing and caring.

251

The revival of virtues-based personality finds renewal in Divine scriptures such as the Holy Qur'an, the Bible. And the Torah, the Old Testament. Manifestly, concern for ethical character runs throughout the Revealed Text of the Holy Qur'an and the Traditions back up the Commands of Almighty God. We must grasp the Majestic reality of our creation and to prudently act in given circumstances. We should teach universally applauded characteristics in our adolescents, and indoctrinate caring acuities to make them morally robust for withstanding unethical worldly fascinations. Our kids, well equipped with prudence and sagacity, would be instrumental in bringing pleasantness in others' lives by making sound judgments and equitable decisions. More focus is placed on admirable behaviour and moral grooming of teenagers in the next chapter of this book.

CHAPTER VIII

YOUTH MORALITY & RELATIONSHIPS

Behaviour is the ultimate result of a particular reaction to a specific situation or provocation. Incitement or irritation sometimes causes for the respondent to act instinctively or irrationally, thus displaying unreasonable behaviour. The mode of conduct may be embedded in the soul or ingrained in the physical matter. Youth moral development is influenced by social practices and religious attitudes, albeit modern societies disregard spiritual consciousness due to secular acuities. The children can quickly learn the rules and standards of diverse cultures by intermingling with peers. Even morality has different forms such as liberal families are open to experimentation and allowing youth to learn from social experiences but believe in precaution and fairmindedness. The conservative kinfolk does not stress fairness and objectivity but recognise moral values and family structure. Youth may be immature but mostly, tend to indulge in emotional experiences irrespective of moods and wishes of others. Pure awareness of morality does not make them demonstrate good moral behaviour. They are unsure about right and wrong and cannot make an ethically precise judgement when faced with ethical matters. Intuitive mechanisms frequently determine moral judgements since moral behaviour is rooted in one's subconscious as it affects others in some ways. The young mind cannot always grasp the moral consequences of a particular situation neither he/she can anticipate the reply that might occur. In the process of growth, children do not always acquire parents 'customs and behaviour but may embrace peer culture and values.

Dewey (1922) specifies three aspects of moral behaviour, e.g. people's habits, shaped in a social atmosphere infusing emotional attachment to their lifestyles; secondly impulses that a person inherits and thirdly the reflective action in response to a given situation. However, self-reflection helps in the rectification and refinement of habits through exhilarating experiences. Moral emotions play an indispensable role in inspiring youngsters to act morally. Initially, ethical development theory was introduced by Lawrence Kohlberg in 1969, and Jean Piaget promoted it by observing kids 'intuition about justice that they articulate later in life. In 1980, a renowned psychologist Blasi recognised the motivational power of moral emotions but conceded that emotions could not be a motivational force for moral actions. (Blasi, 1999). However, intentions could be the primary strength of moral actions. A distinguished scholar Haidt (2001) asserted that the moral emotions are concerned with the well-being of others. Moral sentiments leave a significant impact on the youth's behaviour. Adolescents possessing strong ethical values are more likely to demonstrate a morally correct action. Those youngsters rejecting falsehood, deception and trickery in favour of truth, honesty and accuracy are role models of moral values. Morality has different meanings in various societies, but many elements are similar, although dissimilar in practices and applications.

The youth moral foundations are built on either autonomy and liberty or authority and inviolability. The former group emphasised equality and justice for all whereas the latter group stress sanctity, loyalty and respect for the administration. In European countries. Multicultural communities greatly vary in their application of moral standards because youth emotional experiences occur outside the family circles. As far as their ethical behaviour is concerned, their actions are based on situational encounters and specific reactions. Such measures result from an interaction with the environment, i.e. parental values and moral norms of the society. Ethical, moral conduct is the result of insightful thought and refined intuition augmented by innate virtues. John Dewey had played a vital role in shaping the Turkish education system when he was officially invited in 1924 by the ruler Kamal Ataturk. He submitted two comprehensive reports for the reformation of schools across the country.

Youth Interpersonal Relationships

The unchallenged assumption is that friends share everything in common. Aristotle (384-322 BC) in his "Nicomachean Ethics", for without friends no one would choose to live, though he had all other goods. He declares three types of friends, e.g. useful friends, friends of pleasure and virtuous friends, and they all mutually assist each other to improve their character, cultivate joy in life and flourish as human beings. Francis Bacon (1561-1626 A D.) deliberates that friendship is a necessary component of life because friends help nurture peace in our emotional lives and also, help each other to work through difficult decisions. C.S. Lewis (1898-1963 A D.) elaborates further and comments that friendship is a type of love between two or more people, standing shoulder to shoulder, inspired by and pursuing the same truth. It is a joy sharing experience, building capacities and understanding other's sensitivities. According to Mary Hunt (born 1951 AD.), friendship has a physiological dimension of relationships;

- Spiritually, which emphasises deep interconnections with others.

- Love emphasises emotions and commitments.

- Friendship is the connection through which we can assess and scrutinise relationships.

- Robust relationships bring relaxation and pleasure, relieve anxiety, prevent seclusion and aloneness.

The cyber-world lacks the personal touch and offer little help in distress, sorrow and pain. Online companionships are superficial and rarely lead to in-depth emotional intimacy. Good friends accept cultural diversity, respect opinion and share interests, hobbies but show no curiosity to discover closely-held secrets. Everlasting friends take time to form and even more time to mature. In certain exceptional circumstances, simple text messaging or telephonic conversation turns into a valuable friendship naturally depicting trust and reliability, care and compassion. It further progresses into intimate relationship through thoughtfulness, kind-heartedness and eventually falling in love with the qualities, physiognomies and virtues. Friendship chemistry can be irrefutably magnetic that unpredictably transpires between two individuals.

Time is a precious commodity if appropriately utilised; one can excel in the pursuit of chosen career paths whether it may be engineering, sports, showbiz, media, medicine, fashion design, or teaching and research. Life and time are the two beautiful teachers because experience teaches us to make effective use of time and time shows us the value of life. Charles Darwin declared 'A man who dares to waste one hour has not discovered the value of life' (Darwin, 1887). The culture of timekeeping and time management is exemplary in European countries and the worst in many developing countries. People in general waste plenty of time in worthless distractions, futile diversions, lavish entertainments and petty amusements.

Friendship has to be spontaneous, exciting, profound and consistent that might entail revealing a certain amount of vulnerability. Parental concern has always been for the kids to prosper, develop good habits, high moral, and refrain from immoral practices. They should build up capacities to differentiate between ethical and non-virtuous activities. Virtue is developed and sustained by a community in possession of firm beliefs in the laws of nature. The worthy youth would share what he has with his/her peers, compatriots, companions, friends and broader communities. Maternal affection and love instil confidence and trust that helps kids to become considerate, patient and respectful. Any act that causes hurt to another person or breaking a promise, bringing home office notepad, ink or rubber from school amounts to the immoral deed. Similarly, some acts fall in the jurisdiction of rude manners such as smoking in the presence of no-smokers, burping and belching within a group, and laughing that intimidates others. It is undesirable to make inapposite personal comments about somebody's outfit, hair shade and general appearance. Any kind of stealing, theft, pilfering and shoplifting is morally wrong and intolerable. Both the human-made regulations and Divine laws condemn such acts and designate rightful punishment depending on the enormity and magnitude of the crime that has a deplorable impact on society. Some of the immoral acts are unpardonable, while others are unacceptable in a given culture.

Apart from the family's harmonious environment, the moral atmosphere of the school is fundamental to a child's moral development. Kohlberg (1983), affirms that beliefs of teachers have high relevance to moral education, but Hand (2014, p.520.) reiterates the implementation of moral education should be dependent on individual teachers' practice of ethical training. It should raise kids' moral maturity and understanding that the failure to observe norms invites punishment. The youth are vulnerable to one another since their limited capacity for sympathy and limited supply of needed or wanted resources to make it inconvenient to comply with moral standards. Carr and Landon (1998) interviewed Scottish teachers from six schools and summarised their responses. Moral education, the teachers asserted, should be a separate area of study within the mainstream curriculum. They supported a middle line between moral authoritarianism and moral permissiveness. In England, there is a degree of respect for the religious beliefs of believers from multicultural backgrounds. Upon parental request, the children get an exemption from attendance in specific assemblies. As values are the core beliefs concerning moral and immoral, so the justice, equality and individual freedom are emphasised in classroom lessons. Human life is considered sacred, and views of those opposing abortion are respected but not accepted in secular societies. There is a noticeable difference between the moral stance and emotional reaction to any particular situation, episode or occurrence.

Youth Feelings and Reflections

Ethically, a youngster may know what is wrong and what is right, which is different from the emotional response that delineates what makes him/her feel good or bad about a given setting? Ethical decision-making has been discussed in great detail by Wainryb and Turiel (1993). Emotions impact moral decisions as much as morals influence emotional reactions. For instance, cows are sacred to Hindus, and they despise beef eaters in India but cannot loath Westerns in Europe for eating beef. Likewise, a mortgage is morally wrong in some religious humanities, whereas it is a standard practice across the globe without which only a few would be able to own properties. Professor Michael Hand of the University of Birmingham states that children should learn to follow moral standards and realise the importance of speaking truth and the implications of telling lies that would be a "violation of moral norms".

Either ethical behaviour can provide emotional feedback or vice versa. However, emotions unconsciously have a bearing on human thinking, which are persistently experienced in terms of feeling happy, sad, blissful or miserable. Moral improvement sways kids' emotions as they learn through family values, peers, friend, educational settings and society. The kids learn a lot by observing parents, teachers and the social environment, by respecting feelings of others and exhibiting positive reactions to unreasonable episodes that do not instigate or offend others emotions. Actions and reactions have both pleasant outcomes and at other times, irritating ramifications.

Replication and reflections can conceptualise the self-awareness of youngsters. A young person should become aware of his/her relationships and communication with school fellows and friends in a social environment. Reflecting on relationships and experiences, teenagers develop their self-consciousness and learn to control emotions. They develop self-restraint and do not instantly show the reaction to certain events evolving feelings, moods, and temperaments. Reflection foretells emotive growth and maturity as it relates to the candidness to experience mannerism and reflects tangibly. Self-awareness makes a youth exceedingly realistic about himself/herself thereby modifying behaviour, improving friendly interaction with peers, raising self-confidence, visualising self-emotions, feeling positive, objective and developing a deeper understanding of others.

A renowned German Professor of Psychology Allan Fenigstein (1979) states that 'self-awareness makes us creative, confident, sound decision-maker, effective communicator'. It is indeed, rare quality and employing internal self-awareness, we can observe our aspirations and values and how do we fit with an environment and understand our thoughts, strengths, weaknesses and behaviour. With external self-awareness, we discover how others perceive us and value the opinion of others. Paul Silva (2002) declares that self-awareness clarifies internal states such as sensations, emotions and attitudes. May (1967, p.9) in an esteemed book 'Psychology and human dilemma' says that self-awareness might influence emotions on the input end of the initial appraisal. High self-awareness predictably leads to more inner provenances for both positive and adverse incidents. Somehow, self-awareness minimises selfishness and enriches assessment power. In more senior secondary schools, the educational atmosphere should create a caring youth community and the teaching should promote a culture of intellectual enquiry focused on personal growth, integrity and the exploration of diverse fields of knowledge for human fulfilment. Congenial environment for teaching and learning invigorates youth social growth, mutual respect, and relational intimacy.

Ethical Education in E.U. States

Present-day open society displays peculiarities of diverse humanities, and modern societies have created uncertain, blurred and non-transparent domains. Multicultural civilisations are deficient in social conventionality, unquestioning obedience and religious uniformity. The child upbringing in obscure and muddy settings has serious connotations which do not allow teachers to impart ethical instructions in a friendly manner. Traditionally, closed societies offered atmosphere which helped teach values, morals and ethical behaviour in adolescents. It has been intensely debated in Germany how to re-establish the outmoded qualities of obligation and obedience and how to tackle the complex issues of socialisation and morality? Diverse societies comprise varied segments of immigrants, evacuees and expatriates and refugees. In contrast, ethnic communities with different cultural, linguistic and religious backgrounds do not comprehend the challenges and changes of the modern world.

After World War II, the social welfare and nation-building were at the forefront of all educational initiatives, although ethical substance was given priority for achieving ideals of high culture. The school pupils aimed for senior social positions and the materialistic values were predominant. In the process, the youth broke away from parental constraint and teachers' highhandedness in disciplining them for unacceptable behaviour, albeit indulged openly in social relationships. Consequently, the marriage institution unconsciously got replaced by the culture of living together. The German policymakers from 1995 onwards diverted their attention to address the future of humanity and tackle the ecological crisis of the globe. Owing to the first School Reform Act (Schulreformgesetz) of 1990, religious education as a subject was introduced in schools, basically intended to raise the morale spirit of teenagers. Since the beginning of 2000, educationists have been debating the restoration of old values and virtues directed at kids' moral training. The families exert indelible impact on children's behaviour and principled outlooks and wield domestic power overvalue directions. Dieter Claessens in his esteemed publication entitled "Familie und Wertsystem" (1967) proclaims that the diffusion of family values permits the child respect those values and ethical norms but also allows to misbehave and contravene the boundaries without any trepidation of accountability. The norms of family behaviour are somewhat different from the formal school regulations where moral education emphasises through teaching the adherence to standard rules of conduct. There has been an overlap, and some confounding perplexity in moral consciousness and moral development declares Kohlberg and states that 'social education is moral. Both Piaget and Kohlberg believe the socialisation and morality inhibit in the daily conduct of human beings. When pupils socialise with peers and freely forge relationships without expecting any ethical constraints, the moral, educational instructions have little significance in their everyday behaviour. Rousseau once mentioned that there was no place at all for moral education in childhood. How can you envisage a teenager to have a sufficiently developed moral perception and behave in a manner that does not infringe ethical rules? It is a very systematic and slow process to infuse virtues in the hearts and minds of innocent children to promote moral feeling for others. Keeping in view the parents' own experience, they simply cannot impose morally sensitive norms or set boundaries that are likely to be hindered largely due to multi-polar open modern societies. The school are under obligation to back up the freedom of the individual child and to reinforce self-awareness for bearing liability for their actions.

In the post-war decades, both the Catholic and the Protestant Church in Germany have played the commendable role for the incorporation of Christian religious instructions in the curriculum of public schools across the country. For the children belonging to other faith clusters, ethical lessons are imparted based on conceptual impartiality. But the question remains as to how to meet demands of moral competence, critical reflection, social engagement and responsibility, personal awareness and insight into what is good and what is bad? Both German scholars Gilligan and Hoffman emphasise the promotion of the emotional and psychodynamic fruition and support Heinz Schmid's selective four task-fields of moral instruction namely a) The self, concerning others b) Social structures and processes c) Meaning of Life and Orientation within life d) Theories of ethics. The kids' moral development could proceed in stages ranging from 2 to 6, 6 to 8-year-olds, 8 to 12 years and then teenagers. The children receive lessons about the meaning of life and the understanding of social structures and ethics, including the differentiation between intentions and activities, inclinations and intuitions. Schmidt asserts that moral education demands consensual forms of practice since ethical matters are multifaceted and debatable because children cannot comprehend the inherent intricacies of good behaviour.

In the first two stages of grooming, the grandparents' involvement is crucial as they build up unique relations with kids. They take them on short vacations, create a sense of belonging and uniqueness through uttering interesting episodes that demonstrate the benefits of patience. While visiting grandparents, the children learn gardening, foraging, shoe shining, developing cognitive skills in a relaxed atmosphere. The time spent with grandparents helps learn discipline, regulations and boundaries. They acquire skills to save energy by switching off unnecessary lights, turning off water taps to conserving water, washing hands before a meal, brushing teeth in the morning and obeying instructions. The grandmothers are particularly compassionate and caring, ignore minor faults, and praise grandkids a lot. Grannies smilingly get involved in enjoyable activities such as collecting stamps or old coins, knitting, painting pebbles, drawing pictures, painting and playing with all sorts of educational toys. The parents in general, reprimand kids for certain mischiefs and do not ignore acts of disobedience. Kids in the age range of 8 to 12 do not like dressing-downs and telling-off for acts of naughtiness and impishness. They feel uncomfortable for pickiness and vacillation. The small children turn edgy and irritated and mistreat peers at school unless parents prevent them from becoming jittery and oversensitive by empathetic explanations about central concerns.

Our approach to ethical education should be fitting for making real-life decisions. Amazingly in the Republic of Ireland, religious institutions run and manage,96 per cent of primary schools. Many of them belong to the Catholic faith, and religious instructions are part of the core syllabus. In Norway, teachers do impart proper training covering the philosophy of life and ethics, but no faithful preaching occurs because the teaching at schools is impartially and independently. Morality has different meanings in different cultures because the social environment and values define human moral conduct. In the West and to some extent in the East, individuals enjoy sufficient freedom to explore their capacities and learn moral values through trial and error. They are reluctant to accept the strict imposition of moral norms and psychological paradigms. They do need excellent skills applicable in day-to-day affairs. The classroom environment can promote flexible, honest practices and realistic insight to enhance and foster thriving in children's societal development. The moral atmosphere of a school has an everlasting impact on children's ethical behaviour and values edification shapes pupils' notion of society. Most teachers in the U.K. have been willing to attend the refresher course for refining their moral expertise. In

2007, Revell and Arthur interviewed 1000 British teachers concerning their attitudes and experiences about character education and found them prepared to improve ethical education skills. Temli et al. (2011) conducted a survey in Turkey in which 824 primary school teachers responded to the questionnaire regarding excellent skills and social issues. The teachers strongly supported moral education and agreed about the necessity of imparting values such as forbearance, reverence, respect and decency. They recognised the vitality of family influence and family values for kids' ethical development. It is only through social experiences and shared interactions that the youngsters can make appropriate moral decisions in various situations.

ETHIKA EUROPEAN PROJECT evolves structure of moralities, doctrines, virtues, epitomes and beliefs that shape youth lives in a multicultural, multi-ethnic and multi-lingual society. Ethical education comprises all facets of human life dimensions—moral teaching impacts human behaviour, societal norms, beliefs and practices, customs and traditions.

EU researchers and educationists have been instrumental in addressing the challenges of modern and multicultural societies and the imperative necessity of integrating ethics in the schools' educational curriculum. In April 2014, two initiatives simultaneously came to light, e.g. the ETHIKA Project and the Teacher Manifesto for the 21st Century produced by the Council of Europe, Strasbourg. The primary aim was to equip teachers with relevant knowledge and skills to implement ethics and value s education, the participants in ETHIKA Project included Austria, Croatia, Germany, Italy, Slovenia and Spain. Apart from Italy, all other countries offer ethics/ethical or religious education in schools. However, the Federal Republic of Germany is the only EU state providing formal instructions in ethics and moral education as a core subject at primary and secondary schools. In other countries, some segments of ethics form part of teaching within mandatory items such as Homeland Culture, Social Values and Civics. The German secondary school curriculum is very comprehensive covering, topics and themes, e.g. Conduct of Life; Values and Norms; General Ethics; Ethics and Religious Education; Ethical Education; Ethics and finally Philosophy with Children. In the countries surveyed, the instructions commence at Kindergarten level about multiculturalism, tolerance and willingly helping others. The European population is in, increasingly diverse, which requires bicultural integration with respect for shared values, mutual respect and openness towards others. The EU teachers themselves should have uninterrupted access to integrated super quality education through which they become well capable of transmitting ethical values, peacefulness, solidarity and education for peace. They can promote meaningful, engaged learning at schools. It shows EU determination to develop inclusive societies, democratic values, intercultural competencies and respect for human rights.

Happy Kids' Behaviour and Attitudes

Teenagers experience physiological changes, social demands, emotional challenge and peer pressures in the course of which they discover self-worth, and the possible consequences of personal relationships. With robust adherence to family values, morally stable youngsters act as inspiration for others and are capable of persevering in the face of unpredictable social encounters. They can:

- Cope with unpleasant situations

- Resist peer pressure at social gatherings and pleasurable activities

- Refrain from attending undesirable venues and indulgent parties

- Avoid the unnecessary company of permissive peers

- Demonstrate the courage to disengage with friends without causing resentment

- Show compassion to others but choose likeminded friends

- Understand media power, media distortions and fake online intimidation

- Accept responsibility for their actions and outcomes

- Reflect on social involvements to make decent moral judgements

- Transmute challenges with relationship and fun-loving activities

- Access delicate situations and be assertive in response to persuasion

- Set ethical standards and boundaries for oneself

- Stay strong despite abrupt rejection in a circle of friends

- Endure relationship breakup with dignity

Happy children are well equipped with positive qualities, optimistic perceptions and beautiful characteristics. They share with others, valuable rich experiences, build understandings, and express feelings of love, affection and tenderness without expecting any reward or recompense. Happy kids are upbeat, constructive, and confident sharing knowledge and participating gleefully in social activities. They are hopeful in adversity, offer help to the needy, cooperation to friends, and inspiration to others. They distribute happiness by making others happy through acts of kindness, gentleness, and benevolence. They demonstrate self-restraint, respect boundaries, and show dignity in intimate relationships. Happy children use common sense derived from family legacy, parental training, and teachers' instructions to make morally apt judgements. In short, happiest teenagers are models of stimulation, paradigm of motivation, and an example of impetus for classmates and friends. Happy kids set standards to be followed, patterns to be shadowed, and values to be adored. They are observant and conscientious, pragmatic and meticulous, practical and vigilant in matters of vital importance, impacting their own and other members of the society.

Our adolescents absorb better in an inspirational setting in which they enjoy freedom and display discipline without undue restraints. A teenager performs an act of benevolence, exhibiting compassion and kind-heartedness, it becomes a beautiful character that turns into an attribute. He/she can overcome emotional blackmail and practice abstinence. The girls, in particular, are well protected by moral laws, safeguarding integrity, honour and self-esteem. Lassies despise being harassed, mentally intimidated and emotionally humiliated whether at school, college or in any social gathering. Individual state laws and U.N. human rights conventions offer complete protection to teenagers. Whether male or female, the older the child would be, the more ingrained the behaviour since teenagers invariably possess increased emotional baggage. The progression to a higher class means building a rapport with new peers and making new friends having a diverse family background with varying cultural and moral acuities.

Both the school setting and social environment have considerable influence on youth perceptions, moral outlooks and social connections. We can teach ethical principles and virtues in forming relationships includes helpfulness, caring for others and loyalty in social affiliations. The Persian mathematician Ibn Siena attached importance to emotions and moral attitudes of individuals in face-to-face encounters. Different eventualities create a distinctive child in the same membrane because many hereditary and ecological circumstances come together in a common effect. Fundamental causes of behaviour are traits of character as some are stay-at-home types, whereas others are outgoing socialisers. The kids' behaviour is reinforced by its impact on others and positively influenced by genetic endowment. The youth behaviour may change in the limelight of culture, fascinations of luxury, comfort and illicit attractions of modern living. Ghetto culture and similar surroundings harm a young mind.

The school is an arena that shapes young lives, feelings and behaviour and the shaping of young mind exposes how our surroundings shape them as it mediates youth identity. Once Sir Winston Churchill remarked, 'we shape our buildings, and afterwards our buildings shape us'. Clearly, our school buildings, yards, tennis courts, gyms and corridors define pupils personally, socially and communally. The youngsters are unlikely to gain anything in isolation but learn more in coordinated social adventures, exploits and escapades. Even they learn more from mistakes and then exercise prudence in future encounters. Modern multicultural societies allow freedom of thought and expression of feelings so that the youngsters feel good about themselves in multi-ethnic and multi-lingual surroundings. They hold on to moral principles, recognise good and evil, and exercise control over egotistical moods, instincts, faults, fantasies and naughty cravings. Inevitably, openness, liberalism and broad-mindedness help nurture appreciative traits as long as the school environment does not become a social hub for sensual intimacies and unripe permissiveness. The obligation rests on the families and the teaching staff who can transform the emotional, social and psychological health of their kids. Parental guidance along the morality lines help improve child perceptions about equality and justice, fairness and tolerance. For instance, Bulgarian children appear to behave remarkably well due to parents' compassionate upbringing and caring manner.

Globally, most cultures are based on material acquisitions as youth desire luxury and comfort and aspire for happiness, peace and pleasant environment. Proper pleasure interrelates to our deepest feelings of contentment and personal serenity.

Almost a decade ago, a UNICEF report revealed. Dutch children were the happiest and far ahead of other E.U. countries in wellbeing. Unsurprisingly, the U.S. A. came 26th, but the U.K. achieved 16th place in making school-going youth happy and comfortable. The survey took into consideration the kids' general health, safety, education and behaviour. It discovered the Netherland topped the list in Europe and the kids were happy, smiling with a higher level of contentment. The Dutch have a reputation of being socially liberal, easy-going and relaxed people raising children in a family-oriented environment. The U.S. parents and caregivers have varied modes of upbringing children. Some kids exhibit fear, sadness, and frustration on account of cultural peculiarities, turbulent parental relations, and general home atmosphere. The parents in many countries across the globe appreciate unique and rewarding profession for their children. The Dutch are different in a sense, as they consider that happiness cultivates achievement. Confidence to move forward rather than running away, an attitude of embracing life rather than denying it, gives the youth reflective cheerfulness at the cost of sometimes denying oneself of sensual pleasures. The happiness is related to the mental state of youngsters because warm, empathetic and loving feelings generate heartfelt optimistic motivation. Most teens are well aware of the fact that anger and hated are negative emotions and lead to pain and distress, sufferings and discomfort. Character education is a means of gaining knowledge about what leads to happiness and what exactly causes agonies and heartbreaks. Character education is a means of internal transformation and engagement in constructive activities that bring about discipline within young minds. A calm and caring frame of mind has a social impact on the emotional and physical wellbeing of adolescents.

An illustrious 17th-century philosopher Thomas Hobbes viewed the human race as being violent, savage, in continual conflict and concerned only with self-interest. Another Spanish philosopher George Santayana proclaimed that generous, caring impulses are typically feeble, predictably ephemeral, and unstable in human nature. Still, beneath the surface, there is a ferocious, persistent, overwhelmingly egotistic man. Sigmund Freud (1856-1939) asserted that the inclination to aggression is an original, self-subsisting instinctive character. In the later part of the twentieth century, the pessimistic view of humanity underwent a drastic change as Seville in 1986 acknowledged that violent behaviour does occur. Still, the human being does not have the inherited tendency to perform acts of violence which are not part of human nature. Conclusively, all youngsters of diverse hues, cultures, beliefs and races have the potential to develop into caring people. Dr Linda Wilson, a professor of sociology, stated that altruism might be part of our basic survival instinct, but working together to help each other tended to ward off later psychological issues. The forming of close social bonds with classmates, acting for the welfare of others as well as oneself is acutely ingrained in human nature. As Confucius, a Chinese philosopher (551 BC- 479 BC) states, "Everyone is born with an innate sense of what is right", but he/she still commits errors or even blunders owing to brought up conditions and environmental settings, surrounding culture and childhood experiences.

Rina Mac Acosta and Michele Hutchinson have conjointly narrated exciting and intriguing research findings of the happiest children. They declare that "[Dutch parents] raise the world's happiest children, so it is time you shared the cost" (The Telegraph, London, January 7, 2017.). The following features set Dutch children apart from those in the United Kingdom and the United States:

"Dutch babies get more sleep

Dutch kids have little or no homework at primary school

Dutch children are not just seen but also heard

Dutch youth are trusted to ride their bikes to school alone

Dutch adolescents are permitted to play outside unsupervised

They enjoy family meals together

Parents consistently spend time with broods

They feel happy and contented with inexpensive toys

They get pleasure in simple activities

The kids are satisfied with chocolate sprinkles for breakfast."

There are lessons to be learnt from the family-oriented training pattern in which freedom, liberty, trust, confidence, time management, social, physical and recreational needs are paramount for developing emotionally stable, healthy and academically successful children.

The Dutch parents seem to be courteous and polite in their attitude towards kids, allow them sufficient freedom for playful activities, and encourage them to participate in supplementary events at school. Dutch society appears to have excellent tolerance for petty theft, although minor incidents of shoplifting do occur. The same situation prevails in most countries around the world. Dutch parents avoid arguing in the presence of young children as that the innocent broods do not get emotionally disturbed and unnecessarily distressed.

Family-steered grooming produces children who act only after careful consideration of the possible consequences, whereas other kids might be reckless and hasty. When youth begin to ponder over their behaviour and therefore, conduct self-examination, they start to think who they are? Practice improves, and an element of unselfishness creeps in future actions. Altruism is an invaluable attribute that reflects the behaviour patron of youngsters. A teenager reinforces his/her conduct while discovering how the classmate feels about a particular issue. If he/she misbehaves and then determines how the affected individual thinks about it, the self-evaluation helps improve future actions. Time and again, it has been averred that there are two significant behaviour influencing factors, the genetic endowment and secondly, the domestic and external environment. If we take children outdoor on a short vacation or even a day trip to ocean views, spring plants and shades of trees, these are sources of nourishment and wield effect on their ability to think. Also, subtle ecological landscapes have an impact on attitudes. Presumably, relocating the school's tennis court can affect kids' behaviour. The children must feel safe in the shared spaces within the school. Equally important is the safety mechanism in local parks and sports centres where CCTV cameras may act as an unnoticed watchman so that children move around without any fear and apprehension.

In New York City, small triangles of roadsides encircled by fences are called parks. The prohibition rues are displayed on big billboards which must be obeyed by the public. These rules are as follows:

Littering and Glass bottles, bicycles, scooters, skateboards, roller skates, pets, using illegal drugs, alcohol, smoking, disorderly conduct, feeding birds and squirrels, standing on swings, barbecuing and open fires.

The parents can improve children's behaviour by acting as role models and also, by offering incentives for definite chores and performance of educational tasks. If a child behaves well, get a treat and gains points for gift purchase. Surprisingly, a Dutch study of 32,800 children aged 10 to 12 years revealed that those born to older parents tended to have fewer externalising behaviour problems such as aggression than the children of younger parents. In Western countries, the cohabiting couples either get married in their late twenties and early thirties or delay having children until early or mid-forties. An observational study of school-going children in Asia, Arabia and the West, the present writer proclaims that extravagant way of living, excessive luxuries and unconditional love produces egocentric kids with behaviour issues at school. They also face difficulties in interpersonal communication with peers, teachers and friends partly due to scarcity of self-accountability and self-consciousness. They are accustomed to seeking excitement, pleasure and self-satisfaction.

The children mention Dr Larry Scherwitz, who do not have close social relationships seem to suffer from vulnerability to anxiety and high level of desperation.

Nevertheless, the seed of compassion will flourish given the suitable atmosphere both at home and in the school and beyond at community gatherings. The environmental conditions and social climate must be fitting for the seed of care and compassion to grow in the hearts of children. The character education lessons should focus on the kids' need to understand the meaning of their lives and the value of human qualities for leading meaningful and satisfying lives. A child should be free to share his/her deepest feelings and concerns with either parents or grandparents and openly seek solace, empathy and affirmation. Freedom of thought, expression and speech are the fundamental rights of a young soul, the use of mind, body and dealings in society carry specific responsibilities and restraints. The self-restraint, self-accountability and willpower set the moral criteria for character development. Moral values, either genetically inculcated in kids or learn in school laboratories through experimentation. Decent beliefs are invaluable facets in developing unblemished comportment, improving conduct in social communication and building strong character.

The youth behaviour is the ultimate result of innate qualities, habits, values, customs and beliefs.

The following diagram illustrates the transformation of youth behaviour and its features.

The pain is said to be a natural facet of human life, but its intensity can be unbearable for many youngsters. When privileged children reach out to help the underprivileged or become volunteers in various community projects, they are highly likely to enhance self-worth and derive tremendous happiness and satisfaction.

In secondary schools, character-building should be an integral part of all educational and extracurricular lessons. It helps improve youth behaviour when the values such as kindness, truthfulness, obedience and responsibility are embedded, which then, transform attitudes, develop positive feelings, instigate thinking and stimulate intrinsic motivation. In New Zealand, for example, from year one to six, the values are taught in a manner that kids can joyfully learn character strengths by real-life experiments, and whole episodes. Do they practice how to think rather than what to think? They learn about sharing thoughts and feelings with peers, listening attentively, and reflecting solicitously. In mostly Catholic-run schools throughout the U.K. quotes from the Holy Bible, disciple narrations relate to enlightening kids' moral and inner feeling of love and compassion. Likewise, in Islamic faith schools throughout Europe, quotes from the Holy Qur'an, sayings of the Prophet and anecdotes of his learned companions are re-counted to develop teenagers' behaviour, morals and character. All schools can teach the significance of youth responsibility and respect for elders. (Lickona, 1991) just as New Zealand schools teach character building through values. (Heenan, 2002). In less developed Afro-Asian countries, the character-building task is very involved in the face of oppression, corruption, widespread bribery in every governmental department, contaminated food, poverty and exploitation. The innocent teenage girls in colleges and universities are sexually harassed, bullied and exploited not only by male students but also by lecturers and professors who blackmail them for not heeding to their illicit and immoral advances. On the contrary, the laws in Western countries offer more excellent shield to girls from all types of sexual harassment, verbal abuse and emotional intimidation. These laws guarantee protection from online social coercion, verbal abuse, inappropriate texting and bullying.

The school and college classroom is the right forum for open dialogue and frank discussion among teachers and learners. The teenagers can take part in the morally challenging discussion, transmitting personal experiences, reflections and outcomes. They

Since the beginning of the present century, the less developed Afro-Arab and Asian countries are becoming increasingly open societies, banning physical punishment at schools and allowing more freedom to the young population in their career choice or social practices. In the West, there are better conditions for acceptance of ethnic minorities in all spheres of human endeavour. All parents and teachers need to develop kids' emotional and social skills, explicitly respecting peers from diverse backgrounds, beliefs and cultures. The children build willpower to stem desires and overcome feelings, help others in need, curtail unlawful yearnings and forge sturdy attachments based on mutual compassion. They learn to make the right choices and right decisions for sustaining relationships. If solitude nurtures creativity and spiritual enrichment, deep, meaningful social connections are necessary for mental and physical health. Equally important is the understanding of social dilemmas of youth facing deprivation, poverty and moral deficit leading them to resort to substance abuse, theft, shoplifting and begging.

CHAPTER IX

SOCIAL EDUCATION

Community ingenuities directed at the personal, emotive and social development of teenagers do make a visible difference in their acuities, motivations, and dreams. Affluent members of the society and compassionate multinational companies have introduced many initiatives in several Western countries for the wellbeing of youngsters. There is plenty of room for imitation and replication of such comprehensive, thought-provoking programmes by philanthropists who believe in "Giving something back" to the deserving and deprived juveniles. We can dramatically improve their living conditions, through right incentives, well-meaning encouragements and robust material support. The society can achieve more for hard-to-reach and deprived kids by designing educational projects, sharing resources, allocating funds, and involving local communities. Many children in the West equally deserve care, affection and consistent emotional help due to lack of parental love caused by family tragedies, health-related incidents and natural catastrophes.

It would be ideal to involve kids in service-oriented activities ranging from feeding pigeons, ducks, swans to designing greeting cards for house-bond people, to making birthday cards and wrapping gifts for the destitute individuals. Making others feel better is an indispensable part of social education for youth personal development. Just as school social clubs engage pupils in sewing, knitting, drawing, painting and singing activities, the community- created social groups can arrange visits to homeless youth shelters, libraries, museums, art galleries, orphanage and handicapped youth facilities. It would be potentially useful to accompany kids to faith centres to attend short talks on the role of spirituality in their daily lives.

Learning social skills is a significant part of social education, enabling young learners to grasp necessary life skills utilising exciting lessons. Children get inspired through exhilaration activities such as theoretical performances within the socially sustainable school atmosphere. It has been the usual practice of schools in the European countries to hold live performances in which students participate that shows their creativity and motivation. Until recently, the present writer's visit to Doha, Qatar (January 2020) and interaction with educationists revealed tremendous support for enactment of dramas and theatricals presentations to promote social and life skills of secondary school students. The Ministry of Education & Higher Education had organised School Theatre Festival at Abdul Aziz Nasser Theatre primarily designed to discover the dynamism of students and develop their artistic skills. The Theatre of the Qatar Scouts and Guides Association located in Doha subsequently performed the thrilling episode attracting a vast audience. Socially electrifying events tremendously help pupils polish linguistic skills, increase vocabulary, and refine moral, social and cultural values. The kids who participate, and those who watch live theatrical acts have better speaker power are very expressive and audacious in social communication.

Dr Ibrahim Saleh Al-Nuaimi believes classroom theatre helps convey pictorial and auditory learning and sharpens kids' memorisation skills. He further stated that "theatre is the most prominent educational institution due to its pioneering role in building nations and promoting moral values" (The Peninsula: Doha Today, [English daily]23 January 2020). Amina Ibrahim Al-Hail, Doha based education psychologist commented, 'theatre teaches students shouldering responsibilities and love for teamwork". Maryam Numan Al-Emadi, Director of Al Ruqaiya Preparatory School for Girls, Doha mentioned that her school was successfully running a drama theatre and witnessed significant personality improvement. With the moral and material sponsorship of Education Ministry, drama shows are continually being held at Souq Waqif in which groups of pupils from several state schools enthusiastically compete and learn many vital facets of social and morally appropriate undertakings. Some renowned poets, artists, authors and composers reflect on real-life problems, emphasising the value of self-restraint and patience. They learn about the consequences of the dangerous driving, hasty road crossing, spreading litter and hurting peers.

Notwithstanding that, telling lies and deceiving others or depriving someone of a chance to succeed in any sports activity amounts to a moral deficit caused by impending inequalities in the society. The social education teaches fairness, objectivity and even-handedness in day-to-day dealings with others. Offering help to the elderly crossing the road, lifting a heavy bag for an elderly lady or vacating a bus seat for a senior citizen are the practical lessons of social education. These small but vital acts of kindness purify inner self-setting examples of pleasant manners and desirable attributes that are likely to be emulated by the on-lookers and mimicked by youngsters.

Socialisation Impact on Learning

Socialisation facilitates understanding of concepts, hypotheses, and theories when peers contribute to the knowledge co-construction process during classroom lessons. Social proximity makes learning more pleasant, studying pleasurable and thinking productive. The pupils amiably share thoughtful ideas, hold a constructive conversation and improve their problem-solving dexterities. Social collaboration improves critical thinking and decision-making proficiencies. Lindeman affirmed in 1926 that learning is a social activity and then Dewey in 1963 expressed his view about knowledge acquisition through engagement and participation. Hurst et al. (2013, p.376.) asserted that students learn more when they can talk to one another and be keenly involved. Glasser (1993) believed one of the basic human needs is to have fun and enjoy studies. Social communication inspires peers to reflect, speak, resolve and accomplish more in groups rather than in isolation. By such mode of social learning, they become prolific writers, creative thinkers, and confident orators. Pupils' involvement in education is a predictor of personal development, and such students say Astin (1999, p.518.) allocate substantial energy into studying and interaction with class fellows and faculty. Social relationships created during college years' asserts Wayt, (2012, p.50.) have an invaluable impact over their success in academic studies. Social engagement with college mates edifies their sensitivities about social values, and social interactions and achieve desirable outcomes.

We impart social education to change youth habits, practices and lifestyles and positively enumerate cross-cultural differences. The welfare and wellbeing of youth, say, Max Weber, a German sociologist, depends on the cultural values and civility. For instance, the choice of words in interpersonal communication can either soothe or insult the individual. Unnecessary gossips and backbiting about peers and friends lead to displeasure and resentment in social circles. Just as charitable deeds boost moral and social standing; loving words act as a panacea for socially perturbed youngsters. So, reaching out to others, serving the destitute and containing self-emotional reactions are acts of unique benevolence. Social education cultivates youth to become men of integrity who would be anxious to assist, support and contribute to the betterment of others and building an amiable, just, equitable and peaceful society.

Classical Social Literature

The study of classical social English literature provides invaluable modules for the teenagers of today, and historical episodes enlighten and socially educate the young brains. The present writer recalls the thoughtful reading of Dickens' literary pearl "Oliver Twist" in the Degree classes as a part of English literature studies. Charles Dickens enumerates social issues during the Victorian era on account of class disparities, manipulation of the poor and youth workforce. The central character in this book is an innocent boy called 'Oliver' representing struggle in the abandoned lives of children. He was born in a workhouse where his mother died and then, he fell into the hands of an artful dodger who made him a thief. He gets caught but acquitted in court. A decent English gentleman Mr Brownlow adopts Olive and gives him love and care. It is a social novel, a pure Dickens' Classic that indicates social environment has a substantial impact on a child's life and how it is conceivable to overlook these influences. This distinguished work was initially published in 1839 under the title 'The Parish Boy's Progress,' as a monthly serial from February 1837 to April 1839 by Robert Bentley of London. Another female English novelist Casey Watson in her work entitled "Too hurt to stay" demonstrated how Spence- an eight-year-old kid misbehaves that no one dares to accept him as a full-time regular foster parent. In this literary thriller, published in 2012 in London, Casey Watson, being a foster mum herself, narrates the accurate and moving tale of a troubled and problematic child's desperate search for a loving home. The emotionally upset child displayed abnormality with a deplorable history of absconding and to get into trouble with the law. Sometimes the enormity of what a child does in terms of mischief is beyond our sympathetic imagination. Even though you catch him red-handed and red-faced, he flatly denies the wrongdoing with a pack of lies and arrogance. Whether the kid comes from a professional background or his/her roots are unashamedly working class, their behaviour can still be challenging, seeking pleasure by inflicting pain on other children. They develop odd ways of hurting street children and classmates, especially if they are born into belligerent and muddled families. They seem very hesitant to form social bonds with foster carers. They do know that the families taking care of them are not real biological parents. Social responses are the reflections of emotions, and how they affect others, which actions are right and which actions can make others feel uncomfortable. If social settings change, social responses would be changed too due to social assessment.

Social Thinking Platforms

Inspiring conversation topics based on real-life conditions stimulate youth interest and enhance attentiveness. Reading nights at local libraries promote reading habit and notes taking sessions during socially amusing lectures foster writing skills. Open dialogue and free talking at social-thinking platforms kindle speaking power and debating skills that boost youth confidence. Real-life bondage among youngsters should be encouraged, and social media remote contacts must not undermine the credibility of interpersonal relations. In 2018, South Koreans established Salons for small social gatherings in which youth from poor to upper-middle-class hold salon meetings to intermingle and increase socialisation. In rural areas, they have created "Don't Worry Villages" for the social wellbeing of youngsters. Professor Ha Ji-Hyun, a Korean psychiatrist at Konku University, Medical Centre, Seoul, asserts that depression is at an all-time high among Korea's youth and mainly has an incongruent impact on low-income broods, but delinks socialisation with wealth and material resources.

Social communication happens when young people share space with others which may be in a theatre, classroom, playground or an amusement park. They learn about the social world through movies, T.V. dramas, live plays, history and romantic novels and personal face-to-face contact. They learn about the feelings of others and how others feel about them in an informal chatter as conversation reflect emotions and physical gestures, depict sentiments and social behaviour. Adolescents emphatically require broader social awareness of the society's social norms, social boundaries and relationship limitations, opportunities and possible social and moral consequences.

Social Awareness and Relationships

Moral dimensions and values help solve social problems with social competence. Female pupils tend to have better self-social restraint and demonstrate a relaxed and responsible social response in intimate affairs and social connections. Kids' coping strategies determine and facilitate social development. Socio-economic conditions exert influence on social perceptions, Girls

291

mature earlier than boys and possess better social skills that augment decision making in delicate social situations. Also, collaborative learning and knowledge -sharing enhances rapport and instigate positive social relations. Open debates organised by competent teachers offer an opportunity to all students to raise concerns, discuss social issues, describe personal experiences and socialisation processes. They present perspectives on various problems, express viewpoints and narrate exciting stories. Frank dialogue tremendously helps all participants in developing social skills. Positive connections with parents cultivate self-esteem in broods which leads to productive links with peers. The youth dispositions impact social relationships and consequently, social relationships influence youth character and personalities. The variability of social involvements and peer social experimentation unravel nature and have mutual influence over time. During such social encounters, feedback occurs depending on the intensity of feelings, relationship closeness, level of poignant and psychological attachment and the duration of the interaction. Each interaction triggers social conduct, emotional expression and nature of proximity. Mutual first impressions are vital that show manners, physical attractiveness, personality traits, warmth and cheerfulness.

Concerning social relationships, Michelle Harris and Ulrich Orth (2019) scrutinised 52 research studies involving well over 47000 participants, including children, teenagers, and adults. One of the studies examined 311 students aged 18 to 39 (171 girls) from various departments at Johannes Gutenberg University in Mainz, Germany. Starting with the students' social behaviour in the initial phase of acquaintance, they examined interpersonal sensitivities and evolving relationships in a round-robin design. They conducted a further appraisal of students' perceptions of dating and mating potential. Some of the student statements were: " I am a person who is generally trusting", I am a person who tends to find fault with others", I am an honest and trustworthy person" "I am helpful and like to help others". Other eye-opening comments include " I like to be accepted by fellow students", " I am easy going and like to do new experiments", "I am a sociable and easy-going person", " I tend to do things without thinking". Some female students remark " I act impulsively", " I am a self-controlled individual", " I am optimistic", "I am satisfied with myself", "I am satisfied with my appearance", " I want others to accept me". A few girls say that " I like to enrich others' lives", " I am the caring person". Concerning sensation-seeking tendencies, the authors found, many female and male students admitted trying new and exciting things and preferred to work in a group rather than working alone and also endorsed social talking freely to peers. They tended to be friendly, outgoing and interested in making new friends. Both Michelle Harris and Ulrich Orth discovered that positive social relationships, social support, and social acceptance help shape the development of self-esteem in youth over time. Student life embodies a pivotal developmental phase in learner's maturity and peer relations mirror a significant mode of social connection. Social rapport processes motivate the expression and mutual influence of personality and promote positive social relationship in that phase of youth life.

Voluntary assignments are an informal segment of demonstrative social learning for youngsters. Experience of undertaking work without remuneration advances the objective of helping others in need and develops tender feelings for communities and individuals who may be less fortunate, facing hardships, relationship breakdowns, social isolation or moral deprivation. The higher secondary school pupils should have a taste of inspirational voluntary work during winter or summer vacations. The venues for placements can be charity shops, care homes, libraries, art galleries, supermarkets, entertainment outlets or faith institutions. These unpaid assignments would enable teenagers to learn about the practicalities of real work, modes of talking, and feasibilities of the social environment. Upon completion of noble missions, the kids should be awarded certificates by nationally authorised institutions that would be an asset in the advancement of academic or vocational careers. The teens outdoors, have the chance to view people's social behaviour, learn the importance of leisure time, observe glamour, perceive opulence, and recognise the time as a precious commodity. Social adventures such as climbing, cycling, running, and boating are equally exciting for teens to cool off and relieve frustration. Since teenagers crave for affection and love, both parents and teachers need to build and sustain amicable relationships that kindle coherence and harmony. Proper sleep and consistent healthy eating habits are essential aspects of social education. The teenagers have unique social congeniality's and dislike, but parents should stay connected to overcome any social issues or social anxieties. During mealtimes, there should be no social distractions such as T.V. phones or music.

Creative Education During Covid-19.

Parents are facing a daunting prospect of educating and entertaining children for long hours in a small house or a single bedroom apartment. Self-isolation makes it even worst to retain their attention for creative or intelligent exercises. On the one hand, we are suffering from monotony within the residential boundaries, unable to visit the park or a shopping centre. At the same time, a door has opened for developing analytical minds with creative imagination for the creation of invaluable fresh ideas. Remarkable ingenuity is a merely subjective ability invoking imaginative hikes and innovative spikes. We have the opportunity to transmit knowledge that stimulates the inquiring mind, improves stimulus for learning and divergent thinking. We can make home tutoring a wonderful experience and give our adolescents a chance to create multiple solutions to identical problems.

Remote learning is undoubtedly a pleasant experience for teachers and pupils facing movement restrictions for virus protection. While online teaching is progressing, the students need to be aware of internet strainers to block wicked websites and the parents to seek advice through Childnet, Internet Matters, and Safeguarding and Social Care for children networks. Other helpful sites include Educate Against Hate, Let's Talk About It, Net-aware, Anti Bullying Alliance, and Tootoot designed to address complaints about abuse, harassment, and emotional exploitation. Although social platforms have introduced censors to ward off paedophiles, parents still have to be watchful about kids' online activities, and the teachers should avoid sharing contact details when emailing lesson content to a group of pupils. It is equally essential to follow Coronavirus (COVID-19) risk assessment guidance and regulations for Supporting your Children's education during this epidemic.

We have a complex task of keeping children at home throughout the day and night, during which time, frustration, boredom, and edginess affects morale and wellbeing. It increases the responsibilities of single mothers and caregivers. They need much more resilience and suppleness to thwart dullness by providing in-house pleasurable activities and simultaneously monitor the excessive use of mobile devices. The parents should watch out what adventures are freely available online for keeping kids busy, happy, and joyful. For example, U.K. National Literary Trust sponsors "Online Zone." disseminating reading and writing skills, interesting book lists, and videos. Katherine Rundell, an award-winning author, provides a free reading of her book, "The Book of Hopes: words and pictures to Comfort, inspire, and entertain children in Lockdown." The book comprises 100 stories written by children and profusely illustrated to make it an impressive read. Exemplar Education allows free access to the online math tuition programme for 5 to 16-year-old children. Other free for all amusing and academically promising web services include:

Purple Mash - aimed at 3-11year olds, displaying animation, coding, spelling, and grammar

Activity Village - offering colouring pages, puzzles, crafts, and worksheets.

All Kids Network - presents themed colouring pages and snack ideas for parents and teachers in primary and secondary schools.

Bamboo Learning - A voice-based application covers academic subjects, listening comprehension, and social studies.

Black Box Education - It exhibits digital and interactive resources for drama, theatre, and dance.

Home School For ME- Freely available for downloading worksheets depicting educational activities that enable children to focus on the completion of tasks.

Twinkl - Given the necessity to educate children during school closures, a privately-run educational platform, "Twinkl" has prepared 630,000 home learning packs for free distribution to parents enabling them to keep up with school studies. The kit consists of activity sheets, interactive presentations, information packs, online games, and videos. Each package caters to different age levels ranging from the early years' foundation stage to GCSE.

Code Break Programme - It is a free computer science programme for children and adults.

Roblox - Learn to Design Roblox Games. It is a collection of online multiplayer games; each game is coded and designed by the player who can share with other players online.

Learn How to Draw - It hosts drawing classes for kids. Steve Harpster hosts classes via his Facebook page and YouTube channel every day intended for teaching families how to draw cartoons.

Ask her more - a Social Media Platform. Jennifer Siebel runs it, and her second successful launch is "Smart Girls Ask."

There are numerous amusing online activities for children to follow, get involved, and enjoy in the comfort of their home:

Minibeasts - a shadow matching activity in which children observe the shape of the shadow and select the picture of the common minibeast.

Multiplication Tables Check Practice evolving Time Table Practice Quiz.

Pizza Fractions Matching Interactive Activity - It shows images of pizza and pupils by dragging and dropping the proper fraction to match each picture.

Parts of a Flower - It is an interactive plant eBook for teachers to instruct the class about the different processes which make up the life cycle of plants. The teacher can set pupils some research questions asking children to access eBook to look for answers.

Fake News interactive quiz - It enables kids to distinguish between true stories and fake news. This exercise helps to teach online safety to vulnerable children.

Ramadan Interactive Word Search – It is a quiz in which children learn about unique Islamic festivals.

Arithmagic Interactive Colouring Activity - It is a mental adventure for 6 to 11-year-olds to reinforce skills and key math facts.

Circulatory System Labelling Activity - It is for teachers to impart lessons on human biology as the kids learn to locate the parts of the human circulatory system.

William Shakespeare Self-Marking Reading Comprehension - Reading comprehension is designed for developing the critical reading skills of retrieval, inference, prediction, and vocabulary. It improves pupils' reading capabilities aimed at a wide range of ability levels.

Physical fitness is paramount for a healthy and vibrant, imaginative mind as we can take advantage of "P.E. With Joe." Joe Wicks is a Body Coach hosting free workouts directed at kids live on his YouTube channel. It is a 30-minute live intensive workout; anyone can stream via a mobile device or the tablet. Eileen Phillipa Rose Fowler (1906-2000) came to my mind when I was living in London throughout the 1970s. She was a "Keep Fit Craze" physical exercise instructor and a founder of the British Keep Fit Association (1956). Every morning at 6.45 a.m., the exercise lovers (including myself) would switch on the radio and exercise with her radio broadcast. She injected fun into the exercising cycle and introduced her catchphrase, "Down with a bounce; with a bounce, Come Up." It was a hilarious and physically pleasant early morning experience to tune with Eileen Fowler before heading to the University of London.

We cannot afford to waste precious time in meaningless chores since our kids are the human capital and a useful resource for a better future. With some parental attention and affection supported by teachers' online instructions, our youth may expand their horizons of thinking and imagination for creating a peaceful, accommodating, and the caring world as many of us will hopefully witness a rejuvenated shaping of the universe after the COVID-19.

Social Learning

Social Dilemmas are common in developing countries where social welfare systems do not exist owing to the scarcity of determination to improve the social and economic conditions of deprived communities. Any person visiting one of these destinations would find mendicants occupying particular spots at the shopping malls, train stations, bus terminals, traffic signals, amusement parks and cinema houses. It is challenging to discriminate between genuine vagrants and professional beggars. Among them are many drug addicts, alcoholics and gamblers who knock on the glass window of every car, forcefully appeal to a passer-by and pester passengers at the railway stations to give alms. Some beggars hold placards with pitiable slogans displayed to entice innocent individuals to part with cash at the cost of creating traffic jams.

Social learning has become a significant part of creative education at the Glasgow School of Art in cooperation with the Castlehead High School in Paisley, Scotland. The studio-based, practice-led model is geared to the aspirations of youth who can build confidence, practice teamwork and improve social thinking across different subjects. The Director of GSA Professor Tom Inns explicitly remarked that these innovative teaching and learning methods would improve attainment through creativity and enhance the quality of life and expand the young mind. (GSA, Nov. 2017). Social learning is about whether begging is right in a welfare state, and how the fake beggars could be apprehended and punished in the court of law? In a classroom, students may debate the social issue and put forward ideas to deal with nuisance epidemic. The pupils' thoughts, feelings and social opinions could be discussed in which class teacher might act as a mediator and moderator. Such deliberation and pupil discourses would improve knowledge and enhance the debating capacity of the participants.

Traditionally held social norms have transformed since the beginning of the twentieth century. The Western liberalisation of societies impacted the social values of youth in many Asian and African countries, especially the states administered by the French, British, Dutch and Spain. The U.S. Revolution in 1776 and the French Revolution in 1791 permitted citizens of respective countries to enjoy freedom as human rights were guaranteed in the constitution. Three social values namely justice, the rule of law and democracy became recognised at all levels during the eighteenth and nineteenth centuries. The teachers training included value education to promote love for the nation, improve diligence and endorse optimism. The notion of liberty, democracy and fairness created social awareness and the concept of independent thought and acquisition of personal goals. Several Afro-Asian nations adopted the Western education system to keep pace with modernisation and comfortable way of life. This youth wakefulness made the fulfilment of self-directed social desires a way of life free from socially binding family values. Youngsters preferred academic goals over morality and ethical perceptions. Since the beginning of the twentieth century, moral and social issues became complex affecting coherent families and conservative values. During the last few decades, the need for social education has gained attention from thinkers, sociologist, psychologists and educators across the globe, including Singapore, Japan, Europe and Australia. In the United States, Jefferson Centre for Character Education,

Josephson Institute of Ethics and Heartwood Institute, Wexford have specially designed moral values-oriented curriculum for high school students.

Social values are intangible and more abstract than attitudes as values may change with life experience in a multicultural society, and with the emergence of new roles and responsibilities. (Feather, 1994; Kahle and Timmer, 1983). Determination, independence and imagination are three social value assets that make a youth succeed in life whereas parents develop their perceptions about raising them based on their cultural socialising. (Julian et al., 1994; Lee & Zahan, 1991). The process by which youth are educated or trained with the manners, morals, and conduct of society, is an integral part of social education.

For example, U.S. culture, albeit secular in all hues stems from Judo-Christian roots and Chinese culture twigs in Confucianism. (Tu, 1990; Wu & Tseng, 1985). Value is a piece of cultural evidence (Opler, 1954), a way of life (Morris, 1956) or a criterion for performance or justification for social behaviour (Williams, 1968, 1970). Value is an element, common to a series of situations which is capable of arousing an understandable response in the individual. (Linton, 1945). The status and social class of parents has an impact on child upbringing. In Kohn's view, differences in parental values result in large measure from differences in the conditions of life experienced by parents at a different social-class level. (1979, p.45.). Lynds (1929) enumerates social class structure in a classic community study, and also, Melvin Kohn (1976, p.538.) evaluated Wright and Wright's (1976) appraisal of the relationship between social class and parental values. The professional social class endorses the view that the social situation is full of trials that can be encountered rather than evaded. The social class level disparities engender differences in social emotions, impacting the formation of interpersonal relations in an educational environment. Conclusively, social class variations have their roots in economic unfairness and deplorable living conditions of large segments of societies.

Social values of individuals in a group may have more extensive diversity owing to family social practices. Still, youth may adopt some of those traits or adapt for acceptance that cluster with renewed social identification. Social background, economic standing and stability of family life have a considerable influence on youngsters' social behaviour. The parents take their children for a banquet and expect them to sit still and enjoy the meal; and yet they move around dropping ketchup, opening sugar sachets and emptying pepper shakers. Also, the kids scatter tissue paper and play around, thus upsetting other people. These children are emotionally unsettled and socially disturbed due to domestic and social environment in which they are raised, nourished and educated in mannerism. Perceived inequalities have a disproportionate impact on teen social behaviour, but social rejection harms their self-worth. Social education is all about cooperative learning, managing behaviour through self-control and shared experiences. Indeed, social values are impalpable thoughts and intangible feelings that are subject to adaptation depending on communal experiences. Social control is self-restraint in holding back undesirable social emotions, politely rebuking unwanted and detrimental social advances and evaluating personal movements before indulging in illicit actions. Informal social pressure exerted by family members, friends, peers and neighbours work wonders in preventing prohibited conduct and despicable behaviour. Youth tend to form small social groups for gossips and blathers, fun and enjoyment. If anyone proves to be a misfit due to typical habits, he/she faces exclusion and consequential isolation. Persistent use of foul language that violates the group's social norm may result in shaming the youth.

We move forward with positive perceptions and optimistic acuities, ignoring unpleasant voices, respecting diversity and extending heartfelt collaboration. Everyone, youth in particular, thoughtfully contributes, conjoins, and participates in productive processes, permeating true spirit of shared values. Together, we build a tolerant and open-minded society embracing diversified hues and opinions, recognising beliefs and admiring acceptance. Youth character revolves around facets of gratification, satisfaction, and pleasure, desiring realisation of aspirations, aims and hopes. Just social system provides opportunities for self-fulfilment and offers support for community unification. Adult wisdom enlightens young minds and inspires rightful thinking for a constructive role to bring peace, tranquillity, and happiness in the global village. Our past may be different from the present but hope for the better future never fades.

Youth Sports Engagement

It is virtually difficult for any kid to aim for a career in a somewhat distinguished field of sports without active encouragement, help, and moral support of parents at home and teachers at schools. Currently, over fifty million children (National Council of Youth Sports) take part in numerous competitions. Youth sports organisations are not adequately financed and always require volunteers, monetary sponsors, campaigners, and guides to support their initiatives. Enthusiastic parents get personally involved in the kid's time management, eating schedule, exercise timetable, and suitable sleeping needs. Physical and mental fitness is a prerequisite to participation in productive training for learning new skills. Involved fathers and loving mothers readjust their work and personal programmes to accommodate children's sporting arrangements. They happily drive them to the training venue, provide nourishing food, keep watch on their physical fitness, and continuously offer encouragement.

German Psychologist Siegfried Bernfeld (1892) says social origins determine youth life-courses, their actions, but mindsets differ according to their performance in the playground. In 1934, he arrived in the United States, continuing research and advancing the idea of progressive education. During amateur sports practices, the transition from childhood to youth occurs gradually with a change of attitudes and behaviours, approaches, and manners. The biological process relates to the body, physical strength, and stamina. The psychological process refers to the functioning of the brain, thinking, and reacting to the environment. Stanley Hall (1844) valued youth above the adult. He says, 'Youth, when properly understood, will seem to be not only the revealer of the past but of the future, for it is dimly prophetic of the best part of history which is not yet written because it is not yet transpired.' It has been quoted in Meyer Spacks, Hall, 1904, p.233) The biological procedure forms the basis of development for youth relations and social activities. Both at school and playgrounds, peer-group socialisation dissolves family-bonds and diminishes ties between families and the youngsters. Youth transition to adolescence and adulthood is supposed to be the most significant moment for social stability. Parents at this crucial stage of grooming must pay thoughtful attention to the genuine socio-psychological needs of youth. They should initiate a shared decision-making process with complete kids' involvement and participation. Teenagers unable to comply with measurable performance goals would require increased parental support, demonstrating courage, patience, and tolerance.

Social freedom and sports passion generates interest, promotes positive conduct, and minimises negative behaviour. Positive attitude reflects kids' discipline at school playgrounds, where they tend to get on well with classmates. Regular involvement in sports inculcates in them the habit of curiosity, the desire to educate and improve oratory skills. The refinement of sporting skills brings meaning into their lives. Their appetite to do better increases engagement and ensures presence in the sports venues. Youth sport has the potential to keep children off the street and create excitement in a safe environment. The schools can focus on giving youth a chance to join one or more indoor or outdoor games in which they can build skills, talents, and efficacy. The kids will prove their usefulness and worth with precipitous tenacity and absolute determination. The local Government's financial incentives and support to strengthen training programmes can raise the aspirations of deprived communities. Youth voice should be valued in all matters pertaining to sport participation and empowerment, and their engagement should reflect enjoyment in every activity.

Regular reassurance and praise motivate kids to improve their performance with tenacity and vigour. A few inspirational words boost children's morale, strengthen dynamism, and rejuvenate confidence. Most children rightly consider sport as entertaining, making them excited and animated. The collection of memorabilia and souvenirs is a passion for most kids who earnestly obtain autographs of famous sportsmen and women. Purchase of baseball caps, shirts, and pictures of top footballers such as Ronaldo, Messy, Neymar, and Harry Cane is just proof of youngsters' craving for soccer. The photographs and paintings of the highest goal scorers on bedroom walls create thrill and joy for broods.

Assurance enhances their optimism and revitalises commitment paving the way for setting high targets. The signs of improved focus begin to appear on his/her face, indicative of progression in the competitive environment. Mothers are ardently involved in the practical help necessary for their children to feel safe and comfortable. Mindful fathers indeed remain on board and attend to a child's genuine requirements, including the purchase of uniforms, sporting equipment, and related apparatus. They make sure on-time payment of sporting club fees and miscellaneous expenditure. If a child does not perform well initially, praise must not be withheld, and admonition should be avoided under all conditions. Sporting genius is not produced overnight, but it is a slow process demanding patience and endurance. Kid's sporting stamina is built with meticulousness and diligence over time. In the sporting environment, children feel a sense of freedom and accept responsibility, learn self-control, and develop an individual identity. They make better choices and get prepared to deal with the consequences of choices. Sportsmanship sharpens qualities of compassion, judiciousness, and care.

Many successful sportspersons have contributed a considerable chunk of their fortunes for charitable causes. They become role models for the younger athletes by establishing a charity platform to promote noble endeavours for uplifting the plight of poor and subjugated. Three-time N.B.A. Champion Le Bron James, a Black American born in Ohio, invited Don Lemon of CNN for a tour of his project "I Promise School." So far, Le Born James Family Foundation has spent over forty-one million dollars to pay for the tuition fees for all high school young residents of Akrorn, Ohio. Serena Williams is another black American girl, the Queen of Tennis, who has given lavishly for the welfare of deprived communities. Curtis Granderson, also black American, is a baseball philanthropist who has built sports complex for inner-city youth in Chicago. A white American lady Ronda Rousey is a famous name in the sphere of charity. Everybody knows the Brazil National Team and Barcelona Football hero Neymar who loves charity and looks after 2400 disadvantages kids. He says the love from kids and conversation with them gives him the strength to return to Barcelona after the holidays. Neymar recently gave £770,000 to a charity for fighting Coronavirus pandemic. Mesut Ozil, a Turkish Football player, has donated £237,000 to a children's hospital, whereas Hector Bellerin, an Arsenal defender, offered colossal money to compensate Grenfell Tower fire victims. Likewise, Mohamed Salah has set up a charitable foundation, donating £234,000, and then giving £2.5 million to the National Cancer Institute in Egypt. He also consistently contributes money to fund 450 families by providing each of the monthly allowances. However, Cristiano Ronaldo, a goal scorer football legend, prominently surpasses many players in advancing charitable ambitions throughout his career. He is the most generous and most charitable sportsman today who donated the entire sum of UEFA Team of The Year Award in 2013 to the Red Cross, followed by £450,000 to another charity in 2014. Ronaldo is the ambassador of three notable charities, Save The Children, UNICEF, and World Vision. With his goal-scoring spree, he entertains millions of young and old who gleefully watch him play first at Manchester United, then Real Madrid and now in Italy.

Sportspersons are famous for raising their voices against injustice and unfairness. For example, in the United States, 28-women footballers on the National Soccer Team have filed a Gender Discrimination Lawsuit against the United States Soccer Federation. These women play more games and win more matches than men, but get far less paid. Muhammad Ali lost his boxing licence for refusing to join the army to fight in the Vietnam War, which he believed was unjustified. In May 2020, the Boston Red Sox team rejected the Presidential invitation to visit the White House. In June 2020, U.S. Women Football Team refused to meet the president at the White House. Some bold sports persons always speak out on issues related to social injustice, inequalities, and discrimination. Unfortunately, racism is not only prevalent in the West, but it is also rampant in the Arab world, teasing dark-skinned people on the Television screen. Comedian shows make fun of these people that are utterly against the norms of any religion. For example, a T.V. serial "Azmi We Ashgan" in Egypt makes a mockery of black people throughout the series. It is a deplorable and dreadful programme, infuriating right-thinking viewers who believe in the racial equality and dignity of all human beings. Other Egyptian movies include disgraceful dialogues such as "Did someone burn this apartment before or What." Anti-black racist language is involved in many drama series for the entertainment of mostly white

Egyptians, humiliating people with darker skin. The negative portrayal of black people is also practiced in Kuwaiti dramas and comedy serials entitled "Block Ghashmara" (the block of Jokes), an entire episode of actors in blackface depicting Sudanese people as indolent and sceptical.

Many parents enrol their children in various after-school sports clubs to keep them fit, relaxed, and busy. Recreational activities at school enable pupils to enjoy, laugh, and have fun with fellows and friends. Such exciting events are the means of relaxation and refreshment. A few kids supported by mother or father join local clubs for extra training at weekends and summer holidays. Among these enthusiastic children, the lucky and ambitious go on to enter under 12 and 15 professional clubs. With sheer tenacity, training, dedication, and polished skills, some extraordinarily competent and brilliant children outshine and play for the national teams. While others participate in local, national, and international competitions, winning silver, gold, and bronze medals. They bring home awards and mementoes, glorifying the national flag. Parents should be aware of the professional coaching clubs and their training programmes for preparing kids for future enrolment. In the U.S.A., they have On Track Development Progression training programme for swimmers offering three hours per day, six days a week schedule. (Making a Move. Los Angeles Times- Daily Pilot e-newspaper, July 8, 2020). This training helps improve speed, suppleness, and stamina for prospective swimmers. Girls Football Club is known as "WILDCATS" cater to girls aged 5-11, offering a chance to practice and develop their skills. There are 165 cricket clubs in Somerset, welcoming children as young as 4 to 18 years old. The Harrow Cricket Club looks after 300 children in two categories, under 7-years and 17-years, offering encouragement and training.

Most children participate for enjoyment and refreshment while some are exceedingly ambitious to become superstars. Likewise, Tennis Oxfordshire, 'Tennis For Kids," is a beautiful club giving between 4 and 11-year-old kids an opportunity to attend tennis sessions to augment fair play, concentration, and teamwork skills. City of Peterborough Tennis Club initially offers free lessons to 5-11 year old followed by 6-weeks training. Youth Triathlon in Scotland aims at under 16-year old children, combining running and swimming and inspiring ambitious kids to succeed in entering national competitions. In Germany, youth can join hockey, tennis, handball, Boxing, rugby, and basketball clubs as well as Curling, Ice-Hockey, and Volleyball Clubs. There are over 87000 clubs affiliated with the German Sports Federation; most are managed and run by unpaid volunteers. Since 1998, Ursprung Basketball Academy has been successfully training German youth and produced some remarkable players.

Teenage girls are increasingly missing out on the terrific benefits of sports due to puberty issues arising as early as at the age of ten. Participation in a football game is inspiring and rousing for girls who give incredible performance by winning trophies and shields. In European competitions, British girls bring home medals and golden plaques. They feel empowered and get emotional rewards by exhibiting splendid talents. Sports engagement fuels their sense of achievement, but sudden puberty brings emotional upheaval, causing anxiety and disengagement. The girls in the U.K. prefer to try out new things and gain experience with different activities, including baking a cake, walking in the woods, and playing hide and seek in the local parks that offers happiness and pride. Any form of self-expression is worthwhile as long as it is rewarded with emotional feedback and social satisfaction. In a survey covering America and Europe, it is revealed that more than one-third of youngsters aged 10-17 drop out of the sport due to social and psychological factors. (Crane, et al. 2015). A vast majority of young boys and girls withdraw from team sports owing to personal and family circumstances. (Rottenstein et al., 2013). They do not feel connected, coupled with the lack of motivation, leads to stepping aside. Regarding drop out and sport, there are 38 published studies conducted between 1980 and 2015. Overwhelming drop out reason appears to be the disputes with coaches, pressure from peers, occupation with social life and relationships, lack of fun, and plenty of boredom. (Monteiro et al., 2017).

Surprisingly, youth participation in sports has been on the decline in Canada owing to the coaches exerting pressure on athletes and their families to respect the training schedule. Some youth pull out of the sports due to intolerance, racism, and lack of fair play. The teenage girls withdraw from training on account of harassment and emphasis on winning the competition. The Canadian coaches often complain that the parents are either over-involved or under-involved that disrupts their programme. The kids have reported various forms of bullying, physical, and mental abuse during training sessions. Amongst the most popular games are tennis, cycling, skiing, baseball, soccer, and golf. The kids often express disquiets and apprehensions that they do not like sitting on the bench for the winning team and would prefer to play for the losing side. There is a shortage of volunteers who run practices and coach games for the youth because it takes many years to become a qualified coach. Sport participation crises for children under the age of 13 have worsened. Hyper-competitive environment and setting high standards have dissuaded the kids from remaining in training. They have stepped away before 13-years of age and have hung up their sneakers plimsolls, and cleats for good. The coaches pick up the best players too soon, leaving low performers disgruntled and demoralised. They have no viable option but to quit altogether. An Exclusive rigid selection based on excellent performance backfires on coaches and parents with stunningly high dreams for kids. Concerning gratuitous parental expectations, Karri Dawson, Director of the True Sport Foundation, Canada, asserts that those who excel and are seen in the Olympic teams have distinguished themselves through tremendous struggle, tenaciousness, and passion. She tells parents, "They were multi-sport athletes, they played hockey in the winter, soccer in the summer, and they participated in different sports at school. They cross-trained, and they exercised all kinds of different muscles and abilities that one day made them gifted at a particular sport". Besides, the steeply rising cost of sport dissuades most children for participation that equally demands plenty of time and distraction from serious studies.

However, during the last three years, the Canadian Government has injected funds to support the training of female coaches in hockey, soccer, and tennis and also to eliminate gender-based violence, helping increase girls' participation. Several organisations, including ParticipAction, Motivate Canada, Physical Health Education Canada, Go KidSport, Canadian Tire Jumpstart, and Le Grand Defi Pierre Lavoie, are actively promoting participation in sport throughout the country.

For encouraging youth to choose a particular sport as a career, there is a need for youth-parent-teacher collaboration. The trio affinity will co-jointly discuss, consult, and design comprehensive economically affordable programme feasible for children from diverse backgrounds and multicultural communities. During the process of implementation and training stages, youth opinions, voice, and empowerment would act as useful tools to facilitate enrolment, engagement, and practice. The more regularity is achieved at the training sessions, the better would be the outcome, raising youth morale, interest, and cooperation.

A well-thought-out youth sports programme carries tremendous benefits for the mental, biological and psychological wellbeing of youngsters. Health benefits include the burning of calories, better hand-eye coordination, and increased enjoyment. Moreover, it expands focus and motivation, energising brainpower, embedding desire for learning. Youth become caring and helpful, accepting defeat and setbacks with forbearance. Obesity in adolescence is penetrating at a staggering rate, creating laziness and sluggishness. Idleness is the playing field impacts overweight children who do not make substantial progress in any sport. For instance, running develops bone density in female participants and prevents osteoporosis later in their lives. Physical activity positively affects the brain physiology by increasing cerebral capillary growth, oxygenation, blood flow, and better growth of nerve cells in the hippocampus. The kids become more conscientious of their fitness, follow instructions, enjoy training, and avoid using harmful drugs. They can distinguish between accurate and wrong, truth and falsehood, justice, and unfairness. They cooperate with friends and mates at school and playing field, reach out to help the injured and console the losers.

Youth athletes view sport as a positive leisure involvement leading to psychological maturity and social capital. It increases robustness and eliminates surplus body fat in boys and girls. In 1995, Borra and Colleagues conducted a Gallup Survey "Food, Physical Activity, and Fun" in which they discovered that the American children have a positive attitude about food nutrition and physical activity. Since that time, many psychologists and sociology Professors have researched youth attitudes and behaviour in the field of sports, health, and fitness.

Through sports, children can stay in shape, polish motor skills, and make new friends. They learn endurance, capable of withstanding danger and hardships, and persevere in all weathers and conditions. The youth find a sport an outlet for socialisation and an opportunity to demonstrate sporting talent, build self-image, and enhance academic competence. Winning creates feelings of accomplishment and jubilation since competing, and getting a trophy is a hard-earned privilege. In present-day sports, victory brings fame, dignity, honour, and above all, financial reward. When youth gains world recognition, he/she becomes a role model for aspiring amateurs, acting as an inspiration. Eminence makes a youngster celebrity dishing out autographs, delivering talks, and appearing on television shows. Almost all sports commentators are sportsmen and women who have excelled in their chosen fields. They understand the true spirit of play, rules of the games, and rewards of achievements. Women participate in masculine sports and produce excellent results, winning world cup hockey and football competitions.

Youth engagement programmes involve exciting adventures ranging from amateur sports to bird spotting in coastal areas of various countries. The Young Birders of New Zealand have introduced online sessions for kids to develop their knowledge of numerous birds, migration patterns, and breeding practices. Predator-Free Motusara Island Bird Sanctuary is a bird lovers paradise and home to Blue Penguine, Kereru Bellbird, Yellow-Crowned Parakeets, N.Z. Falcon and South Island Robins. Youth bush walk tours take them on to the top of the Island, where the teenagers enjoy the viewing of white-fronted terns and Australasian Gannets. Norwegian school kids receive encouragement from parents to join officially arranged tours of coastal areas to study and watch unique birds, take down notes, and capture photographs with their smartphones. They can make sound recordings of bird sounds from a considerable distance, bring home videos for others to enjoy, and gain knowledge of ornithology. Bird watching is a breath-taking and pulsating pastime for the youngsters to broaden their perception of beautiful bird varieties, hues, and singing descriptions. Similar Ornithological societies exist in the U.S.A., Canada, Europe, and Australia, especially for youth engagement who learn to work on academic assignments exploring the history, origin, and breeding environment of birds. Kids learn through bird watching the wonders of nature, broadening their knowledge of marvellous creations. The sight of flora and fauna and rare exotic species of seabirds revitalises youth memories and improved thinking power.

Youth possess lovely ideas and exciting opinions requiring validation, a sympathetic ear, and a compassionate response. The meaningful participation and sustained involvement of kids in recreational activities make them more confident, composed, and self-reliant. They like to be heard and perceived, responsible for making choices and accepting the implications of such decisions. A high degree of perfection and excellence in a sport is gracefully unpredictable. Tenacious and strenuous training energises youth technical talents, invigorates ambitions, and rejuvenates physical capacities. Accuracy in the playground develops overtime; confidence comes by surmounting hurdles and vanquishing misgivings, doubts, and hesitations. The supportive parent is logical partners in youth engagement, nurturing the strengths, abilities, and knacks. Parents, teachers, and trainers infuse trust, permeate conviction, appreciate progress, and praise achievement.

Let us permit kids, youth, and adolescents to choose the path, express the voice, make a choice, shoulder responsibility, and bear the consequences of their actions. Let them learn through experience and errors, minimising interference, supporting perseverance, and offering purposeful guidance, direction, and interaction.

LIST OF PLATES

Notice board Initiatives: Displaying community information

Learning Support: Manager Paul helps Draw & Paint

Promotional Initiatives: Free Reading Book Gifts

Creative Activities: Granddaughter Colouring

Controlled Behaviour: Keeping in line For the Bus

Eating Etiquettes: Grandmother & Granddaughter

Family Etiquettes: Talking and Consulting

Environmental Behaviour: Teenagers Littering

Collaborative Learning: Young Readers

Explorational Learning: Young Scholars

Committed Learning: A Serious Reader

Parental Learning: Parent and Child Reading

Online Learning (Botany): Parts of a Flower

Online Learning (Maths): Pizza Fractions

Online Learning (Science): Human Biology Lessons

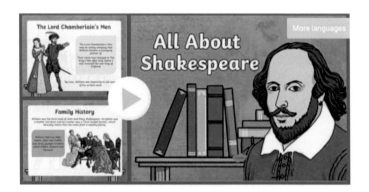

Online Learning (Literature): William Shakespeare

Skilful Learning: Plumbing & Joining Pipes

Experimental Learning: Science Lab Experiments

Targeted Bullying: Boy Being Bullied at School

Isolated Bullying: Three isolating One

Confrontational Behaviour: Boy Teasing Girl

Physical Bullying: Girl Enduring Physical Bullying

Conspired Bullying: Two Conspiring against Third

Playful Activities: Kids with Pompoms at school

Aerobic Workouts: Playing on Trampoline

Isometric Activities: Horse Riding

Learning Activities: Pony Riding

Aerobic Activities: Cycling

Functional Exercise: Rope Pulling

LIST OF PUBLICATIONS BY
THE AUTHOR

1. Science & Technology: A select bibliography. London: Southwark College, 1975.

2. Building Technology: an annotated bibliography of critical path analysis. Surrey, England, Crown Books, 1976.

3. Man-Powered Flight: Its History and Progress. Surrey, Crown Books, 1977.

4. Structure of Education and Libraries in a Developing Society. Lahore: Sang-e-Meel, 1983.

5. Academic Libraries. Lahore: Qadriya Books, 1984.

6. University Library Practices in Developing Countries. London; Boston, Melbourne, Kegan Paul, 1985.

7. Indexing Newspapers: Subject Analysis. Birmingham: NAAF Tec, 1991.

8. The Illumination of Heart. Birmingham: ACS Publications, 2001.

9. Virtuous Life of Imam Ali: The gateway of Knowledge. Birmingham: Radiant Valley, 2010.

10. Karwan-e-Zainab bint Batool. Birmingham: Radiant Valley, 2011.

11. Sufferings of the Sacred Family: Karbla Atrocities, Birmingham: Radiant Valley, 2012.

12. Karb-e-Hafsa. Lahore: Nida-e-Haq, 2012.

13. Manzoomat Dr Nazir Ibn-e-Zainab. Birmingham: Radiant Valley, 2013.

14. History of Arabic and Persian Printing. Birmingham: Radiant Valley, 2015.

15. Collection of Poems.[Allah ka Qurb] Birmingham: Radiant Valley, 2016.

16. The Sacred Land of Jordan. West Midlands: Radiant Valley, 2017.

17. The Refinement of Spiritual Potential: illumination of soul and mind. West Midlands: Radiant Valley, 2018.

18. Challenges of Raising Youth: Nurturing teenagers in a Digital World. Birmingham: Radiant Valley, 2020.

19. Emotional Wellbeing: Emotional Attachments Shape Our Lives. Birmingham: Radiant Valley, 2021. [Printing in Progress]

20. Literary Memoirs: a Collection of English Poems and Chronicles. [to be published in 2021]

21. Family Memoirs: an Illustrated biography with Poems and Photos. Birmingham: Radiant Valley, [to be published in 2022.]

REFERENCES

Akubra girl Dolly's bullying suicide shocks Australia. BBC News, 10 January 2018. [bbc.co.uk/news/world-australia-42691208]

Alavi, H. R. (2007). Al-Ghazali on moral education. Journal of Moral Education. 36(3), 309-319. [Imam Ghazali is a great world scholar of Islam]

Alberti, R.E. & Emmons, M.L. (1970) Your perfect right: a guide to assertive behaviour. Oxford: Impact, 109p.

Althof, W. and Berkowitz, M.W. (2006). Moral education and character education: their relationship and roles in citizenship education. Journal of Moral Education, 35(4), 495-518.

Amato, P.R. (2000). The consequence of divorce for adults and children. Journal of Marriage and the Family, 62(4): 1279-1287.

Amato, P.R. & Fowler, F. (2002). Parenting practice, child adjustment, and family diversity. Journal of Marriage and Family, 64: 703-716.

Anderson, D.R. (2000). Character education: Who is responsible? Journal of Instructional Psychology, 27: 139.

Aries, Elizabeth and Seider, Maynard (2010). The role of social class in the formation of identity: a study of public and elite private college students. *The Journal of Social Psychology*, 147(2), 137-157.

Arthur, J and Carr, D. (2013). Character in learning for life: a virtue ethical rationale for recent research on moral and values education. Journal of Beliefs and Values. 34(1), 26-35.

Astin, A.W. (1999). Student involvement: a developmental theory for higher education. Journal of College Student Development, 40(5): 518-529.

Atherton, O.E., Tackett, J.L., Ferrer, E. and Robins, R.W. (2017). Bidirectional pathways between relational aggression and temperament from late childhood to adolescence. Journal of Research in Personality, 67: 75-84.

Atik, Gokhan, Ozmer, O. & Kemer, G. (2012) Bullying and submissive behaviour. Journal of the

Bandura, A (1986). Social foundations of thought and action: a social cognitive theory. Englewood Cliffs, NJ: Prentice-Hall.

Barboza, G.E., Schiamberg, L.B., Oehmke, J., Korzeniewski, S. J., Post, L. A., and Heraux, C.G. (2009). Individual characteristics and the multiple contexts of adolescent bullying: an ecological perspective. Journal of Youth Adolescent, 38(1): 101-121.

Baumrind, Diana (1971). Harmonious parents and their preschool children. Developmental Psychology, 4: 99-102.

Baumrind, Diana (1991). The influence of parenting style on adolescent competence and substance use. Journal of Early Adolescence. 11: 56-95

Baumrind, Diana. (1966). Effects of authoritative parenting control on child behaviour. Child Development, 37: 887-907.

Berkowitz, M. W. (1999). Obstacles to teacher training in character education. Action in Teacher Education, 20(4), 1-10.

Berkowitz, M.W., Battistich, V.A. and Bier, M.C. (2007). What works in character education? In Nucci, L., Krettenauer, T., Nucci, L.P. and Narvaez, D., Handbook of moral and character education. New York: Routledge.

Bertoia, C, and Drakich, J. (1993) The fathers' rights movement: contradictions in rhetoric and practice. Journal of Family Issues, 14(4): 592-515.

Blaise, A. (1980). Bridging moral cognition and moral action: a critical review of the literature. Psychological Bulletin, 1: 1-45.

Blasi, A. (1980). Bridging moral cognition and moral action: a critical review of the literature. Psychological Bulletin,1, 1-45.

Blasi, A. (1999). Emotions and moral motivation. Journal of the Theory of Social Behaviour, 1, 1-19.

Brendgen, M., Poulin, F. (2018). Continued bullying victimization from childhood to young adulthood: a longitudinal study of mediating and protective factors. Journal of Abnormal Child Psychology, 46(1): 27-39.

Bucciarelli, Monica, Khemlani, S. and Johnson-Laird, P.N. (2008). The psychology of moral reasoning. Judgement and Decision Making, 3(2), 121-139.

Bun, J.R., Louiselle, P.A., Misukanis, T.M., and Mueller, R.A. (1988). Effects of parental authoritarianism and authoritativeness on self-esteem. Personality and Social Psychology Bulletin, 14(2): 271-282.

Burgess, A (1997). Fatherhood reclaimed: the making of the modern father. London: Vermillion

Bushway, A and Nash, W.R. (1977). School cheating behaviour. Review of Educational Research, 47; 623-632.

Campbell, E. (2008). Teaching ethically as a moral condition of professionalism. In D. Narvaez and L. Nucci (Eds), The International handbook of moral and character education. (pp.601-617). New York, NY: Routledge.

Campbell, Marilyn A., (2005). Cyberbullying: an old problem in a new guise. Australian Journal of Guidance and Counselling. 15(1), 68-69.

Churchill, L. R. (1982). The teaching of ethics and moral values in teaching: some contemporary confusion. The Journal of Higher Education, 53(3), 296-306.

Churchill, R., Ferguson, P., Godinho, S., Johnson, N., Keddie, A., Letts, W., and Vick, M. (2013). Teaching making a difference. 2nd ed., Milton Australia: Wiley.

Claessens, Dieter. (1967). Familie und Wertsystem. Eine Studie zur zweiten, sozio-kulturellen Geburt des Menschen. Verlag Duncker and Humblot 2. Auflage Berlin.

Colby, A, et al., (1977). Secondary school moral discussion programmes led by social studies teachers. Journal of Moral Education, 6(2): 90-111.

Collier, R and Sheldon, S. (2016). Fathers' rights, fatherhood and law reform-international perspective, in A. Collier and S. Sheldon (eds) Fathers' rights activism and law reform in comparative perspective. (pp1-27) Oxford & Portland, OR: Hart Publishing.

Cooley, J.L. and Fite, P.J. (2016). Peer victimisation and forms of aggression during middle childhood: the role of emotion regulation. Journal of Abnormal Child Psychology, 44(3): 535-546.

Corrigan, D., Cooper, R., Keast, S., and King, D. T. (2010). Expert science teacher's notion of scientific literacy. Paper presented at the 1st International Conference of STEM in Education. The Queensland University of Technology, Brisbane, Australia.

Cowie, H., (2013). Cyberbullying and its impact on young people's emotional health and well-being. *The Psychrist.*, 37(5): 167-170. [https://doi.org/10.1192/pb.bp.112.040840]

Coyne, S.M., Archer, J., & Eslea, M., (2006). We are not friends anymore! Unless...the frequency & harmfulness of indirect, relational & social aggression. Aggressive Behavior, 32, 294-307.

Crane, T., Temple, V. (2015). A systematic review of dropout from organised report among children and youth. European Psychological Education Review, 2; 1-18.

Crothers, L.M. & Levinson, E.M. (2004). Assessment of bullying: a review of methods and instruments. *Journal of Counselling & Development,* 82(4), 496-503.

Crown, D and Spiller, M. (1998). Learning from the literature on college cheating: a review of empirical research. Journal of Business Ethics, 17:683-700.

Currie, D.H., Kelly, D.M. and Pomerantz, S. (2007) The power to squash people: understanding girls' rational aggression. *British Journal of Sociology Education*, 28(1), 23-37.

Dahl, Roald (1984). Boy: tales of childhood. Puffin Books.

Dahlsgaard, R., Peterson, C., Seligman, M.E.P. (2005). Shared virtue: the convergence of valued human strengths across cultures and history, Rev Gen Psychology, 9: 203-213.

Daly, M and Wilson, M.I. (1994). Some differential attitudes of lethal assaults on small children by stepfathers versus genetic fathers. Ethnology and Sociology, 15(2): 205-217.

Daneygier, Rafaela M (2013) Immigration and Conflict in Europe. *The Journal of Politics*, vol.75, no.3; 1-2.

DDCMS (2019) the UK to introduce world-first online safety laws. Department for Digital, Culture, Media & Sport, Home Office, London. [https://www.gov.uk/government/organisations/home-office].

De Guronski, Adam (1857). America and Europe. New York: D. Appleton and Co., pp.380-381.

De Tocqueville. Alexis (1990). Democracy in America. Vol.2, translated into English by Phillips Bradley. New York, Vintage. P.192.

Dehue, F., Bolman, C., & Vollink, T. (2008). Cyberbullying: Youngsters' experiences' and parental perception. *Cyberpsychology & Behavior*. 11(2): 217-223. [https://doi.org/10.1089/cpb.2007.0008PMID; 18422417]

Dermott, E. (2008). Intimate fatherhood: a sociological analysis. London: Routledge.

Devine, F (1992). Affluent Workers Revisited: Privatism and the Working Class. Edinburgh: Edinburgh University Press. P.9.

Dewey, John (1922). Human nature and conduct, In the Middle Works, 1899-1924., J.A. Boydston (ed). Carbondale: Southern Illinois University Press.

Dewey, John (1922). Human nature and conduct, in The Middle Works, 1899-1924, J.A. Boydston (ed.), Carbondale: Southern Illinois University Press.

Dewey, John (1932). The moral self. From Ethics (1932), in L.A. Hickman & T.M. Alexander (eds.) (1998), The essential Dewey Volume 2: ethics, Logic, Psychology. Pp.341-354.

Dewey, John. (1963). Experience and education. New York: Collier

Dickens, Charles (1941). Oliver Twist. New York: Dodd, Mead & Co. 541p

Digital Charter (2019). [https://www.gov.uk/government/publications/digital-charter]

Doris, J.M. and Stich, S.P. (2005). As a matter of fact: an empirical perspective on ethics, In Jackson F. and Smith, M. The Oxford handbook of contemporary philosophy. Oxford: Oxford University Press.

Doucet, A. (2006). Do men mother? Fathering care and domestic responsibility. Toronto: University of Toronto Press.

Ellis, Mark (2019). School blades crisis: five knife incidents per day. Daily Mirror, 16 October 2019.

Erikson, E.H. (1959). Identity and the life cycle: selected papers. Psychological Issues, 1, 1-171.

Evans, A.D., Xu, F, Lee, K. (2011). When all signs point to you: lies in the face of evidence. Developmental Psychology, 47: 39-49.

Faculty of Educational Science, 45(1), 191-208.

Fass, Paula S. (2014). How Americans raise their children: generational relations over two hundred years. 27th Annual Lecture of the GHI, Washington D.C., Bulletin of the GHI - German Historical Institute,(54), Spring 2014. Pp1-19.

Featherstone, B. (2003). Taking fathers seriously. British Journal of Social Work, 33(2):239-254.

Feng, W., Ramos, D.E., & Chan, S.R.; & Bourgeois, J.A.(2017). Internet gaming disorder: trends in prevalence, 1998-2016. *Addictive Behavior*. 75: 17-24.

Fenigstein, Allan (1979). Self-consciousness, self-attention and social-interaction. Journal of Personality and Social Psychology, 37 (1); 75-86.

Flood, Michael (2012). Separated Fathers and the Fathers' Right's' Movement (2012). Journal of Family Studies, 18(2-3): 235-245.

Friedman, Lawrence M. (1977). The legal system-Donald Black, the behaviour of law. Law and Society Review, 129: 1977-1978.

Frosh, S. (2002). Characteristics of sexual abusers, In K. Wilson and A. James (eds) The handbook of child protection. Edinburgh: Harcourt.

Gadlin, H. (1978). Child discipline and the pursuit of the self: a historical interpretation. In H.W. Reese and L.P. Lipsitt (eds) Advances in child development and behaviour. 2: 231-261.

Galloway, Rod. (2004). Determining the place of character education in New Zealand schools. N.Z. Foundation for Character Education.

Gava, Marie-Jose (August 16, 2019). Most bullying-whether the verbal, physical or psychological-takes place in college. https://www.connexionfrance.com/practical/family/700-000-pupils-suffer-at-hands-of-bullies-every-year

Geertz, C (1973). The interpretation of cultures. New York: Basic Books.

Gehring, D. and Pavela, G. (1994). Issues and perspectives on academic integrity. Washington, D.C.: National Association of Student Personnel Administrators.

Giddens, A. (1992). The transformation of intimacy. Cambridge: Polity Press.

Gillian, C. (1980). Justice and responsibility: thinking about the real dilemmas of moral conflict and choice. In Chr, Brusselmans (ed), Toward moral and religious maturity. Morristown.

Gino, F., Ayal, S. and Ariely, D. (2009). Contagion and differentiation in unethical behaviour. Psychological Science, 20(3): 393-398.

Glasser, W. (1993). The quality school teacher. New York: HarperCollins.

Gobry, Pascal-Emmanuel (March 14, 2012) The truth about French parenting (and I would know).

https://www.theatlantic.com/health/archive/2012/03/the-truth-about-french-parenting-and-i-would-know/254521/

Goldin, Claudia (2006). The quiet revolution that transformed women's employment, education, and family. American Economic Review, 96(2):1-21.

Goldthorpe, J.H. & Lockwood, David (1963) Affluent and the British Class Structure. *Sociological Review*, 11; 133-163.

Gorzig, A., & Olfasson, K., (2012). What makes a bully a cyberbully? Unravelling the characteristics of cyberbullies across twenty-five European countries. Journal of Children & Media. 7, 9-27. https://doi.org/10.1080/17482798.2012.739756.

Gorzig, A.,(2011). Who bullies & who is bullied online! EU Kids Online- a short report. London: London School of Economics & Political Science.

Graham, J, Nosek, B.A., Haidt, J. Iyer, R, Koleva, S and Ditto, P.H. (2011). Mapping the moral domain. Journal of Personality and Social Psychology, 101(2), 366-385.

Graham, J., Haidt, J., Koleve, S. et al. (2013). Moral foundations theory: The pragmatic validity of moral pluralism. Advances in Experimental Social Psychology, 47: 55-130.

Green, J.D., Paxton, J.M. (2009). Patterns of neural activity associated with honest and dishonest moral decisions. Proceedings of the National Academy of Sciences. 106(30): 12506-12511.

Green, S.P. (2004). Law and philosophy. 23: 137-185.

Greene, J.D., Sommerville, R.B., Nystrom, L.E., Darley, J, M, and Cohen, J.D. (2001). An fMRI investigation of emotional engagement in moral judgement. Science, 293: 2105-2108.

Greic, Joseph. (2013). Virtue theory, relativism and survival. International Journal of Social Science and Humanity, 3(4); 416-419.

Griffin, R.S. & Gross, A.M. (2004). Childhood bullying: Current empirical findings and future directions for research. Aggression & Violent Behavior, 9, 379-4

Gross, E.F., Juvonen, J & Gable, S.L., (2002). Internet use and well-being in adolescence. *Journal of Social Issues*. 58(1): 75-90. [htpps://doi.org/10.1111/1540-4560.00249]

Grotpeter, J. K., and Crick, N. R., (1996). Relational aggression, overt aggression and friendship. *Child Development*, 6, 2328-2338.

Guignon, Charles (2004). On being authentic. New York: NY, Routledge.

Guryan, Jonathan, Hurst, Erik H., Kearney, Melissa (2008). Parental education and parental time with children. Journal of Economic Perspectives, 22(3):23-46.

Haidt, J. (2001). The emotional dog and its rational tail: a social intuitionist approach to moral judgment. Psychological Review, 108, pp.814-834.

Haidt, J. (2007). The synthesis in moral psychology. Science, 316: 998-1002.

Halstead, J.M. (2007). Islamic values: a distinctive framework for moral education? Journal of Moral Education, 36(3), 283-296.

Hand, M. (2014). Towards a theory of moral education. Journal of Philosophy of Education, 48(4): 579-532.

Hand, Michael. (2014). Towards a theory of moral education. Journal of Philosophy of Education, 48(4)

Hand, Michael. (2018). A theory of moral education. London, Routledge

Harris, Michelle and Orth, Ulrich (2019). The link between self-esteem and social relationships: a meta-analysis of longitudinal studies. Journal of Personality and Social Psychology.

Hartshorne, H. and May, M.A. (1928). Studies like character. New York: The Macmillan Company.

Haslam, N, Bain, P, Neal, D. (2004). The implicit structure of positive characteristics. Personal Social Psychological Bulletin, 30; 529-541.

Heckman, James J. (1974). Effects of child-care programs on women's work effort. Journal of Political Economy. 82: S136-S169.

Heenan, L. (2002). Building character through cornerstone values- how schools can teach attitudes and values. New Zealand Foundation for Character Education.

Hemenway, D. Kennedy, BP., Kawachi, I, Putnam, RD. (2001) Firearm prevalence and homicide. *Annals of Epidemiology*. 11: 484-490.

Herrenkohl, T. L., Catalano, R. F., Hemphill, S.A., and Toumbourou, J. W. (2006). A longitudinal examination of physical and relational aggression as precursors to later problem behaviours in adolescents. *Violence and Victims*, 24(1), 3-19.

Herz, L., and Gullone, E. (1999). The relationship between self-esteem and parenting style: a cross-cultural comparison of Australian and Vietnamese Australian adolescents. Journal of Cross-Cultural Psychology, 30(6): 742-761.

Hillman, Mary., Adams, John, Whitelegg, M. (1990). On false move: a study of children's independent mobility. London: Policy Studies Institute.

Hoffman, M.L. (1994). Discipline and internalization. Development in Psychology. 30: 26-28.

Hoffman, M.L., (1979). Eine Theorie der moralentwicklung im jugendalter. In : L. Montada (Hrsg.) Brennpunkt der Entwicklungspsychologie. Stuttgart.

Hosley, C.A., and Montemayor, R. (1997). Fathers and adolescents: the role of the father in child development. In M.E. Lamb (ed.) The role of the father in child development. (3rd ed.) New Jersey, Hoboken; John Wiley and Sons. 162-178.

Howard, J. (2001). Mothers and sons: bringing up boys as sole parents. Port Melbourne, VIC Lothian. Pp.156-162.

Hume, D. (1978). A treatise of human nature. 2nd ed. Oxford: Oxford University Press, (first published in 1739)

Hurst, Beth, Wallace, Randall, Nixon, Sarah. (2013). The impact of social interaction on student learning. Reading Horizons, 52(4): 375-398.

Hursthouse, R (2012). Human nature and Aristotelian virtue ethics. Royal Institute of Philosophy Supplement, 70: 169-188.

Hutton, P. (2006). Understanding student cheating and what educators can do about it. College Teaching, 54: 171-176.

In Australia, guns are a privilege, not a right. (2019). The New York Times, 10 October 2019. [https://www.nytimes.com/2019/03/21/world/gun-laws-australia-uk-germany-canada.html]

Jackson, Stevi and Scott, Sue. (1999). Risk anxiety and the social construction of childhood. In Deborah Lupton (Ed.). Risk and sociocultural theory. Chapter 4, pp.86-108. Cambridge: Cambridge University Press.

James, V.H. and Owen, L.D. (2005). They turned around like I wasn't there: an analysis of teenage girls' letters about their peer conflicts. School Psychology International, 26(71), 71-88.

Jamieson, L. (1998). Intimacy: personal relationship in modern societies. Cambridge: Polity Press.

Jeffee, SR, Moffitt, TE, Caspi, A, Taylor, A (2003). Life with (or without) father: the benefits of living with biological parents depends on the father's anti-social behaviour. Child Development, 71(1): pp.109-126.

Jones, K.C.(2009)Facebooknamesincyber-bullying-suit. [http://www.informationweek.com/shared/printableArti cleSrc]

Jones, L.M., Mitchell, K.J. & Finkelhor, D (2013). Online harassment in context: trends from three Internet Youth Safety Surveys. Psychology of Violence, 3(1), 53-69. DOI:10.1037/a0030309.

Journal of Interpersonal Violence. 26(17): 3542-3560.

Julian, T.W., Patrick, C, McKenry & Mary W. Makelvey. (1994). Cultural variations in parenting: perceptions of Caucasian, African-American, Hispanic, and Asian-American parents. Family Relations, 43(1): 30-37.

Juvonen, J, Gross, EF. (2008). Extending the school grounds? Bullying experience in cyberspace. Journal of School Health. 78(9): 496-505.

Juvonen, J., & Gross, E.F., (2008). Extending the social grounds? - bullying experiences in cyberspace. Journal of School Health. 78(9): 496-505. [htpps://doi.org/10.1111/j.1746-1561.2008.00335xPMID:18786042]

Kammerl, R. & Hasebrink, U. (2013). Media and information literacy policies in Germany. [http://ppemi.ems-cachan.fr/data/media/colloque140528/rapports/GERMANY-2014]

Kant, I. (1959). Foundations of the metaphysics of morals and what is enlightenment? Translated by L.W. Beck. Indianapolis: Bobbs-Merrill. (first published in 1785).

Kartal, H. & Bilgin, A. (2009). Bullying and school climate from the aspects of the students and teachers. EgitimArastirmalari- Eurasian Journal of Educational Research, 36, 209-226.

Karzer, C., Fetchenhauer, D., & Belschak, F. (2009). Cyberbullying: who are the victims? A comparison of victimization in internet chatrooms and victimization in school. Journal of Media Psychology. 21: 21-25.

Kearney, Melissa and Levine, P.B. (2012). Why is the teen birth rate in the United States so high and why does it matter? Journal of Economic Perspectives, 26(2):14-63.

Kepenekci, Y.K. & Cinkir, s. (2006). Bullying among Turkish high school students. Child Abuse & Neglect, 30, 193-204.

Kiemer, K., Groschner, A., Pehmer, A.K. and Seidel, T. (2015). Effects of a classroom discourse intervention on teachers' practice and students' motivation to learn mathematics and science. Learning and Instruction, 35: 94-103.

Kohlberg, L. (1958). The development of modes of thinking and choices in years 10-16. PhD Dissertation.

Kohlberg, L. (1963). The development of children's orientation towards a moral order. Vita Humana, 6(1-2) 11-33.

Kohlberg, L. (1981). Essays on moral development: vol.1; the philosophy of moral development. San Francisco: Harper & Row.

Kohlberg, L. (1984). The psychology of moral development: the nature and validity of moral stages. San Francisco: Harper & Row.

Kohlberg, Lawrence, (1967) Moral and religious education and the public schools: a developmental view. In T. Sizer (es). Religion and public education, Boston. Pp166-167.

Kohlberg, Lawrence, (1976). This special section in perspective, vol.40, 4: p.213

Kohn, Melvin L. (1976). Social class and parental values: another confirmation of the relationship. American Sociological Review, 41(3): 538-545.

Kraft, E, Wang, J. (2010). An exploratory study of the cyberbullying and cyberstalking experiences and factors related to the victimization of students at a public liberal arts college. *International Journal of Technoethics.* 1(4): 74-91.

Krahn, J.H. (1971). A comparison of Kohlberg's and Piaget's type 1 morality. Religious Education, 66 (5): 373-375.

Kraut, R., Patterson, M., Lundmark, V., Kiesler, S., Mukophadhyay, T., Scherlis, W. (1998). Internet paradox: a social technology that reduces social involvement and psychological wellbeing? *American Psychologist.* 53(9):1017-1031.

Krug, EG, Mercy, JA, Dahlberg, LL, Powell, KE. (1998). Firearm-and-non-firearm-related homicide among children: an international comparison. *Homicide Studies.* 2: 83-95.

Krug, EG, Powell, KE, Dahlberg, LL. (1998). Firearm-related deaths in the United States and 35 other high- and upper-middle-income countries. *International Journal of Epidemiology.* 27:214-221.

Kutlu, F. (2005). The effect of bullying management training on bullying behaviours of elementary school students. (PhD. Thesis, Middle East Technical University, Ankara). Turkey.

Lehr, R and MacMillan, P. (2001). The psychological and emotional impact of divorce: the noncustodial fathers' perspective. Families in Society, 82(4): 373-382.m

Lesko, Nancy. (2012). Act your age: the cultural construction of Adolescence.2nd ed. New York: Routledge.

Letendre, J., (2007). Sugar and Spice but not always nice: Gender socialization and its impact on development and maintenance of aggression in adolescent girls. *Child and Adolescent Social Work Journal*, 24(4), 353-368.

Levine, Madeline (2012). Teach your children well: parenting for authentic success. Harper Collins Publications.

Li, Q. (2007). New bottle but old wine: a research of cyberbullying in school. *Computers in Human Behavior*, 23(4) 1777-1791.

Li, Qing (2006). Cyberbullying in schools. *School Psychology International*, 27(2), 157-170. DOI:10.1177/0143034306064547.

Lickona, T. (1991). Educating for character: how schools can teach respect and responsibility. New York: Bantan Books

Lickona, T. (1996). Eleven principles of effective character education. Journal of Moral education., 25(1): 93-100.

Lindeman, E.C. (1926). The meaning of adult education. New York: New Republic.

Livingston, S. &Helsper, E.J. (2013). Children, internet and risk in comparative perspective. *Journal of Child Media*. 7; 1-8.

Lockwood, David (1960) Archives Europeenes de Sociologie. Vol.1, no.2. pp.250-251.

Lockwood, David, (1958) The Blackcoated Worker: A Study in Class Consciousness. PhD. Thesis. Oxford: Oxford

University Press. [available in the Oxford University Library]

longitudinal studies. Development Review, 49, 31-40.

Lukianowicz, N (1972). Incest. British Journal of Psychiatry, 20: 301-313.

Madlock, PE, Westerman, D. (2011). Hurtful cyber-teasing and violence who's laughing out loud?

Martinez, I., Garcia, J.F., and Yubero, S. (2007). Parenting styles and adolescents'self-esteem in Brazil. Journal of Psychological Reports, 100:731-745.

Mason. K.L. (2008). Cyberbullying: a preliminary assessment for school personnel,

Matsunaga, M., (2009) Parents don't know their children have been bullied: child-parent discrepancy on bullying and family-level profile of communication standards. *Human Communication Research*, 35, 221-247.

May, R, (1967), Psychology and the human dilemma. New York: Van Nostrand Reinhold.

Maynard, H. & Joseph, S. (2000). Development of the multidimensional peer-victimization scale. Aggressive Behavior, 26, 169-178.

McCabe, D and Trevino, L. (1993). Academic dishonesty: honour codes and other contextual influences. Journal of Higher Education, 64, 522-538.

Mckenan, K.Y. & Bargh, J.A., (1999). Plan 9 from cyberspace: the implications of the Internet for personality and social psychology. *Personality & Social Psychology Review*. 4(1): 57-75. [https://doi.org/10.1207/S15327957PSPR0401_6]

McManamon, Catherine (2017). Imitating Mary's 10 amazing virtues. [https://www.getfed.com/imitating-marys-10-amazing-virtues-6169/ assessed 28 December 2019]

Michael, S. (1987). Are sons and daughters treated more differently by fathers than by mothers? Developmental Review, 7:183-209.

Milevsky, A, Schlechter, M., Netter, S., and Keehn, D. (2007). Maternal and paternal parenting styles in adolescents: association with self-esteem, depression and life satisfaction. Journal of Child and Family Studies, 16: 39-47.

Ministry of Education, Singapore (2019). Cyber Wellness: what is cyberness? [moe.gov.sg/education/programme/social-and-emotional-learning/cyber-wellness.]

Mischel, W. and Peake, P.K. (1982). Beyond déjà vu in cross-situational consistency. Psychological Review, 89(6): 730-755.

Monteiro, D., Cid, L., Marinho, D.A., Moutao, J., Vitorino, A., Bento, T. (2017). Determinants and reasons for dropout in swimming: Systematic Review. Sports, 5(3): 50.

Morgan, D.H.J. (1996). Family connection: an introduction to family studies. Cambridge: Polity Press.

Murray, Charles (1984). Losing ground: American social policy, 1950-1980. New York: Basic Books.

Murray, Charles. (2012). Coming apart: the state of White America, 1960-2010. New York: Crown Forum.

Newsom, Jennifer Siebel. The Representation Project.org/film/miss-representation-film]

Niaraki, Fahimeh.Rezai. and Rahimi, Hassan. (2013). The impact of authoritative, permissive and authoritarian behaviour of parents on self-concept, psychological health and life quality. European Online Journal of Natural and Social Sciences, 2(1): 78-85.

Niemiec, R. M. (2018). Character strength interventions: a field guide for practitioners. Boston: Hogrefe Publications. 299p.

Nixon, Elizabeth Bringing up babies: the cultural divide. Irish Times, November 10, 2019. (Rosita Boland asks parents in Ireland about their attitudes to breastfeeding, childcare and discipline). https://www.Irishtimes.com/life-and-style/health-family/bringing-up-baby-the–cultural-divide-1.685567.

No more Snapstreaks and autoplay- a new American law wants to ban them. BBC Newsround, 2019, 31 July: https"//www.bbc.co.uk/newsround/49175442.

North, Anna, (June 18, 2019). Elizabeth Warren just introduced her childcare plan in Congress. Vox.com/policy-and-politics/2019/6/18/18683527.

O'Brien, M (1982). Becoming a lone father: differential patterns and expressions, In McKee and M. O'Brien (eds). The father figure. London: Tavistock Publications Ltd, (pp.184-195)

O'Moore, M., & Kirkham, C. (2001). Self-esteem and its relationship to bullying behaviour. *Aggressive Behavior.* 27(4); 269-283. [https://doi.org/10.1002/ab.1010]

OECD (2017). PISA 2015 Results (Vol.III): students' well-being, PISA, OECD Publication, Paris. [http://dx.doi.org/10.1787/9789264273856-/en]

Olweus, D. (1993). Bully/victim problems among schoolchildren: long-term consequences and an effective intervention program. Journal of *Mental Disorder and Crime.* 2: 317-349.

Olweus, D. (1993). Bullying at school: what we know and what we can do. Oxford: Blackwell.

Olweus, D. (1996). The revised Olweus Bully/Victim questionnaire for students. University of Norway, Berge, Norway.

Once I am gone the bullying will stop, Rochelle Pryor. Mail Online, 20 January 2019. [dailymail.co.uk/news/article-6613221/girl-14-cry-help-social-media-ending-life.html]

Oppenheimer, L. (2004). Perception of individualism in Dutch society: a developmental approach. International Journal of Behavioral Development. 28: 336-346.

Oppenheimer, Valerie K. (1977). The sociology of women's economic role in the family. American Sociological Review, 42: 387-406.

Ortega, R., Elipe, P., Mora-Merchan, J.A., Genta, M.L. & Brighi, A. (2012). The emotional impact of bullying and cyberbullying on the victim: a European cross-national study. Aggressive Behaviour. 38, 342-356. https://doi.org/10.1002/ab.21440.

Peterson, C and Scligman, M. (2004). Character strengths and virtues: a handbook and classification. Oxford: Oxford University Press.

Piaget, J. (1965). The moral judgement of the child. New York: Free Press. (first published in 1932)

Piaget, J. (1965). The moral judgement of the child. New York: Free Press. [originally published in 1932]

Piff, P.K., Kraus, M.W., Cote, S., Cheng, B., and Keltner, D. (2010). Having Less, giving more. The influence of social class on prosocial behaviour. *Journal of Personality and Social Psychology*, 99, 771-784.

Piskin, M (2010). Examination of peer bullying among primary and middle school children in Ankara. Education & Science, 35(156), 175-189.

Popenoe, D. (1996). Life without father: New York: The Free Press, pp.139-163.

Price, M and Dalgleish, J. (2010). Cyberbullying experience. Impact and coping strategies as described by Australian young people. *Youth Studies Australia*, 29(2), 51-59.

Protecting kids and communities. (2019). Keeping our schools safe: a plan to stop mass shootings and end gun violence in American schools. [https://everytownresearch.org]

Psychology in the School, 45(4), 323-348.

Raenkl, A. (2014). Towards an institutionally oriented theory of example-based learning. Cognitive Science. 38: 1-37.

Raz-Yurovich, Liat (2012). Application of the transaction cost approach to households- the demographics of households' make or buy decisions. MPIDR Working Paper WP 2012-025, August 2012. Max Planck Institute for Demographic Research. Rostock, Germany. Pp.1-54. http://www.aemog2.mpg.de

Rebecca, P.A. (2006). Effects of parenting style on personal and social variables for Asian adolescents. American Journal of Orthopsychiatry, 76: 503-511.

Reisinger, A.J. (2012). Histories. In N. Lesko and S. Talburt, (Eds.) Key words in youth studies. Oxford: Routledge.

Revell, L. and Arthur, J. (2007). Character education in school and the education of teachers. Journal of Moral Education, 36 (1), 79-92.

Rickard, M. (2002). Children of Lesbian and single women Parents Research Note no.41, June 4, 2002. Canberra: Department of Parliamentary Library, Commonwealth of Australia.

Robinson, CC, Mandelco, B., Frost Olsen, S and Hart, CH. (1995). Authoritative, authoritarian, and permissive parenting practices: development of a new measure. Psychological Reports, 77: 819-830.

Rosenfeld, R., Baumer, E, Messner, SF. (2007). Social trust, firearm prevalence, and homicide. Annals of Epidemiology. 17: 119-125.

Rottenstein, C., Laasko, L., Pihalaja, T., Kontinne, N. (2013). Personal reasons for withdrawal from team sports and the influence of significant others among youth athletes. International Journal of Sports Science Coach, 8; 19-31.

Rudy, D. and Grusec, J.E. (2006). Authoritarian parenting in individualist and collectivist groups: associations with maternal emotion and cognitive and children's self-esteem. Journal of Family Psychology, 20(1): 68-78.

Safer Internet Centre. European Union. (February 2019). Better Internet for kids: how it is done in The Netherlands. [www.saferinternetcentre.nl]

Sahin, M. (2017). John Dewey's influence on the Turkish education system in the early republic era. European Journal of Education Studies, 3(6): 622-632.

Sam, David L., Bruce, Delphine, Agyemang, Collins B., Amponsah, Bejamin and Arkorful, Helen. (2019). Cyberbullying victimization among high school and university students in Ghana. Journal of Deviant Behavior, 40(11): 1305-1321.

Schafer, ES. And Bell, RQ. (1958). Development of a parental attitude research instrument. Child Development, 29: 339-361.

Schenk, A, Fremouw, W (2012). Prevalence, psychological impact, and coping of cyberbully victims among college students. *Journal of School Violence*. 11(1): 21-37.

Schmid, Heinz Didaktik des Ethikunterrichts, vol. II, pp.30-72.

School violence, Oslo, Norway. (2017) The Independent Barents Observer, September 28, 2017. https://www.newsinenglish.no/2017/09/28/school-violence-shocks-minister/

Schwartz, Judith D. (1993). In the mother puzzle

Schwartz, S.H. and Sagiv, L. (1995). Identifying culture-specifics in the content and structure of values. Journal of Cross-Cultural Psychology, 26(1): 92-116.

Sentile, D.A., Bailey, K., Bavelier, D. et al. (2017). Internet gaming disorder in children and adolescents. *Paediatrics*; 140[suppl. 21: 581-585.

Shapira, NA, Lessig, MC, Goldsmith, TD, Szabo, ST, Lazoritz, M, Gold, MS, et al. (2003) Problematic internet use: proposed classification and diagnostic criteria. Journal of *Depression and Anxiety*. 17(4): 207-216.

Shazam, Daniel (2018) Shazam confronts cyberbullying in Singapore. Digital Market Asia News, 23 April 2018. [www.digitalmarket.asia/shazam-confronts-cyberbullying-Singapore/]

Silverstein, LB, Auerbach, CF. (1999). Deconstructing the essential father. American Psychologist, 54(6): 397-407.

Silvia, Paul J. (2002). Self-awareness and emotional intensity. Cognition and Emotion, 16, 195-216.

Smith, Helena (2002). Slaves in the land of the free. New Statesman, September 9, 2002.

Smith, PK, Mahadiv, J, Carvalho, M, Fisher, S, Russell, S, Tippett, N. (2008). Cyberbullying: Its nature and impact in secondary school pupils. *Journal of Child Psychology and Psychiatry and Allied Disciplines*. 49(4): 376-385.

Smythe, M and Davis, J. (2004). Perceptions of dishonesty among two-year college students: academic versus business situations. Journal of Business Ethics, 51: 63-73.

Souto, Anne-Marie (2011) Racism increasingly aimed at children and aimed at teens. teens[yle.fi//osasto/news/racism_increasingly_aimed_at_children_and_teens/5387317]

Spock, Benjamin (1973). Baby and Child Care. New Ed. New York, Pocket Books.p.1.

Stattin, H., Janson, H., Klackenberg-Larsson, I, and Magnusson, D. (1995). Corporal punishment in everyday life: an intergenerational perspective. In J. McCord (3d.) Coercion and punishment in long term perspective. New York: Cambridge University Press, 315-347.

Stokes, A. and Newstead, S. (1995). Studies of undergraduate cheating: who does and why? Studies in Higher Education, 20(2): 159-172.

Storm, P and Storm, R. (2007). Winter. Cheating in middle school and high school. Forum, 71: 105.

Straus, M.A. and Paschall, M.J. (2009). Corporal punishment by mothers and the development of children's cognitive ability: a longitudinal study of two nationally representative age cohorts. Journal of Aggression Maltreatment and Trauma. 18: 459-483.

Suzuki, K, Asaga, R, Sourander, A, Hoven, CW, Mandell, D. (2012). Cyberbullying and adolescent mental health. *International Journal of Adolescent Medical Health*. 24(1): 27-35.

Swart, Cecile, All4women.co.za/137411/lifestyle/social-media-attacks-and-cyber-bullying-among-teens-on-the-rise]

Temli, Y., Sen, D. and Akar, H. (2011). A study on primary classroom and social studies teachers' perceptions of moral education and their development and learning.

Educational Sciences: Theory and Practice, 11 (4), pp.2061-2067.

Tokunaga, R.S. (2010) Following you home from school: a critical review and synthesis of research on cyberbullying victimization. *Computers in Human Behavior*. 26(3), 277-287. [https://doi.org/10.1016/j.chb.2009.11.014]

Totura, C.M., MacKinnon-Lewis, C., Gesten, E.L., Gadd, R., Divine, K.P., Dunham, S., and Kamboukos, D. (2009). Bullying and Victimization among boys and girls in middle school: The influence of perceived family and school contexts. *The Journal of Early Adolescence*, 29(4), 571-609.

United Nationals Educational Scientific and Cultural Organisation. (1991). Values and ethics and the science and technology curriculum. Bangkok, Thailand: Asia and the Pacific Programme of Educational Innovation for Development.

Valentine, G. (1996). Angels and devils: moral landscapes of childhood. Society and Space, 14: 581-599

Van, Geel., Goemans, A., Zwaanswijk, W., Gini, G., and Vender, P. (2018). Does peer victimization predict low self-esteem or does low self-esteem predict peer victimization? meta-analyses on longitudinal studies. Developmental Review, 49; 31-40.

Van Lange, P.A., De Bruin, E., Otten, W. and Joirman, J.A. (1997). Development of prosocial, individualistic, and competitive orientations: Theory and preliminary evidence. Journal of *Personality and Social Psychology*, 73, 733.

Van Oudenhoven, J. P., De Raad, B., Carmona, C., Helbig, a. K., Van der Linden, M. (2012). Are virtues shapes by national cultures or religions? Swiss Journal of Psychology, 71; 29-34.

Victoria- Building respectful and Safe Schools. [http://www.eduweb.vic.gov.au/edulibrary/public/Stum an/wellbeing/respectfulsafe.pdf]

Violence rising at primary schools, Oslo, Norway. (2019) The Independent Barents Observer, March 20, 2019. https://www.newsinenglish.no/2019/03/20/violence-rising-at-primary-schools/

Wainryb, C and Turiel, E. (1993). Conceptual and informational features in moral decision making. Educational Psychology, 28, 205-218.

Walker, D.L., Roberts, M.P., Kristjansson, K. (2015). Towards a new era of moral education in theory and practice. Educational Review, 67(1): 79-96.

Wayt, Lindsay (2012). The impact of students' academic and social relationships on college student persistence, M.A. Thesis, University of Nebraska, Nebraska.

West, Emily (2018). Understanding authenticity in commercial sentiments: the greeting card as an emotional commodity. Emotions as Commodities, Capitalism, Consumption and Authenticity, 59, edited by Eva Illouz, pp.123-144., NY, Routledge.

Weyns, T., Verschueren, K., Leflot, G., Onghena, P., Wouters, S., and Coplin, H. (2017). The role of teacher behaviour in children's relational aggression development: A five-wave longitudinal study. Journal of School Psychology, 64: 17-27.

Wheaton, Oliver (May 26, 2018) Self-service checkouts scams. The Independent, English Daily London.

William, K.R. and Guerra, N.G. (2007). Prevalence and predictors of internet bullying. *Journal of Adolescent Health*, 41, S14-S21.

Willingham, Catherine (2018). Cyberbullying in Singapore: a guide to new online laws. [http://expatliving.sg/cyber-bullying-in-singapore-guide-to-new-online.laws/]

Wright, J.C. and Mischel W, (1987). A conditional approach to dispositional constructs: the local predictability of social behaviour. Journal of Personality and Social Psychology, 53: 1159-1177.

Young, A., Hardy, V., Hamilton, C., Biernesser, K., Sun, L., Niebergall, S. (2009), Empowering students: Using data to transform bullying prevention and intervention. *Professional School Counseling*, 12(6), 413-420.

Zevenbergen, AA, Haman, E, Olszansko, AA (2012). Middle-Class Polish and American mothers' beliefs regarding parent-child narratives. Journal of Cross-Cultural Psychology. July 28, 43(6). Pp.979-998. https://doi.org/10.1177/0022022111416005.

ABOUT THE AUTHOR

Parental affection, timely attention, tenacious guidance, and precise social management assist youngsters in keeping on track despite life hindrances, hurdles, and obstructions. Time is a precious commodity and self-discipline is an invaluable treasure for a teenager to succeed and carve a place in the intellectual sphere. The journey is arduous, demanding time management, a degree of self-restraint and moderation in a socially alluring atmosphere. An academic expedition is challenging in a competitive world. Excellent school teachers, inspiring university professors, and pleasant study mates make the learning exciting and exhilarating.

One has to be stoutly ambitious to surmount difficulties and overcome diverse concerns to achieve higher accolades. Best teachers and cordial class fellows both in Manchester and London facilitated shared learning and group activities. Interestingly, student social clubs were practically knowledge co-construction hubs, holding debates on topics of literary importance and scholarly significance. Meaningful conversations reflected mannerism, respect, and gesticulation among members of the student unions. Occasional giggles, mild laughs, and harmless jokes rejuvenated the Manchester Polytechnic social club environment. The Polytechnic later became Manchester Metropolitan University. A few names stand out in the academic pursuit such as Tim Baxter, Barry Mills,

Michael Sharkey, Barry Cheale, Ian Goldie, and Mrs Patricia Coleman. They were vigorous participants in extracurricular undertakings.

Having earned Post-graduate MCILIP from Manchester Metropolitan University, Dr Ahmad served as Research Assistant in the School of Oriental and African Studies, University of London. He gained admission at University College London for an intensive MPhil Degree programme. He had the opportunity of studying under Professor Ronald Staveley, Professor B.C. Vickery and Professor James. D. Pearson. In monthly postgraduate seminars, doctoral students were invited to give talks on topics ranging from research strategies, human ideals, the significance of archives, to understanding principles of psychology and philosophical doctrines. Dr Nazir presented a paper in the presence of Professor Bernard Lewis, Professor Ronald Staveley, Professor J.D. Pearson, B.C. Bloomfield, K.C. Butler, B. Wallace, and Mr Driskel, entitled " Psychology of Interpersonal Communication", receiving an encouraging feedback and scholarly guidance for producing other research papers. At the university level, professors invigorated all students to help each other, share knowledge and research findings for the common good and mutual benefit.

After the successful acquisition of an MPhil degree, Dr Nazir Ahmad subsequently earned a place for Doctoral studies at the University of London. He pursued his studies and research with relentless resilience for four and a half years and finally, the University of London awarded him a Ph.D. degree. In the course of studies at Manchester Metropolitan University, Dr Ahmad benefited from awe-inspiring lectures by Professor Alan Duxbury, Professor Alan. G. Pate, Professor K.W. Neal and Professor Keith. C. Lund

In the course of his professional career, Dr Ahmad served London Borough of Sutton, Southwark College London and then for a couple of years, King Faisal University, Dammam, Saudi Arabia. While working for the Inner London Education Authority, he attended an interview at Saudi Embassy, London for the position of a Professor at King Abdul Aziz University, Jeddah, Saudi Arabia. He accepted the offer and proceeded to Saudi Arabia where he had the opportunity of teaching both undergraduate and Master degree students for fifteen years. Some of those bright students have now become professors in various Saudi universities. Dr. Ahmad still remembers with affection and gratitude the traditional Saudi hospitality and friendly atmosphere. Saudi colleagues such as Professor Dr Abdul Jalil Tashkandy [now retired], Professor Dr. Muhammad Amin Marghalani, Professor Dr Hasan Al-Sereihy and Professor Dr Muhammad Jafar Arif were kind and hospitable. Dr Abdul Ghafoor Bukhari, Dr Abdurrashid, and Dr Sharaf Al-Jefri displayed a good sense of humor.

Among my former students still serving as Professors in King, Abdul Aziz University includes Dr Nabil Qumsani, Dr Qahtani, and Dr Atif Gattan. Dr Atif, being from Holy Makkah, kept up the supply of Zam Zam and never let it run out. Dr Hasan Al-Sereihy, being from Holy Madina, showed Dr Ahmad some ancient Islamic monuments near the Holy Mosque of the Holy Prophet. [Allah's blessings and peace be upon him]. Dr Faisal al-Haddad was my excellent Master Degree student who went on to earn his PhD degree abroad. Dr Faisal al-Haddad is now Director of Strategic Studies, King Abdul Aziz University, Jeddah, Saudi Arabia. I worked closely with Dr Marghalani, then the Chairman of the Department and also, Dean of the Faculty, on a number of research projects in the sphere of information management.

Renowned for my time-keeping, I delivered carefully timed lectures, sometimes on behalf of my colleagues such as Dr Abdul Aziz Al-Nihari (who passed away 7 June 2020) and Dr Abdul Jalil Tashkandy. I also conducted semester exams when they were away on academic assignments. I taught female Master's degree students via CCTV, allowing them remote access to ask questions over the phone. In addition to my scholarly commitments, I rendered academic guidance, admission facilitation, and maintained liaison with U.S. and British Universities for securing acceptance in doctoral programmes for our top student scholars.

While at Manchester Metropolitan University, I had specialised in the indexing, abstracting, and information retrieval discipline. Given my expertise, one of my colleagues Professor Dr Hashim Abdu Hashim (who was also Director-General of the Okaz Organisation, publishing an Arabic and English' Saudi Gazette' newspapers), engaged me for the task of indexing Saudi Gazette- an English daily. I dexterously indexed the backlog, devising thesaurus, assigning subject headings, and produced 25-volumes covering twenty-five years period from 1976-2000.

In the course of my MPhil studies at University College London, one of the significant assignments was the "Psychology of Student Behaviour in the Classroom" that had provided me with an insight into the significance of sustaining a learning environment for university students. I applied my social psychology skills at King Abdul Aziz University classroom settings, keeping my students engaged, smiling with little harmless puns, and making the learning a pleasurable experience. My lectures were envisioned to be a subjective manifestation of knowledge, gleaned from reading, research, and strengthened by the needs of courses. I used multilingual Arabic-English proficiencies to facilitate absorption and retention for mostly Arabic speaking students.

At Southwark College London, I collaborated with Don W. Wendon, Director of Information and Learning Resources, to plan and prepare a comprehensive User Instruction programme for both pure sciences and Humanities students. We partly implemented Ralph Waldo Emerson's notion of 'urging colleges to appoint Professors of Books' (1840) to imbue in students the spirit of scientific enquiry, search strategies, and information retrieval capabilities. In cooperation with Professor H.G.L Davis, Head of Science department at the college, I prepared a series of lectures on research methods for science students. I taught research methodologies to final year physics, biology and chemistry students. While serving at King Faisal University Damam, I devised research methods course in collaboration with Abdullah Driskel (formerly Michael Driskel) who was the Chief of the Medical Library. It was a series of lectures we both delivered in the beginning of each semester to medical students.

Likewise, my most intelligent student Dr Gabriel Arish is now Dean and a Professors at King Saud University, Riyadh. Another former student Dr. Ibrahim Kamaluddin Arif is a Professor at Ummul Qu'ra University, Makkah Al-Mukarrama. Sad-Uddin Sharitha was an steadfast Master degree student who is now serving Ummul Qur'a University, Makkah.

While serving King Abdul Aziz University, it was a very rewarding spiritual experience to pay frequent visits to Holy Ka'aba in Makkah Al-Mukarrama and the sacred shrine and the Holy Mosque of the Prophet Muhammad [PBUH] in Madina Al-Munawwara. As the present writer returned to London after serving King Abdul Aziz University for 15 years, his son Dr. Adeel Ahmad joined King Faisal Specialist Hospital Jeddah as Consultant, Family Medicine. Again, with the blessings of Almighty Allah, the author, and his wife Farah Ahmad spend most of their time in Jeddah regularly visiting Makkah and Madina Al-Munawwara. Dr Adeel has now moved to King Abdullah

University of Science and Technology as a Medical Director and Consultant, Family Medicine.

Dr Nazir Ahmad has written a considerable number of research articles published in professional journals of Europe, Turkey, U.S.A., Australia and South Asia. He authored more than twenty books in the field of emotional psychology, youth nurturing and social media, digital learning, Islamic literature, knowledge management, and composed a comprehensive collection of English poems.

E-Mail: drnahmad3@hotmail.com
1442 Hijra / 2020